COGNAC

*"A well-written, informative page-tu....ci that's
definitely worth the investment."*
Jancis Robinson

*"This book is the most up to date literature that can be found about
cognac; the drink and the region, and certainly makes for a 'must read' for
anyone who pays homage to the wonder that is eaux-de-vie."*
CognacExpert.com

*"If you're looking to understand the world of cognac this is
one book worth investing in."*
diffordsguide.com

On previous editions of Cognac

*"Combines history, geography, human interest, business, marketing, controversy
and of course cognac the drink in an account that is racy, witty and entirely
without pomposity."*
Judges of the Deinhard/Wine Magazine award

*"This season's stand out is Cognac ... Faith artfully demonstrates how
the history, geography, sociobiology, politics and economics of the
town come together."*
New York Times

*"Here, one feels, is a wine journalist who is prepared to probe
beneath the surface."*
Wine & Spirit

"His evocation of the past is as convincing as his judgment on the present."
The Times

*"An imaginative and well-researched account of cognac ...
a jolly good read it certainly is."*
The Independent

THE CLASSIC WINE LIBRARY

There is something uniquely satisfying about a good wine book, preferably read with a glass of the said wine in hand. The Classic Wine Library is a series of wine books written by authors who are both knowledgeable and passionate about their subject. Each title in The Classic Wine Library covers a wine region, country or type and together the books are designed to form a comprehensive guide to the world of wine as well as an enjoyable read, appealing to wine professionals, wine lovers, tourists, armchair travellers and wine trade students alike.

The series:
Port and the Douro, Richard Mayson
Cognac: The story of the world's greatest brandy, Nicholas Faith
Sherry, Julian Jeffs
Madeira: The islands and their wines, Richard Mayson
The wines of Austria, Stephen Brook
Biodynamic wine, Monty Waldin
Spirits distilled, Mark Ridgwell
The story of champagne, Nicholas Faith
The wines of Faugères, Rosemary George

——————————— ℮♉ ———————————

Nicholas Faith was for many years a senior editor on the business pages of newspapers including the *Sunday Times* and *The Economist* and was a regular contributor to the *Financial Times*. He is best known however, for the books and hundreds of articles he has written on wines and spirits over the past thirty years. His first book on wine, *The Winemasters*, won the André Simon award. He also edited the prestigious magazine *L'Amateur de Bordeaux*. In 1996 he founded the International Spirits Challenge, now recognized as the world's leading competition devoted to alcoholic spirits of every description. In September 2010 Nicholas Faith was the first recipient of the Lifetime Achievement Award given by the Bureau National Interprofessional de Cognac.

COGNAC

THE STORY OF THE WORLD'S GREATEST BRANDY

NICHOLAS FAITH

First published in 2013 by

Infinite Ideas Limited
36 St Giles
Oxford
OX1 3LD
United Kingdom
www.infideas.com

This edition 2016

A CIP catalogue record for this book is available from the British Library

ISBN 978–1–908984–76–0

Front cover photo © BNIC/Jean-Yves Boyer
Illustrations on pages 8, 21, 32, 40 and 112 courtesy of Courvoisier/Beam Global/Anne Cochet
Back cover, bottom, photographs on pages 16, 17, 47 and 198 © BNIC/Stéphane Charbeau
Photographs on pages 18, 31, 36, 41, 42 (Pierrette Trichet), 106 and 122 courtesy of Rémy Martin
Photograph on page 20 courtesy of Hine
Back cover, top row, photographs on pages 29, 42 (Yann Fillioux), 73, 74, 81, 118 and 147 courtesy of Hennessy
Photograph on page 43 (Patrice Pinet) courtesy of Courvoisier/Beam Global
Photograph on page 108 courtesy of Frapin/McKinley Vintners
Photographs on pages 43 (Benoit Fil), 68, 97 courtesy of Martell

Text designed and typeset by Nicki Averill Design

Printed in U.S.A.

CONTENTS

Appendix I: THE LAW

Appendix II: THE FIGURES

ACKNOWLEDGEMENTS

Thirty years ago my old friend Michael Longhurst suggested that I should write a book about cognac, a suggestion I accepted and have never regretted. Since then I have been able to rely on many friends, old and new, to produce this third – and thoroughly revised – edition. In no particular order they include David Baker, Alain Braastad – who has forgotten more about cognac than I will ever know – Bernard Hine, Colin Campbell, Alfred Tesseron, Georges Clot, David Baker, Benoit Fil, Patrick Leger, Olivier Paultes, Yann Fillioux, Olivier Blanc, Pierre and Jennifer Szersnovicz, Catherine Mousnier, and Catherine Lepage, Agnes Aubin, Laurine Caute at the BNIC, Stephane Feuillet, Luc Lurton at the Station Viticole, Michel and Catherine Guillard who have let me stay in their lovely house so often, as well as my former colleagues at the International Spirits Challenge, most obviously Simon Palmer and Neil Mathieson.

Thanks also to Richard Burton, Rebecca Clare and their so agreeable and professional colleagues at Infinite Ideas.

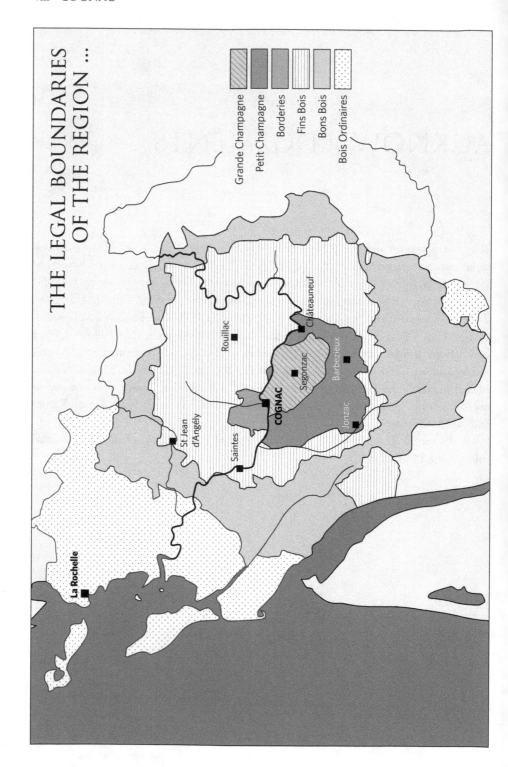

THE LEGAL BOUNDARIES OF THE REGION ...

Grande Champagne
Petit Champagne
Borderies
Fins Bois
Bons Bois
Bois Ordinaires

La Rochelle
St Jean d'Angély
Saintes
Rouillac
Châteauneuf
COGNAC
Segonzac
Barbezieux
Jonzac

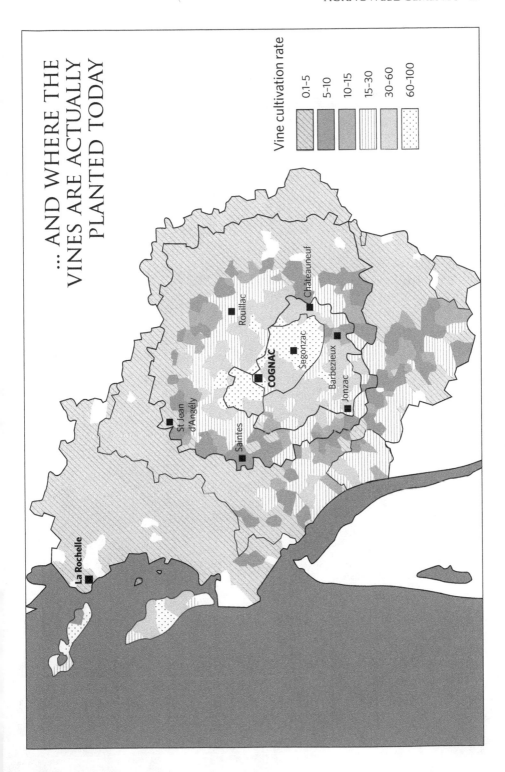

... AND WHERE THE VINES ARE ACTUALLY PLANTED TODAY

Vine cultivation rate

0.1-5
5-10
10-15
15-30
30-60
60-100

La Rochelle

St Jean d'Angély

Saintes

Rouillac

COGNAC

Châteauneuf

Segonzac

Barbezieux

Jonzac

INTRODUCTION
THE UNIQUENESS OF COGNAC

In winter you can tell you are in cognac country when you turn off the N10, the old road between Bordeaux and Paris at the little town of Barbezieux and head towards Cognac. The landscape does not change dramatically; it is more rounded, perhaps a little more hilly, than on the road north from Bordeaux, and the vines are thicker on the ground. But the major indicator has nothing to do with the sense of sight. It has to do with the sense of smell. During the distillation season from November to March the whole night-time atmosphere is suffused with an unmistakable aroma, a warm smell that is rich, grapey, almost palpable. It emanates from dozens of otherwise unremarkable groups of farm buildings, distinguished only by the lights burning as the new brandy is distilled.

Cognac emerges from the gleaming copper stills in thin, transparent trickles, tasting harsh and oily, raw yet recognisably the product of the vine. If anything, it resembles grappa; but what for the Italians is a saleable spirit is merely an intermediate product for the Cognacais. Before they consider it ready for market it has to be matured in oak casks. Most of the spirits, described by the more poetically minded locals as 'sleeping beauties', are destined to be awakened within a few years and sold off as relatively ordinary cognacs, but a small percentage are left to sleep for much longer. Every year expert palates sample them and eliminate – or, rather, set aside for immediate sale – those deemed incapable of further improvement. As the survivors from this rigorous selection process mature, so their alcoholic strength diminishes and within forty or fifty years is down from around 70 to 40 per cent – the strength at which cognacs, old and new, are put on the market. These truly aristocratic brandies are then transferred to the glass jars – *damejeannes*,[1] known to the Cognacais as *bonbonnes* – each holding 25 litres of the precious fluid, and stored, even more reverently, in the innermost recesses of their owners' cellars – the aptly named *paradis* familiar to every visitor to Cognac.

Hennessy has the biggest *paradis* in Cognac itself, but an even more impressive collection

---

1 Hence the English term 'demi-johns'.

is hidden away in the crypt of the medieval church of the small town of Châteauneuf sur Charente, a few miles to the east. The Tesseron family store their brandies in this holy cellar. For nearly a century four generations have supplied even the most fastidious of the cognac houses with at least a proportion of the brandies they require for their finest, oldest blends. The Tesserons' two *paradis* contain over 1,000 *bonbonnes* dating back to the early nineteenth century. I was privileged to taste a sample of the 1853 vintage.

The world of cognac is governed by certain immutable rituals. Even when pouring the 1853, the firm's maître de chai swilled out the empty glass with a little of the cognac and dashed the precious liquid to the floor to ensure that the glass was free from impurities. Astonishingly, my first impression of the cognac was of its youth, its freshness. Anyone whose idea of the life-span of an alcoholic beverage is derived from wines is instinctively prepared for the tell-tale signs of old age, for old wines are inevitably faded, brown, their bouquet and taste an evanescent experience. By contrast even the oldest cognacs can retain their youthful virility, their attack. It seemed absurd: the brandy was distilled when Queen Victoria was still young, and the grapes came from vines some of which had been planted before the French Revolution. Yet it was no mere historical relic but vibrantly alive. But then the perfect balance of such a venerable brandy is compounded of a series of paradoxes: the spirit is old in years but youthful in every other respect; it is rich but not sweet; deep in taste though relatively light, a translucent chestnut in colour. Its taste is quite simply the essence of grapiness, without any hint of the over-ripeness that mars lesser beverages.

But what makes cognac the world's greatest spirit, is not only its capacity to age but its sheer complexity. When the BNIC[2] convened a hundred of the world's leading professionals in early 2009 to discuss the individual tastes associated with the spirit they came up with over sixty adjectives – shown in the Cognac Aroma Wheel on page 150 – to describe cognacs of every age, from the overtones of roses and vine flowers of the young to the leatheriness and nuttiness obvious in the oldest brandies.

For me they reach their peak not after a century but when they are around forty years old. Only then does the brandy reveal its full potential qualities, its nuttiness, above all its sheer concentration and length while retaining its fruitness and floral delicacy. To some connoisseurs the secret of a great cognac lies in its nose, its bouquet. In the words of Robert Delamain, scholar and cognac merchant, what one looks for in a cognac is 'above all a scent, a precious scent that exists nowhere else in nature, not in any flower, not in any herb; a soft aroma that engulfs you in successive waves; a scent that you examine, you explore, in order to uncover other agreeable, if indefinable, aromas.'[3]

The warmth and delicacy Delamain is describing linger long after the glass has been emptied, for in the wine tasters' vocabulary the crucial attribute is that the brandy, like any other alcoholic drink of any quality, is 'long'. At the end of the nineteenth century Professor Ravaz, who did a great deal to help rebuild the cognac vineyard after the phylloxera disaster, claimed that: 'The bouquet of a good eau de vie from the Grande

---

\c's governing body, the Bureau National Interprofessionel du Cognac.
\elamain, *Histoire du Cognac* (Paris, 1935).

Champagne lasts for a week or more.'[4] He was not exaggerating. In the distilleries themselves the aroma lingers on throughout the eight or nine months in every year when the stills themselves are empty. Cognac's essential difference from most other spirits is that its aromatic components derive directly and exclusively from the grape, its quality dictated by the nature of the *terroirs* where they are grown.

Only after tasting a cognac of that age and quality can you appreciate the truly miraculous nature of the whole enterprise and begin to understand how it is that the name of a small town in western France has become synonymous with the finest distilled liquor in the world. As a result, Cognac is by far the best-known French town, Paris alone excepted. A typical story concerns a session of an Episcopal Council.[5] According to the legend Mgr Cousseau, the Bishop of Angoulême, was chatting to neighbours from far-off sees, from North America to Ireland, none of whom had ever heard of his diocese, that is, until he explained that he was the Bishop of Cognac. The whole assembly, bishops, archbishops and cardinals immediately exclaimed 'what a great bishopric'.

Yet even today Cognac has only 30,000 inhabitants, and when it first rose to fame in the eighteenth century fewer than 2,000 people sheltered within its walls. Whatever the town's size, the reputation of its brandy would have been a prodigious achievement, for anyone with access to grapes and the simplest of distillation apparatus can make brandy of a sort. But only the Cognacais can make cognac, a drink with qualities that are enhanced by age until it becomes the very essence of the grapes from which it was distilled.

The success of the Cognacais is due to a multitude of factors – a combination of geography, geology and history. They had the perfect soil, the right climate and the ability to market their products to appreciative customers the world over. At first sight nothing about Cognac, a small town in the middle of an agreeable, albeit unremarkable, landscape, is special. Yet a more detailed investigation reveals that almost everything about the region is out of the ordinary. The most obvious distinction is geological, as it is for the sites producing all of France's finest wines and spirits. But whereas the soils and sub-soils of Bordeaux and Burgundy, if unusual are not unique, as I explain later, the Cognac region includes formations found nowhere else.

Cognac's geography and its weather are both special, though they are less easy to define than its geological peculiarities. Cognac is at the frontier of the geographical divide within France which separates the northern Langue d'Oil from the southern Langue d'Oc. In the later Middle Ages the linguistic boundary passed through Saintes, due west of Cognac, and Matha, a few miles north of the town. The -ac ending, meaning a town in the southern Langue d'Oc, is common in the area but the proximity of the frontier with the Langue d'Oil is shown by the presence only a few miles to the north of towns like Saint Jean d'Angély with the -y ending characteristic of the northern tongue. The change between the two cultures and languages is not as dramatic as in the Rhône Valley, where you are suddenly aware of the influence of the Mediterranean, but it is nevertheless abrupt enough to emphasise that you are in a different world.

---

4 Louis Ravaz and Albert Vivier, *Le Pays du Cognac* (Angoulême, 1900).
5 Ardouin-Dumazet, *Voyage en France* (Paris, 1898).

Travellers have long been aware of the change. In Robert Delamain's words:

For sailors from the whole of northern Europe, the coast of France below the Loire estuary was the region where, for the first time, they felt they were in the blessed South, where the heat of the sun makes life easier, where fruits ripen and wine flows. The Bay of Bourgneuf, and the Coast of Saintonge sheltering behind its islands, were for them the first sunny shores they came across.

Cognac is at the heart of a very special border region, a rough oblong bounded on the north by the Loire, between the Bay of Biscay and the mountains of the Massif Central. The whole area is remarkable for its gentleness. There are no abrupt slopes, no cliffs, no obvious drama in the landscape which can appear dull to the uninstructed eye until one begins to appreciate its subtleties. Its most obvious characteristic is its weather, like the landscape gentle, temperate, but more emollient than further north. Everything is softer, lighter, gentler, and Cognac epitomises those qualities.

Naturally the River Charente, which bisects the area, is a gentle river: 'the most beautiful stream in all my kingdom,' said King Henry IV four hundred years ago. They call it *molle*, the soft, sweet Charente, which twists and turns on its leisurely way to the sea. Bordered by willows and poplars, troubled only by fishermen (and the town's ever-energetic oarsmen), the Charente is an almost absurdly picturesque river. The slopes above, like the river itself, are spacious and gentle. But the Charente is not known as the *rivière de patience* for nothing. There is immense variety, if only because the river changes in width so abruptly. At times it is so narrow that the trees close in, forming a roof, their green echoed by their reflections on the water. It is a complicated stream, with its traps, its numerous weirs, its treacherous sandbanks, its hidden rocks. Moreover, it is so low in summer that only flat bottomed boats can float on it and so high in winter that the waters often reach right up to the arches of its many bridges. But the Charente is not the only river providing excellent drainage, there's the Né, the border between the two Champagnes, and the Seudre, the Trèfle and the Seugne.

As you can see from the map on page ix the heart of the region – where today most of the grapes are grown – is an irregular rectangle, which naturally distils the climatic advantages enjoyed by the region as a whole. It is near enough to the coast for the winters to be mild. To the east it is bounded by the first foot-hills of the Massif Central, and as you move east from Cognac the weather becomes a little harsher, the brandies become less mellow. Cognac itself enjoys the best of both worlds. The climate reinforces the initial advantages provided by the geological make-up of the soil and sub-soil. It is temperate, there is very little rain during the summer months and the winter lasts a mere three months, hence the fear of frosts from mid-March on – the appalling frosts of February 1956 reduced yields by a quarter or more for several years afterwards. The weather closes in during the second half of October, which makes recent earlier harvests an advantage. But the winter is no fun, the rains of 700–850 mm or more in the heart of the region are often accompanied by very high winds of up to 220 kph, often accompanied by floods, as, most recently, in 1982.

Because Cognac is so northerly a vineyard, the long summer days allow the grapes to ripen slowly and regularly, giving them the right balance of fruit and acidity required for distillation purposes. But the sunlight is never harsh, for the micro-climate is unique. Even the most transient visitor notices the filtered light, its unique luminosity – more intense sunlight would result in over-ripe grapes with too much sugar. Many observers, including Jacques Chardonne, the region's most famous novelist, the cartographer Louis Larmat and the scientist Louis Ravaz use the word soft, *doux* or *douce* to describe the region, its weather and above all the light – which Jacques de Lacretelle describes as *tamisée* – filtered. As Jacques Chardonne put it, 'The quality of the light in the Charente is without any parallel in France, even in Provence.'[6]

The weather has another contribution to make after the grapes have been fermented into wine and then distilled into brandy, but only those who live in Cognac can fully appreciate how this quality of diffused intensity extends even to the rain. The Charente region is wetter than many other regions of France, but, in the words of Professor Ravaz, the rain falls 'often, but in small amounts...sometimes it is only a persistent mist which provides the earth with only a little moisture, but which keeps the atmosphere saturated with humidity and prevents any evaporation.' Ravaz's description sounds remarkably like that of a Scotch mist, or a 'soft' day in Ireland. This is no coincidence, for both cognac and malt whisky require long periods of maturation in oak casks and their special qualities emerge only if the casks are kept in damp, cool cellars.

The individual components of the cognac formula could, in theory, have been reproduced elsewhere, but the result is unique. In the words of Professor Ravaz:

The same variety of grape can be grown anywhere and in the same way as in the Charente: distillation can be carried out anywhere else as at Cognac and in the same stills; the brandy can be stored in identical casks as those we employ in our region; it can be cared for as well, or maybe even better. But the same combination of weather and terrain cannot be found anywhere else. As far as the soil is concerned, it is not enough that it should belong to the same geological formations; it must have the same physical and chemical composition. And no one has ever found such a duplicate. In addition, the climate of the region must be identical to that of the Charente, and that is almost inconceivable: there is therefore very little chance that all the elements which influence the nature of the product should be found together in any region apart from the Charente; and thus no other region can produce cognac. The slightest difference in the climate, the soil, and so on is enough to change completely the nature of the brandy; and that is as it should be because there are, even in the Charente, a few spots (small ones, it is true) which produce mediocre brandy. All the trials which have been made all over the place to produce cognac with the same varieties and the Charentais methods have resulted only in failure. And this lack of success could have been foreseen if people had only remembered this one principle: that the nature of products is dependent on a combination of conditions which occurs only rarely.

---

6 In *Le bonheur de Barbezieux* (Paris, 1938).

Even Professor Ravaz omits one crucial element in the creation of cognac – the unique qualities of the people themselves. The combination of conditions that he outlines provide only the potential for making cognac and ignores the human characteristics needed to spread its fame throughout the world. For the potential could be realised only through a very special type of person, combining two superficially incompatible qualities. The making and storage of the spirit demands painstaking patience, a quality usually associated with the peasantry in general and especially marked in a region with such a troubled past as that of the Charente. In the words of Maurice Bures: 'Scarred for a long time by incessant wars, the Charentais became reserved, introverted, discreet.'[7] This combination was precisely the opposite of the open, adventurous, outlook required if cognac were to be marketed successfully the world over. Yet it was always destined chiefly for sale abroad, for the French market has never been a dominant factor.

Their instinctive reluctance to allow anyone to intrude on their intensely private family life is symbolised by the apparently unwelcoming facade of the local buildings with their dour stone walls interrupted only by stout, permanently shut wooden doors that enclose spacious cobbled farmyards surrounded by fermentation vats, still rooms and storehouses. Outsiders find the blank stone walls sad and menacing; the inhabitants find them deeply reassuring. *Cagouillards*, snails, they are nicknamed, shut in their fortresses. This collective introversion, this native defensiveness, is not confined to the countryside but extends to the small country towns – like Cognac itself.

Yet, miraculously, the inhabitants have managed to combine the two qualities. The fusion was best expressed by the region's most distinguished native, the late Jean Monnet, the 'founder of Europe'. He was the son of one of Cognac's leading merchants, and he remembers how every evening 'at dusk, when we lit the lamps, we had to shut every shutter. "They can see us," my mother would say, so greatly did she share the anxiety, the fear of being seen, of exposure which is so marked a trait of the Charentais character.'[8]

Yet in the Monnet household, as in that of many other merchants, guests were not exclusively aged aunts or squabbling cousins but also included buyers from all over the world. As a result, the little world of Cognac provided the young Jean Monnet with 'an enormously wide field of observation and a very lively exchange of ideas…I learned there, or springing from there, more than I could have done from a specialised education.' Moreover he found that abroad the name of Cognac was deeply respected, a sign of refinement amongst the 'rude' inhabitants even in far-off Winnipeg. This combination of a patient peasant obsession with detail and an international outlook is as unusual, and as important, as Cognac's geology and geography.

Cognac is the fusion of so many factors that there is no simple or obvious way to arrange a book on the subject. But it is obviously essential to start with an analysis of the reasons for its superiority and the skills required in its production.

---

7 Maurice Bures, 'Le Type Saintongeais', *La Science Sociale*, vol. 23 (Paris, 1908).
8 In *Mémoires* (Paris, 1976).

PART I
THE MAKING OF COGNAC

Anne Cochet

1

LAND, VINE, WINE

Over the past few years the French have been battling to defend the crucial importance of nature rather than nurture so far as fine wines and brandies are concerned. For them *terroir* – the soil, the climate, the weather, the aspect of the vineyard – is all important, while wine 'experts' mostly from the New World assert that nurture, in the shape of the skills of the wine maker, are the primary influence. Indeed the concept of *terroir* forms the basis for their system of Appellations Contrôlées. They could do worse than call the Cognacais to testify on their behalf. For geological and climatic factors are the only variables in the cognac equation. All the brandies entitled to the appellation are made from the same grape varieties, harvested in the same way at the same moment of the year, fermented in the self-same vats, distilled in the same stills and matured in the same oak.

Nevertheless, the late Maurice Fillioux, the sixth generation of his family to act as chief blender for Hennessy was typical in declaring that 'after cognac has been in cask for ten years, out of all the hundreds we taste, 95 per cent of the best come from the Grande Champagne'. The phrase *Premier Cru de Cognac* seen on many a placard throughout the Grande Champagne is not an official term, merely an indication that the Grande Champagne really is the finest area within the Cognac region. But people still matter for, as one local puts it: 'the Grande Champagne is in the inhabitants' minds and not in the landscape' – and in the mind of at least one grower even this small region includes five different sub-regions!

In theory, as well as in legal status and administrative practice, Cognac's *crus* form a series of concentric circles, with the Grande Champagne as a rough semi-circle at its heart, surrounded by a series of rings of steadily decreasing quality. In geographical reality there are in fact three separate areas (four including the Borderies), not the six indicated on the map. To the west there is the coastal plain, with its vast, ever-changing skies, its marshes, sandy beaches, oyster beds, off-shore islands – and thin, poor cognacs. The heterogenous mass of the Bons Bois, which includes patches of sandy soil especially in the south, is mostly anonymous rolling countryside which could lie anywhere between the Loire and the Gironde, the vines mingling with arable and pasture land.

In its total area – as opposed to the lands under vines – the Borderies[9] are by far the smallest of all the *crus*, a mere 13,440 hectares (52 square miles). The massive and very heterogenous Fins Bois are nearly thirty times the size, 354,200 hectares (1,367 square miles); the Bon Bois are even bigger, 386,600 hectares (about 1,500 square miles); and the Bois Ordinaires are smaller, 274,176 hectares (1,058 square miles). Historically the Bois were even more sub-divided, with the Bois Communs below even the Bois Ordinaires.

But today the legal definition differs from vinous reality. Vinous practice has followed the advice of Patrick Daniou, a leading geographer who in 1983 wrote that: 'it seems eminently desirable, in order to defend the quality of cognac's brandies, to take greater account of *terroir* in a new definition of the cognac appellation, which should be based on scientific criteria and on boundaries that should not necessarily be administrative ones.'[10] By 2000 the vineyard had shrunk from 110,331 hectares in 1976, to a stable figure of about 80,000 hectares. As a result there has been a dramatic change in the importance of the different *crus* resulting in an automatic improvement in overall quality.

The contrast is extraordinary. In 1976 the Fins Bois, Bons Bois and Bois Ordinaires accounted for three-fifths of the total, while in 2011 it was little more than a half. Over 25,000 hectares of vines had been uprooted, including over half of those in the Bons Bois while the Bois Ordinaires lost over three-quarters of their 4,300 hectares. This is not surprising. As a professional tasting guide pointed out in 1973, these brandies 'are coarse and hard and lack any distinction'. The remaining vines are virtually all on the islands of Ré and Oléron, producing cognacs entirely for the tourist trade. And, as Pierre Szersnovicz of Courvoisier remarks 'the salty, iodiney taste of brandies from near the sea makes them totally unsuitable for blending'.

By contrast a few more hectares have been found in the Grande Champagne and the figures are much the same in the Petite Champagne and the Borderies. On the two 'outer' regions growers are concentrating on the best, i.e. chalkiest sites, in the remaining vineyards, are taking more care with fermentation and distillation, and can compete with many vineyards in the Fins Bois. Over half the agricultural land in the Grande Champagne and the Borderies is now planted with vines, a figure which falls to 14 per cent in the Fins Bois. In other words Cognac, by and large, has retreated to the region which first made its brandies famous in the eighteenth century, a mere third of the area to which it had expanded in the pre-phylloxera glory years of the middle of the nineteenth century.

The reduction has been more than matched by the fall in the number of growers, down from 44,000 in 1976 to around 5,000 in 2011, the average size of their vineyards rising from 2.5 hectares in 1976 to fifteen today. The most striking contrast is between the Grande Champagne where three-quarters of the land holdings are of over 10 hectares, an average which goes down to a mere third in the Bois Ordinaires. There are only a handful

---

9 The name derives from the *bordes*, the *metairies*, smallholdings cultivated by sharecroppers who were tenants of the outside investors in the area in the late sixteenth century.
10 *Annales GREH*, 1983.

of growers with under a hectare of vines – what can be called a parcel of vines rather than a vineyard. Not surprisingly the smallholders tend to be old; there are 112 over-65s in the Bois Ordinaires, more than in the Grande Champagne – not including the eighty in the Ordinaires who did not give their ages who were likely to be old! Not surprisingly, in the rest of the region the increased size in the average holding has resulted in a far greater professionalism and an increase in quality in the vineyard, the still-room and the *chais*.

This trend has reinforced the concentration of the vines in a relatively compact, if irregular, rectangle (see page ix), its western limits extending south from Saint Jean d'Angély through Saintes to the Gironde estuary between Royan and Mortagne. To the east it runs from Saint Jean down to the estuary via Barbezieux. The heart of the region remains the Champagnes, Grande and Petite, a landscape unlike the Bois, resembling rather the Sussex Downs, albeit covered in vines and not pasture – indeed Warner Allen described the Champagnes as 'chalky downland' for they have the same mixture of gentle rolling hills and snug wooded valleys – together with the Borderies and the northern and eastern parts of the Fins Bois. The climate reinforces the distinction, for the Champagnes, the Borderies and the northern and eastern Fins Bois enjoy warmer summers than the rest of the region and the Champagnes suffer from fewer of the late summer rains that can ruin a harvest.

The comparison with the Sussex chalk is no accident: 'Cognac is a brandy from chalky soil' is the repeated theme of the standard work on the distillation of cognac.[11] The various formations were first defined by Coquand, the mid-nineteenth-century geologist who did the first scientific study ever undertaken of any wine growing region (before his time all of the chalky soils had been lumped together more generally as Maestrichtien). Coquand, a Charentais by birth, rode right through the vineyard taking samples of fossils – helped by the deep cuttings newly-dug for the railways. He defined the three geological eras, the Conacian of 86–88 million years ago and the slightly more recent Saintonian and Campanian. These three formations are especially rich in chalk, and they produce the best cognacs.

'Most important for the cognac industry,' writes Kyle Jarrard, 'Coquand was accompanied by an official taster whose role was to assess the quality of the eau de vie in any given vineyard... "it is very much worth noting" wrote Coquand in 1862, that "taster and geologist never once differed." '[12] Significantly, in the international language used by geologists the world over these types of soil are referred to by their Charentais names: Angoumois (from Angoulême), Coniacian (from Cognac) and Campanian (referring to the Champagne country of the Charente).

The cretaceous soils are found within the Grande Champagne in an irregular quadrilateral, bounded on the north by the Charente, to the west and south by the river Né and petering out towards Châteauneuf to the east. This 35,700 hectares (38 square miles) in the canton of Cognac, has been devoted almost exclusively to the grapes used for brandy for over 300 years.

These soils are composed of a special sort of chalk, the Campanian. Like all other chalky soils it was formed by the accumulation of small fossils, including one particular species found nowhere else, *Ostrea vesicularis*. In the words of the French Geological Survey, it is

---

11 René Lafon, Jean Lafon and Pierre Coquillaud, *Le Cognac sa distillation* (Paris, 1964).
12 In *Cognac* (NJ, USA, 2005).

'a monotonous alternation of greyish-white chalk, more or less marly and siliceous, soft and incorporating, especially in the middle of the area, faults made up of black pockets of silica and lumps of debased marcasite'. Marcasite is composed of crystallised iron pyrites, and this iron (also found across the Gironde in Pauillac) is important, but it is the sheer intensity of the chalkiness of the soil which is crucial – that and its physical qualities, its crumbliness, its friability.

But the Campanian emerges only on the crests of the gentle, rolling slopes of the Grande Champagne, for it is one of three layers of variously chalky soils which come to the surface in the area. The second best *terroir*, the Santonian, covers much of the Petite Champagne, the belt round the Grande Champagne. It is described as 'more solid, less chalky, but incorporating some of the crumbliness of the Campanian slopes, into which it merges by imperceptible degrees'. (One good test is the density of the presence of fossils of *Ostrea vesicularis*.)

The heart of the Grande Champagne, its backbone, is formed by the ridge between Ambleville and Lignière. But the colouring of the modern geological map is specifically designed to underline how blurred is the boundary between the Santonian and Campanian. As the modern geologists put it: 'The boundaries established by H. Coquand and H. Arnaud have been adhered to, although they are vague round Cognac itself where the visible features are much the same.' The town of Cognac itself is built on the appropriately named Coniacian chalk.

The only *cru* whose boundary is completely clear-cut is the Borderies with its very special mix of chalk and clay, the groies, dating geologically from the Jurassic era. Ever since a tectonic accident which left a geological mess in the Tertiary period some ten million years ago when the Charente was carving out its river-bed, the soil has become steadily more decalcified, but the process is still incomplete and the result is a patchwork of chalk which is breaking down and intermingling with the clay. The mixture produces a unique, and often under-rated, cognac. The best comes from Burie, a commune just north of Cognac itself, where nearly three-quarters of the land is planted with vines, more than anywhere else in the region. The Borderies are slightly cooler than the rest of the region, probably because of the clay in the soil, so the wine is usually a degree or so weaker and moreover the clay means that in hot summers the soil may dry up.

Inevitably, in an area the size of the Bois, the geology is much less well defined than it is in the Champagnes or the Borderies. Moreover most of the chalk is Kimmeridgien and Portlandien,[13] types rather less porous than that in the Champagnes. Even Professor Ravaz was rather vague, saying that the brandies of the Bois were 'produced on slopes formed by compacted chalk or by arable soils covered with sands and tertiary clays the first being better because of the chalk'. The finest pockets in the Fins Bois are the so-called Fins Bois de Jarnac, a slim belt of chalky slopes running to the north and east of the town. The eighteenth century maps of the vineyard show these vines as being part of the Champagne region and their brandies are still much sought after today. So are the equally superior brandies from a separate pocket of chalk, the Petite Champagne de Blanzac ten miles south of the river in the Fins Bois which are exploited by two enterprising firms, Leyrat and Léopold Gourmel.

---

13 They are named after Kimmeridge Bay and Portland, both on the Dorset coast in southern England.

There is also one curious pocket of virtually pure chalk on the east bank of the Gironde extending inland to Mirambeau and Gemozac, whose growers have long wanted re-classification from Fins Bois to Grande or at least Petite Champagne. By the river at Saint-Thomas-de-Conac (one of the many spellings of the name) the 'estuarial' Fins Bois can produce excellent long-lived brandies – as witness the quality of those from the Château de Beaulon. These prove the unfairness of the canard that they are iodiney because of the proximity of salt water – the water in this stretch of the estuary is not salty but fresh!

I have come to believe, however, that the distinction between different *terroirs* – and this applies to other wine regions – is due far more to the physical characteristics of the soil rather than its precise chemical composition. Hence the general suitability of chalk soils, not only in Cognac but also, for instance in Champagne and Jerez. Professor Ravaz himself turned his back on a purely geological explanation of cognac's qualities. As he said: 'The clayey, siliceous soils of the Borderies produce brandies of a higher quality than those of the dry groies or even some of the chalkier districts in the south-west of the Charente-Inférieure. For the geological make-up of the earth itself is not as important as Coquand makes out.'[14] Ravaz emphasised the combination of the chemical and physical constituents of the soil, with the physical predominant: 'the highest qualities are produced from chalky soil, where the chalk is soft and highly porous and where the sub-soil is composed of thick banks of similar chalk' (the topsoil is invariably only a few centimetres thick). In these soils, said Ravaz, 'the subsoil hoards rainwater, thanks to its sponginess and its considerable depth, and releases it slowly to the surface soil and to the vegetation. It is thus to a certain extent a regulator of the soil's moisture content, and so, in chalky soils, the vine is neither parched nor flooded.' As a result the roots of the vine can gain access to moisture in the driest of summers – even in the exceptionally hot and dry summers of 2003 and 2005 yields dropped only a little – and, crucially, chalky soils provide very little nutrient value, which helps the quality of the grapes. This description explains why the Borderies, relatively poor in chalk, produce such good brandies: the soil is friable and is thus physically, if not geologically, perfect.

The same factors apply in the Médoc on the other bank of the Gironde, where the thicker the gravel banks, the better the drainage and the steadier and more reliable the growth as the water seeps through to the roots in a sort of drip irrigation. The parallel extends to the importance of the lie of the land. A well-drained slope is obviously preferable to a flat stretch of river valley, liable to clogging. Obviously, too, north – and west – facing slopes are less highly prized. The sunlight is less strong, and in grey years, when the best southern slopes produce wines of a mere 7°, the northern slopes cannot even manage that.

The politicians and the administrators responsible for defining Cognac's *crus* could not afford Ravaz's fine distinctions and naturally followed Coquand's clearer definitions. Broadly speaking, the classification accords with that established by market forces before the geologists moved in, a pattern found in other regions, like Bordeaux.

There is no dispute about the validity of the distinction between the various categories; only the boundaries are in question. The first, and most obvious, is that because the boundaries

---

14 The former name for the Charente-Maritime.

were administrative the Grande Champagne includes the alluvia of the river bed – legally even the airport at Châteaubernard just south of Cognac is within the appellation. The vineyards begin on the slopes leading up to the little town of Genté on a strip of Santonian chalk that separates the alluvium from the Campanian. But it is the sleepy little town of Segonzac several miles south of the river which is the 'capital' of the Grande Champagne (not surprisingly, the only sizeable merchant located in the town is Frapin, which sells only cognacs from its estate in the heart of the Grande Champagne). The outer boundary, the further bank of the River Né towards Archiac, officially in the Petite Champagne, produces cognac arguably superior to some from parts of the Grande Champagne. But most of the blenders agree with Maurice Fillioux that the Grande Champagne should never produce bad brandy and that its boundaries are broadly correct. Francis Gay-Bellile, then of the Bureau Viticole, did not sound ridiculous when he affirmed that they are 95 per cent accurate.

No one disputes the borders of the Borderies, nor the quality of the brandies they produce, two-thirds of which used to be bought by Martell and Hennessy – though today, Martell's overstocking while it was owned by Seagram has allowed other firms, notably Courvoisier, to take a much increased share. As we saw, the vast region of the Fins Bois has become more clearly defined. None of the best and biggest firms buys Fins Bois from the west of Saintes, brandies they find too 'foxy' – with an unappetizing earthiness. Few reputable firms buy much brandy from the Bons Bois and serious firms concentrate their purchases in a narrow strip to the south around Chevanceaux and Brossac.

If the *terroirs* of the Cognac region vary wildly, the grape varieties used have only changed a couple of times in the past four centuries. When Cognac first made its name the region was largely planted with the Balzac grape, which had several characteristics found in today's favourites. It was highly productive; it was a Mediterranean variety and thus did not fully ripen as far north as the Charente and it was relatively late and thus not susceptible to the region's late spring frosts. Its major rival at the time was the Colombat or Colombard widely planted in Armagnac, now mostly used for making table wine. This reminded Ravaz of the Chenin Blanc grape used in Anjou, but Munier found that 'its wine is the most powerful and is indeed needed to provide backbone for those which lack this quality'. These were 'the fattest, that is to say, the most oily' grapes. Indeed, when Rémy Martin used the Colombard to make 'alembic brandy' in California they found that it produced cognacs that were rich and fruity but relatively short on the palate, though a young Colombard brandy from the chalky slopes of Les Hauts de Talmont, a few miles south of Royan is showing enough promise to be sold, eventually, as a single vintage.

In the nineteenth century the Balzac, and to a great extent the Colombard, were almost entirely replaced by the Folle or Folle Blanche. The Cognacais had already understood the importance of acidity in the wines they distilled. Folle Blanche had been planted before the Revolution and was also a great favourite of the Armagnacais. In the words of Professor Ravaz, its wine is 'so acid, so green, that it is something of a struggle to drink it'. Nevertheless, it is still planted round Nantes – by no coincidence a former brandy-producing region – under the name of Gros Plant and not surprisingly most of the wines are as acid as they come. However, it was the ideal grape for producing fine, aromatic, fragrant cognacs, and brandies made from it are still cherished – not least by me. Ravaz described how 'an old bottle of wine made from the Folle gives off a bouquet which can be detected from far off and which provides an adequate explanation for the perfume of brandies made from this variety. For it produces the softest brandies and the ones with the strongest and most lasting scent.'

But its fate was sealed by the phylloxera louse in the 1870s. When the variety was grafted on to American root stock it flourished so vigorously, its bunches were so tightly packed, that the grapes in the middle were liable to the dreaded grey rot (they are still beyond the reach of modern anti-rot sprays). Today even its supporters have to agree that the variety is still irregular, with a reduced harvest at least twice in every decade. Nevertheless, the Folle Blanche offers aromas which provide an additional roundness as well as innate florality during maturation. A good many over-productive hybrids were planted after the phylloxera, but the brandies they produced smelled foul. As a result since 1900 a single variety has been triumphant, and although other vines are permitted,[15] they now account for only a tiny percentage of Cognac's production – even though over the past few years some intrepid souls have planted some Folle Blanche.

The triumphant variety, covering over 95 per cent of the vineyard, is known in Cognac as the Ugni Blanc or the Saint-Emilion. It's an Italian variety which originated as the Trebbiano Toscano from the hills of the Emilia Romagna around Piacenza. It's a relatively neutral variety and much in demand in Italy as a base wine when blended with more aromatic varieties. The Italians also use it for brandy-making, but even in Italy it matures late, and in Cognac, at the very northern limit of its cultivation, it remains relatively green and acid and produces a different type of juice than when grown in Italy. Its other major advantage is that it starts budding late and so, like the Balzac, is less susceptible to the area's late spring frosts. Cognac's long, light but not hot summers ensure that there is a certain intensity in the juice. Since the grapes are not fully ripe when they are picked, it lacks even the little aroma and bouquet it develops when fully mature.

Until phylloxera, cultivation was higgledy-piggledy. Replanting was carried out either in rows or in blocks. In the last twenty years vineyards have been adapted for harvesting by machine and the vines have been trained far higher than previously. It is easy to see the result with the older, thicker trunks pruned right back, the newer trained up to 1.2– 1.5 metres (4–5 feet) high on trellises. Because the wines do not need to be more than adequate older vines are not important as they are in providing the concentration for fine wine, so the vines are dug up when they are a mere thirty-five or forty years old. The optimum age is between twenty and thirty years, for the younger vines tend to give too much juice which lacks concentration and thus the grapes lack flavour. To help the machines the space between the rows has been doubled to just over 2.8 metres (9 feet), and although the vines are planted more closely, there are still only 3,000 to each hectare, 1,000 fewer than under the old system. High vines help the plants adapt to climate change because in hot weather the grapes are sheltered from the sun.

---

15 Legally Colombard, Folle Blanche, Jurançon blanc, Meslier St François, Montils, Sémillon and Ugni Blanc can be planted. Folignan (a hybrid of Ugni Blanc and Folle Blanche) and Sélect can be used in only 10% of a blend.

Vines are pruned less severely than in Bordeaux, allowing for higher production of inevitably more acid wines because you don't need the 'phenolic maturity' which gives flavours for table wine. Nevertheless, the grapes mustn't be too green, they must have at least 8 per cent of alcohol. But too much manure must not be used and the vines must not be pruned too lightly to produce massive numbers of grapes, otherwise the balance will be disturbed, and the acid level will inevitably be reduced. Nevertheless the 'natural' yield now averages over 100 hectolitres for every hectare of vines, double the 1945 level and even then a fifth below the level recommended by viticulturists.

The Saint-Emilion matures so late that even the relatively unripe Cognac grapes used to be ready for picking only in mid-October – though harvest is now up to three weeks earlier than a couple of decades ago thanks to global warming. The only limit to the date of the harvest is the frost, generally expected in late October, which, in a bad year like 1980, can ruin the quality of the wine. Harvesting machines were a natural choice for the region because the Cognacais are not particularly interested in quality, but with early models the wines were rather 'green' for the very obvious reason that the machines were too violent and sucked in twigs and leaves as well as grapes. Opponents even alleged – incorrectly – that the hydraulic machinery was badly insulated and tended to leak tiny quantities of oil on to the grapes resulting in an oiliness which was inevitably exaggerated by distillation. But today the machines employ flayers which make the vines vibrate and don't maul the bunches of grapes. Oddly, they can now be too selective and thus reject the greener grapes that used to prove useful in providing the right amount of acidity in the blend. They are ideal for harvesting the Ugni Blanc which has a thin skin, making it susceptible to oxidation. And their speed means that they can come in handy when, as in 1989 and 2010 the alcohol

Harvesting – modern machines merely nudge the grapes

levels are rising fast and early – and of course they can also harvest at night when it's cooler.

Until the late 1980s there was a long tradition of treating wine as a mere raw material, the more productive the better – indeed in that sense cognac had never been a traditional wine-making region. Nevertheless, as Roger Cantagrel of the Station Viticole put it 'the wines have always been clean and coming from well-tended vines' – you see far fewer of the straggly patches found in other French wine-making regions. Moreover the nine-fold concentration of the inherent qualities of the wine in the distillation process reinforces the Cognacais' obsession with its purity and reliability.

In the past twenty years there has been a real revolution. 'We didn't worry about vinification' says Yann Fillioux, Maurice's nephew and successor, who is responsible for two out of every five bottles of cognac sold in the world, but 'now we realise every day that the quality of the wine is important.' As so often with such changes there were several factors involved, but the drive to improve cognac reflected the general tendency among French wine-makers to return to the vineyard to improve the final product. It was 1989, a year in which the summer heat extended into October which was the turning point. Hot years are not necessarily a bad thing, 1947 was a case in point, but in 1989 the wines were too strong – well over 11° and the fermentation was too quick. Many of the wines contained too much ethanol with the appley aromas it gives out. As a result of the problems Hennessy hired a specialist viticulturalist, Jean Pineau. He found that the Cognac region lacked what he calls any network of advice about wine-making and the type of technical high school that had proved invaluable in educating the children of growers in regions like Champagne and Burgundy. He analysed thousands of samples of the wines made by the firm's suppliers and persuaded them to install more modern pneumatic presses to ensure that the grapes

Cognac requires a lot of wine, and thus some big vats.

were not squeezed too hard so that the juice contained too much tannic material from the pips and skins. After 1989 yields were reduced, partly by changing pruning methods, while global warming increased the average strength of the wines. Indeed the combination of global warming and the technical advances in grape-growing and wine-making should ensure that unripe or rotting grapes are no longer used. For the experience also concentrated everyone's minds as to the importance of the grapes and as a result the major firms have now focused on this crucial factor in their – increasingly close – relations with the growers.

Even today the wine-making itself is pretty basic. The object is a quick alcoholic fermentation lasting around seven days. As Francis Gay-Bellile the former director of the Station Viticole says, it relies on nature: 'We adapt our wine-making techniques to the needs of the still.' For their aim, as he says, is to 'preserve the interesting elements in the juice'. The must is fermented in vats holding 100–200 hectolitres (2,000–4,000 gallons). Until recently these were made from concrete, but modern wine makers now prefer vats made from soft iron lined with epoxy resins or resins reinforced with glass fibre.

The wine-makers used to rely on native yeasts, but now the Charentais use special yeasts, some from neighbouring regions, approved by the official Station Viticole. Some distillers like Frapin ensure that the temperature of the juice is raised to 16°–17°, a level at which fermentation is almost sure to begin, the temperature is then lowered but rises during the few days the wine is fermenting. The object is to produce wine without the secondary characteristics precious to makers of table wines, but which will be far less susceptible to oxygenation in the short period before it is distilled. At the elevated temperature of 20–25°C (68–77°F) the juice ferments for an average of five days, for the wine has to be free of faults. As one distiller put it 'if you put perfect wines into the still

Until recently presses were pretty labour-intensive.

the distiller can concentrate his efforts on capturing its aromatic components.' The longer a wine remains undistilled the more of its valuable aromatic esters it loses. So distillers have to conserve more of the têtes if they distil too late, which in effect means after the end of February following the harvest, a month before the legal limit of 31st March.

The wines used for distillation are obviously undrinkably acid. They are also very weak, between 8° and 10.5°, for one very basic reason: the weaker the wine, the greater the degree of concentration involved in producing a freshly distilled cognac of around 70°. When the Saint-Emilion is fully ripe its wine will reach 10°–11°. A wine of 10° would be concentrated only seven times; one of 8° (the lower limit of practical distillation) will be concentrated nine times, so it will be infinitely more aromatic. The ideal strength is between 8.5° and 9.5° resulting in wines which provide the right balance of qualities – Paultes tries not to buy grapes with over 9.5 per cent of potential alcohol. In theory wine as weak as 3° or 4° could be turned into acceptable brandy. But the lower the strength, the less likely the grapes are to be wholly sound or even half-ripe. Intriguingly, the very considerable variations in the strength of the wine are not necessarily reflected in the quality of the final product. While the average between decades can vary between 8.3 per cent and 9.1 per cent what matters is the 'greenness' that can be caused by grapes below 8 per cent.

Nevertheless, the wine used for distillation by the Charentais has several advantages. It is so acid it keeps well, does not suffer from bacterial problems and lacks the pectins which can make wine rather cloudy. The need for purity includes a ban on *chaptalisation*[16] – in Charente-Maritime a certificate of non-sugaring must be provided. White wines being prepared for drinking are invariably dosed with a little sulphur to prevent oxidation and deter bacteria. It is simply impossible to use sulphur dioxide (SO2) when making wine for distillation. Even without SO2 the yeasts produce a certain quantity of aldehydes. Encouraged by SO2 they produce up to twenty times as much. The compound formed by the SO2 and the aldehydes decomposes when heated in the still, and the resulting mixture of aldehyde and alcohol produces acetal, giving off a smell reminiscent of hospital corridors.

Before the wine can be distilled it should undergo malolactic fermentation, known in France simply as *le malo*, when the malic acid in the wine is transformed into the softer lactic acid. Fortunately when wines are sufficiently acidic, are free from sulphur and have not been racked, the lactic acids develop very quickly. In most wines this sort of viticultural puberty does not take place until the spring following the fermentation, too late for the Cognacais, who have to finish distillation before warm weather stimulates fresh fermentation. You can distil pre-malo wines, but you must not distil them in mid-maling, as the resulting brandies give off a rather foetid smell.

The date of distillation can vary. In a really hot year like 2003 some distillers waited for weeks to distil the strong, concentrated wines, while they did the same in 2004 to try and strengthen the rather watery wines of the year. But by early December, a mere six weeks after the grapes have been picked, most of the wines are ready for distillation, the single most crucial step in the whole process of making cognac. And the shorter the time the wine is stored the better. As Charles Walter Berry put it: 'an early distilled brandy is the best.'

---

16 Adding sugar during fermentation to increase the strength of the wine.

THE VINTAGE QUESTION

In theory there should be a considerable distinction between different vintages in Cognac, just as there are in Bordeaux. Moreover, the conditions which provide for a lousy year in Bordeaux, when the grapes are acidic and unripe, should prove ideal for the producers of Cognac, unless, of course, they're below 8 per cent in which case, in theory, they'll not be ripe enough. Vice versa, the rich ripe grapes which make fine wine in good years for wine should result in flabby, overly alcoholic brandies. In theory, then, there should be a negative correlation between

Bernard Hine: the tenth generation!

cognac and Bordeaux since the Bordelais are looking for grapes that are not overly acid, a quality greatly prized by the Cognacais. But there isn't. One distinguished distiller believes that 'the best years in Bordeaux tend to be the best in Cognac,' and the general consensus appears to be that in virtually any year a little great brandy can be produced while in others it is difficult to produce a bad one. Bernard Hine, whose firm offers a range of single vintages, believes that you can make a vintage cognac in any normal year. In any case, because so few single-vintage cognacs are available for tasting it is impossible to give the sort of yearly guide which is normal with wines. Instead, as with the choice of any cognac, you have to rely on the reputation of the firm involved.

Even so a handful of – relatively – recent vintages stand out. In 1953 Hine produced one of the greatest cognacs of all time, while the 1964 was reckoned by some as the best of the decade. The late Maurice Fillioux felt that the 1975 was 'all I love about cognac,' while the 1988's provided a 'superb balance between fruit and acidity'. The year 1976 was very hot with too much rain at harvest time, resulting in flat cognacs. Then again, in 1980, late cold resulted in thin and flat cognacs; 1984 was reckoned as poor and 1987's lacked any real depth or intensity, as did 1994's. In contrast, 2002 was an excellent year with complex brandies.

As Eric Forget of Hine points out, both regions are looking for 'balance, acidity and quality,' and because harvests start on average three weeks later than in the Médoc, Cognac has a second chance. It helps that the weather in Cognac is sunnier through the summer and less rainy during the crucial weeks in September. For instance, 1972 was a lousy year in Bordeaux because the weather had been cold and rainy, but there was a warm 'after-season' which led to some very good cognacs and today climate change means that the grapes are harvested up to six weeks earlier than they were twenty years ago.

With a greater concentration on the wine has come a much closer look at the nature of each vintage – particularly as single-vintage cognacs are now becoming increasingly fashionable. The characteristics of each vintage depend on the weather in the month before the harvest. Distillers are looking for the right alcoholic content and above all balance, yet in 1965, a lousy year when the average strength was a mere 6.76° Rémy Martin, for instance, made a lovely vintage. At the other extreme it's just as bad if the grapes are too ripe. They were up to 10.94° in 1989 (allegedly too strong, but the same house offered an excellent single vintage) and 11° in 1955 (a classic Hine year).

Anne Cochet

2

DISTILLATION: THE HEART OF THE MATTER

Wine is the raw material of cognac. Of course it has to be clean and free from any impurities that would inevitably be multiplied in the distillation process but it accounts for perhaps only a quarter of the quality of the final product. Even the newly distilled brandy is merely an intermediate product in the production of cognac but nevertheless, the still has transformed the wine not into any ordinary spirit but into one capable of becoming cognac. 'It is one thing to manufacture alcohol,' wrote Professor Méjane, 'it is quite another to create a high-grade brandy…with the same raw materials, brandies produced in batches are greatly superior to those produced in continuous stills.'[17] This vital improvement in quality justifies all the inconveniences and increased costs resulting from double distillation: increased energy consumption, the need for the distiller's skills, and the reduced, limited, discontinuous flow of spirit from the still.

For even the fiery liquids trickling from Cognac's stills have real, and different, characteristics, some are fuller than others, some obviously have more depth, more potential. By contrast some are showing a hint of mustiness, or rawness, or of smokiness, due to faults in the wine or the distillation process. There is no doubt that the average quality, especially at the basic VS level, has improved over the past thirty years, which is not to say that cognacs are as characterful as they were when they were made in much smaller stills – even though the distinctive qualities found in earlier years were often due to faults in the brandy.

Distillation is a simple enough process, based on the fact that alcohol vaporises at a lower temperature than water. So when a fermented liquor (wine, or the sort of 'mashes' used to produce malt whisky) is heated, the alcohol vaporises and the qualities – or faults – of the wine or other raw materials are concentrated. It is then trapped in a pipe leading

17 *Annales de technologie agricole* (1975).

from the top of the still and cooled. Of course, there are an infinite number of practical factors involved: the shape and size of the vessel, the metal from which it should be constructed, the type and quality of the liquor to be distilled, the shape of the pipe conducting the spirit to the cooler, the moment at which the liquor is acceptable – and the cut-off point after which it is either too weak or too full of impurities (or both). But all these problems are matters of trial and error, and most had been solved by the end of the seventeenth century. Then as now the wines underwent a first distillation into a *brouillis* a half-strength spirit, before the second (*la bonne chauffe*) produced the real stuff. It has always been a matter of pride to the Cognacais that their brandies are produced by a double distillation process. The only other spirits traditionally made in this way are the Calvados of the Pays d'Auge in Normandy and Scotland's malt whiskies. Other, lesser spirits (like most Calvados or Armagnac) are made from a single *chauffe*.

Even the distillation process in Cognac is unlike that used elsewhere. Ordinary distillation involves the separation of the volatile elements in the original liquid according to their boiling points, whereas in *distillation à la Charentaise* the alcoholic vapours simply sweep through the distillation apparatus. In an attempt to ban more efficient but less satisfactory stills, a local author writing at the end of the nineteenth century, compared 'the cooking of brandy to that of pot-au-feu. Who does not prefer a nourishing home-made broth to that made in a restaurant, even though it has been made by steam?'[18] Michel Caumeil, the former research director of Hennessy put it even more simply: 'The production of cognac is simply controlled evaporation.'[19] The process is not completely scientific but is an art, a balancing act between the desire to preserve the character provided by the grapes with the need to eliminate undesirable elements by 'rectification', distilling the spirit to a higher strength. It is at this point that the crucial element of personal judgement, the 'distiller's skills' referred to by Professor Méjane, enter into the equation. For distillation is a complex process involving a number of chemical reactions such as esterification and hydrolysis.

The still has to heat the wines, trap the alcoholic vapours and then cool them. In theory this is simple enough. But, as with the wine-making, every element in the process has to be perfect: the heat has to be about 1,600°C – a higher temperature is favourable only for less volatile components: the heat must be applied uniformly to all the liquid in the container; only the desirable vapours must be extracted; they must flow smoothly; and the cooling process, like the heating, must be gradual and regular. Yet by the mid-seventeenth century the locals, with a certain amount of help from the Dutch, had found solutions, most still valid today, to all these problems.

In terms of size, the apparatus used in Munier's day was a mere pilot plant for the much bigger stills employed today which provide much more standardised, less erratic brandies. Then – and indeed, right through the eighteenth and nineteenth centuries when cognac was distilled by thousands of growers – the *cucurbite* was relatively tiny, with an internal diameter of a mere 53 cm and a height of only 75 cm. The size varied, but overall

---

18 Quoted in: A. Baudoin, *Les eaux-de-vie et la fabrication du Cognac* (1983).
19 *Pour la science* (December 1983).

it held only around 3 hectolitres, which remained the norm until surprisingly recently. After phylloxera the average capacity rose to between 10 and 15 hectolitres, but as late as 1974 it was a mere 16 hectolitres. Indeed it was only with the arrival of gas that capacity – among the *bouilleurs de cru* anyway – went up to 25 hectolitres. Everything else was in proportion: the furnace was 0.9 metres in diameter; the *bec* was only 0.5 metres long; the *serpentin* a mere one metre tall and, according to Munier, the whole apparatus could be contained in a 'small one-storey building, consisting of a single room about three by four metres' – few peasant distillers could have afforded a larger building!

Modern technology has changed all that. The stills used for the *première chauffe* can hold up to 140 hectolitres though legally they can only be filled with 120 hectolitres of wine. By contrast those used for the second *chauffe* are legally limited to a maximum of 30 hectolitres and can be filled only with 25 hectolitres of liquid. If they are any bigger, the brandy they produce cannot be called by any of the sous-appellations (just plain cognac). For the balance has to be preserved: the bigger the still, the more neutral the spirit. In any case there is an absolute limit to size: above a certain point too little of the wine or brouillis is in actual contact with the alembic.

The stove heating the wine has always been crucial. Now, as in Munier's day, it is made of thick masonry, with a large door occupying a third of the front, strong enough to resist the heat of the furnace. Behind it the chimney was of brick, as was the lining of the furnace. Considerable skill was required to ensure that the heat was absolutely steady. In Munier's words: 'Too high a flame upsets everything; with the strong spirit water it carries off acids and oils, which do not have time to mix and which alter the taste of the brandy; too low a fire provides a light, pleasant brandy but one that is too strong, with too burning a taste; it removes neither enough water nor all the bitterness.' Even today if the flame is too high, it over-heats the copper, and the resulting brandy is *rimé* (burned).

For a *bouilleur de cru* distilling his own wine the fuel was by far the biggest cash cost he incurred – two-thirds of a cubic metre (over twenty cubic feet) of wood or 100 kilograms of coal were required to produce a hectolitre of cognac. Until the nineteenth century wood from the Bois or from the forests to the east provided the normal fuel. But wood burns quickly, so the furnace had to be refilled every two or three hours during a distillation season that lasted, day and night, for up to three months. This imposed a colossal strain: James Long recounts how when the distiller wanted a nap he would 'hang a tin on the swan's neck suspended on the end of a piece of string stuck there with wax; so that when the wax melted the tin would fall and wake him up!'[20] Munier insisted that the vat house (*brûlerie*) had to be separate from any other building to reduce the danger of fire, for he had seen 'distillers grown sleepy and careless who had, through sheer clumsiness, lit with their candles the spirit that came out of the serpent'; the fire spread up the 'stream of spirit' and could be stopped only by blocking the outlet at the bottom of the *serpentin* with a wet rag. A nineteenth-century visitor, Henry Vizetelly, was only half-joking when he wrote: 'Various little precautions have to be observed; among others, not to set the premises on fire.'

---

20 *The Century Companion to Cognac and Other Brandies* (London, 1983).

During the nineteenth century wood was gradually replaced by coal, which required less frequent attention, although this meant rebuilding the furnaces to provide increased draught. Fuel oil was tried but proved difficult to insulate from the still. Fortunately, the natural gas discovered at Lacq in the south-west of France in the early 1950s has proved an ideal fuel – reliable, regular and requiring no attention. The change-over to gas was relatively quick for so conservative a community, though it took over twenty years for the infrastructure of pipes and tanks of propane or butane to be fitted to the region's thousands of scattered stills. The gas is adjusted to heat the liquid at the same speed as wood and has many advantages, notably that it provides more regularity – with wood even the strength and direction of the wind mattered because of the change in draught involved. An even more modern heating method, electricity, is strictly forbidden, indeed the alembic has, legally, to be heated by a naked flame. Even today a few traditional distillers still use ash wood which burns slowly when it's newly cut and still green and thus helps to heat the alembic slowly. The increase in the size of stills and the change to gas from coal or wood has probably increased the speed of the process and thus led to the production of less concentrated cognacs.

Distillation needs less heat, and thus less fuel, if some of the heat dissipated in the cooling process is transferred to the wine through a heat exchanger. So during the nineteenth century the idea of heating the wine by using a *chauffe-vin* gradually caught on. The pipe containing the wine was simply diverted through the barrel-shaped cooling chamber. But conservatives like Martell still do not employ a *chauffe-vin*; they are afraid that the more complicated refrigeration chamber could not be properly cleaned, that the pipes would be blocked and the incoming wines over-heated. Supporters of the *chauffe-vin* say that it is simply a mechanical process designed to save heat, but even they admit that it can be dangerous if the wine is heated above 40–45°. The *chauffe-vin* can then cause oxidation, so it is often used only for a few hours during a *chauffe* (usually the last few).

The wine can, of course, be distilled with or without its lees. To outsiders it is surprising that many producers do not utilise at least part of the lees, for they are now forming an increasingly important weapon on the part of wine-makers in their efforts to extract the qualities directly linked to those of a specific *terroir*, especially for brandies destined to spend a relatively long time in cask. This reluctance was often due to the Cognacais' continuing lack of interest in the qualities of the wine. Nevertheless, using the lees is a complex business, for only now are researchers gradually separating the two different types of lees, those from the grapes, their skins and twigs; and the relics of the yeasts. Moreover, allowing too heavy a bed of lees can upset the balance of the cognac. They also need protecting from the air before the wines are distilled and cannot safely be used late in the distilling season, i.e. once the external temperature has risen much above 10°C. Moreover they can stick to the wall of the alembic. And, as one distiller pointed out, using the lees 'means that you need time for the brandies to mature and provide their additional complexity'.

As usual the major firms differ in their approaches. In the early 1950s Rémy separated itself from the other producers by using the lees to produce eaux de vie which were rich and fruity and could cope more easily with the wood, giving them greater fullness and richness. 'The 6,000° heat of the fire cooks the lees and infuses the cognac with their aroma,' Robert Leauté told me. The yeast lees contain a number of esters, including three fatty acids, which turn out to be absolutely critical in giving the cognac its much prized *rancio* quality when it is in cask. For its part Courvoisier 'keeps the lees only when the grapes are clean and free from rot' and uses them only when producing brandies that are strongly structured. Hennessy is pragmatic, insisting on the need for pure wines – an attitude inherited from a production director in the 1960s who disliked the idea. At the other extreme from Rémy, Martell has always set its face against the practice in its efforts to produce purer cognacs. But it is noticeable that virtually all the producers in the Grande Champagne I have come across distil on at least some of the lees, if only because they are producing brandies destined to mature long enough to absorb the resulting richness.

Distillers start work as soon as the wine has completed its fermentation in late November or early December. They are legally permitted to continue distilling until 31st March but try to finish before the end of February to ensure that the wine does not oxidise before an early warm spell awakens the dormant wines. They work day and night, for distillation is a long process, with the first *chauffe* taking eight or nine hours and the second up to fourteen hours for distillers anxious to extract the maximum grapiness from the wines. The first distillation produces a *brouillis* of between 26 and 32 per cent alcohol, over three times the strength of the wine. The first vapours to emerge are much stronger, about 55°, and are removed because they are bound to contain impurities already in the system. At the other end of the cycle the flow is cut off when the hydrometer below the *serpentin* shows that the spirit contains less than 5 per cent alcohol – the instrument serves as a check point not only for the strength but also for the temperature of the cognac. Because the *première chauffe* produces what is purely an intermediate product and one, moreover which is difficult even for an experienced distiller to taste, outsiders assume that it is less important than the second *chauffe*. Precisely the opposite is true: virtually all the chemical reactions that provide the cognac with its final quality take place during the first, not the second, *chauffe*. The professionals all agree that it does 60 per cent of the work and that the *bonne chauffe* merely concentrates the cognac still further.

The stills used for the *première chauffe* are usually bigger, but there is inevitably a short time during which enough *brouillis* is being produced to load up a still for the second, *la bonne chauffe*. Too long a gap can have unfortunate effects. Between 1973 and 1975 there were three enormous crops and not enough vats to hold all the wine, so a great deal was reduced through an early *première chauffe*, and there was some oxidation during storage.

La bonne chauffe, is the glamorous one. But the yield is minimal: the 25 hectolitres provides only 6.8 litres of spirit at Hennessy and 7.2 at Martell – though up to six more hectolitres can be redistilled. 'It simply selects and separates; it is not creative' says Jacques Rouvière, formerly of Bisquit Dubouché. As with the first *chauffe*, a small percentage of the 'heads' the *tête*, never much more than 2 per cent of overproof spirit, is drawn off before the brandy is allowed to flow into the *bassiot*. The point at which the *tête* is cut is not crucial. As Gay-Bellile points out: 'The first 0.5 per cent is used merely to clean out the *serpentin*, which is full of diluted wash, for the *têtes* are eliminated not just because of their strength but also because they are "trouble" – cloudy. After that it doesn't matter too much. There is some difference depending on whether you start allowing the spirit from *la bonne chauffe* through after one or two degrees, but since the *tête* goes back into the next load of *brouillis*, the effect is minimal.' Recently, sophisticated distillers like Olivier Paultes have ensured that the stronger wines resulting from global warning have not affected the quality of the cognac by, for instance, cutting off more of the *têtes*.

By contrast, the point at which the flow is diverted after the roughly 40 per cent of *coeur* has been extracted and the *secondes* are put on one side is a matter of considerable skill. The *bonne chauffe* starts flowing at about 78 per cent alcohol, and the legal maximum for the final spirit is 72 per cent alcohol, but below that point the break is a matter of subjective judgement – though the average is about 58–60 per cent, the crucial point being not the exact strength but the excess of fattiness, of liquorice or other impurities so they can go as low as 52 per cent. The basic criterion is simple enough: the higher the degree of the final spirit, the more neutral and rectified it will be; the lower the strength of the last drops allowed through, the more essential aromas they will contain but the greater the danger of including noxious ingredients. But many of the aromatic compounds liable to be excluded are essential in producing rich cognacs, for they include 'congeners', a word covering all the impurities found in any spirit not distilled to 100 per cent, i.e. rectified with everything else eliminated.

There are literally hundreds of them, including aldehydes, polyphenols and more or less aromatic esters but there is no correlation between their quantity and their importance. Some, often present in tiny proportions, should be cherished, some eliminated, while others are of no importance to the quality of the final spirit. Nevertheless, the need for many of them can be exaggerated. In the early 1980s an international firm specialising in the creation of artificial substitutes for natural tastes concocted an ersatz cognac and smuggled it into one of the routine tastings conducted by the BNIC. It was duly approved. By no means outstanding, said the tasters, but perfectly acceptable. Nevertheless, an element of mystery remains. Michel Caumeil of Hennessy said simply: 'We know how a man is made, but not cognac.' Inevitably, however, cognac is less rich in congeners and other appetising – albeit hangover-inducing – ingredients than Armagnac which is distilled to a far lower strength, often barely more than 52 per cent alcohol.

Using a high proportion of the *têtes*, and thus allowing more neutral spirit, can be a useful precaution in a bad year when the solids may turn out to be particularly nasty. In a good year you can afford to let through more of the nutrients. Even in a good year Martell deliberately cuts both *têtes* and *secondes* early as a matter of style, aiming to produce a dry, clear-cut, relatively neutral brandy that will absorb character from the wood in which it will be housed for so long. At the other extreme was Jacques Rouvière of Bisquit, who tried to extract as many of the secondary elements as possible. The decision is a delicate one: 'Even half a degree makes a difference' he said. Some distillers believe that it is essential not to cut too many of the *têtes* in the Grande Champagne, since you want to include as much of the rich raw material in the wine as possible.

But there is more than one decision to make before the brandies are ready. If the discarded *secondes* are mixed with the wine it is distilled four times and so is more rectified, loses more of the grapes' initial contribution and strengthens the raw material used in the *première chauffe* from 9 to 11 per cent, so the *brouillis* comes out at around 30 per cent. This is useful if, like Martell, you are looking for a relatively neutral result, for some of the wine will be distilled four times. (It is also useful if you are using grapes that are less ripe than usual and therefore low in alcohol.) If the *secondes* are mixed with the *brouillis* then you get a greater depth of aroma, with the brandies extracting the maximum benefit from the original grapes.

For two hundred years the end result has been much the same. In the words of Jean Demachy: 'The liquor flows into the receptacle forming a thread, which thickens imperceptibly; and when this thread is roughly the width of a medium-thick pen, the distillation process is well established.'[21] Even at the outset the brandy has an oiliness, a richness, a degree of grapey concentration that sets it apart from lesser spirits. One distiller said simply: 'it's the aroma of the vine in flower'. The newly-distilled brandy is now ready for the years in oak which will transform it into cognac.

THE STILL – THE SAME AS EVER

The first detailed picture we have of an *alembic charentais*, dating from 1710, would be instantly recognisable to a distiller today. So indeed would that written by Etienne Munier, a well-known engineer whose description, written half a century later, remains our basic source of information about cognac in the later eighteenth century.[22] The still itself, the alembic or *chaudière à eau de vie* (literally a 'spirit boiler'), is surmounted by a smaller *chapiteau* – literally, a circus tent, the 'big top' – to trap the vapours, which are then led down a *bec* (beak) to a cooling coil. The alembic is still housed in a massive square, brick-built oven containing an open fire for, legally, cognac has to be heated from outside whereas most malt whisky is now heated internally through a system of steam-heated pipes in the vat. Only the dimensions of the alembic – and the fuel employed – have changed.

*Hennessy's Le Peu distillery.
Not picturesque, but efficient.*

Then, as now, the whole apparatus was constructed of 'several pieces of red beaten copper, fitted together with copper nails'. Copper is an ideal material for the purpose,[23]

---

21 Jean Demachy, *L'Art du distillateur des eaux-forts* (Paris, 1773).
22 *Essai sur l'Angoumois à la fin de l'Ancien Régime.*
23 Recently it has become so valuable that there's been at least one case of someone stealing bits of a still.

though the copper used today is special, very pure (electrolysed) and polished to smooth out the pores in the metal. Physically it is malleable, easy to work, resists any corrosion resulting from the fire, is impervious to most acids and a good conductor of heat. But copper also has a chemical role to play. It fixes the fatty acids in the wine, as well as any of the sulphurous products in the vapours that would harm the quality of the cognac. Copper reacts with undesirable compounds especially those which are sulphur-related and eliminates most of the fatty acids that would 'diminish' the cognac. Experiments using alternative materials, like steel and glass, were conducted in the early twentieth century. They merely confirmed how ideal copper was for the purpose.

The shape of the apparatus has not changed either. The *cucurbite*, the vat in which the wine is heated, has always been onion-shaped, *un cone tronqué* (a truncated cone). This provides an expansion chamber in which the fumes released by heating can swirl like those in a tornado. They sweep upwards into the *chapiteau*. This is also rounded, the combination resembling an old-fashioned cottage loaf sculpted in gleaming copper. In Munier's day it varied in shape, although it always broadened above the neck, which captures the alcoholic vapour rising from the *cucurbite*. The *chapiteau* prevents the froth from spilling over to the condenser and allows the less volatile elements in the vapour to fall back into the *chaudière*, and thus guarantees the quality of the spirit.

The vapours then trickle down the *bec* or, as it was called locally in Munier's time, the *queue* (tail), which is effectively an extension of the *chapiteau*. Then as now the individual components were not merely nailed together but 'strongly soldered with a compound of tin and zinc', which 'helped to ensure that [the bec] was not blown off by the expansion of the vapours during distillation'. This insistence on the construction of the apparatus was not accidental, for every element had to be gas-tight. Observers of Munier's day thought that his solution resembled a Moor's head (*tête de Maure*). To modern eyes it resembles, rather, a bullet-headed cartoon animal with a long sharp nose. Earlier in the century Claude Masse had suggested bending the pipe, and Munier went further towards the modern idea, the elegantly shaped *col de cygne* (swan's neck) which provides an infinitely smoother flow path for the new spirit than the earlier, more angular designs. It is not surprising that the distillers of Munier's time found the flow problem 'delicate', as some unwanted *mousse* (froth) seeped into the *serpentin*. With the older shape, as Bruno Sepulchre notes: 'You got very personalised brandies. The evolution of the present olive or onion shape of the *chapiteau* also reflects the evolution towards brandies that taste more neutral and standardised because they are rectified by the increased height of the *col de cygne*.'[24]

To correct this problem the biggest *chapiteaux* were only about one-tenth the size of the still itself, indeed if it is any bigger, the vapour gets too strong, too rectified while care was taken that the 'swan's neck' did not arch upwards too much. Nevertheless, the *chapiteaux* used in peripheral regions still capitalise on this point: they are larger in order to block off some of their undesirable *goûts de terroir*. Cognac is a conservative

---

24 *Le Livre de Cognac* (Paris, 1983).

place: it was not until well into the twentieth century that the *col de cygne* triumphed over the much more angular *tête de Maure*. The distillation apparatus was completed by the cooling coil, described by Munier as 'the *serpentin*, which forms five circles in a slope of a metre...submerged into a barrel called the pipe...the spirit flows from the *serpentin* into a circular double-bottomed (*foncé de deux bouts*) tub; it is called a *bassiot*. The *serpentin*...condenses the vapours and cools the vapours before filtration.'

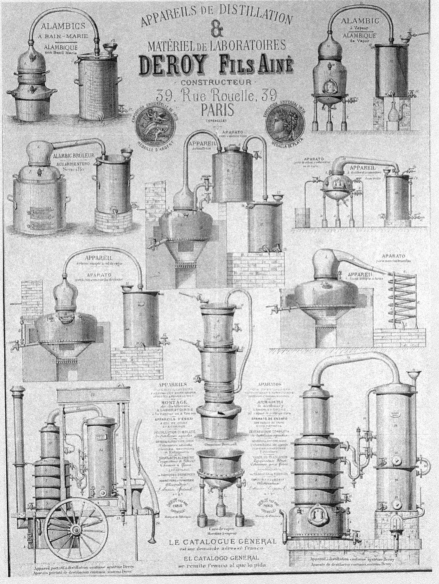

The story of distillation in a single sketch

Anne Cochet

3

BRANDY + AGE + OAK = COGNAC

The thin trickle emerging from the *alembic charentais* is not yet cognac. It needs years of maturation in oak casks. These have always been used by the Cognacais for maturing and storing their brandies and over the centuries distillers and drinkers alike have increasingly appreciated the importance of the role played by the wood. The oak and the spirit react, both physically and chemically. With greater understanding of the complexity of the ageing of cognac has come an enhanced capacity for blenders in different firms to define their house styles more accurately. *Quercus pedunculata*, the common oak, was chosen for casks, originally for its physical properties. In the words of Francis Gay-Bellile, these included:

its strength; elevated density of texture, which increases its strength; its hardness, which protects it from shocks and mechanical tension; its suppleness, which allows the curved lines of the cask to be formed by bending; its water-tightness, which prevents the liquid from leaking; its lack of permeability, which prevents the spirit from being diluted by the humidity in the atmosphere; and its light colouring.

The French are lucky: theirs is still a very wooded country, and oak occupies one-third of all their woodland. Even today *tonnelleries* (coopers) use less than a tenth of all the oak sawn in France. Originally the Dutch imported their own casks made from wood from the Baltic States ('Dantzig oak') but the Cognacais soon found that they could use oak from their nearby forests for both casks and fuel for the stills. Only two types of oak, both French, have ever proved suitable for ageing cognac – the Troncais (sessile) and the Limousin (pedunculata). Even today no foreign wood can furnish the unique combination of physical and chemical qualities required to turn raw-brandy-from-the-Cognac-region into cognac.

LIMOUSIN AND TRONCAIS

The Cognacais use two very different types of wood, the Troncais and the Limousin. The Limousin forests conform to the British idea of oak woods: the trees are widely scattered, thick and sturdy. With their sprawling branches, rough bark and long acorns they form a fifth of all French forests including major growths in the hills to the east of Angoulême – the name derives from the same root as Limoges, the city north east of Angoulême.

The wood is appropriately tough. In his book *The Cooper* Jean Taransaud explained that:

> The oak from the Limousin is a rough, heavy, hard and sinewy wood, with big fat grain up to an inch in size. It is difficult to work and more porous than oak from the Troncais, but it is renowned for its tannic qualities, and if its best recommendation to the merchant is its rate of evaporation, none the less it provides a much appreciated tannin for taming the harshness of cognac.

The first Cognacais to discover the forest of Troncais, until recently the only rival to Limousin wood, was a member of the Martell family. By the 1840s, according to letters preserved in the firm's archives, it was already a regular source of wood. He found it was better-suited to the Martell style than that from the Limousin and was already used by wine-makers on the Loire (of which the river Allier is a tributary) – even though it is more difficult to treat because it is harder. Troncais trees, with their relatively smooth bark, are taller and older as they take longer to mature and come from a man-made forest first planted in the middle of the seventeenth century when the great French statesmen, Colbert, reckoned that the only way to combat the over-mighty warships of Holland and England with their 'Hearts of Oak' was for France to grow its own. These trees were not ready to provide oak until after the Revolution.

The forest is in the Bourbonnais, the very heart of France between Montluçon and Moulins, extending north towards Nevers and east towards Burgundy (Ravaz calls it 'wood from Burgundy'). The forest itself is a major tourist attraction, awarded two stars by the editors of the *Michelin Guide*. The trees are more crowded, and therefore taller and slimmer, than those grown in the Limousin, and thus unfamiliar to British eyes accustomed to naturally grown oaks. Today a great deal of wood from other forests is labelled 'Troncais' for it is now recognised as a type of wood rather than a geographical description. When Jean-Marc Olivier of Courvoisier went looking for *grains fins* in other forests he found them, notably in the Jupilles forest south of Le Mans, which was planted at the same time as the Troncais itself. (There are a number of forests providing wood with fine grain along the Loire – forests which have been carefully tended since before 1789 and which therefore have trees more than two hundred years old.)

The wood from Troncais-type forests is darker than that of its rival, copper-coloured where that from the Limousin is a lighter yellow. In the words of Jean Taransaud, 'Mature clumps of trees provide an oak which grows thin and straight. The wood from it has a delicate and soft grain which is easy to work. It is particularly impervious to alcohol, very unporous. It has an excellent tannin, soft and slightly sweet, which permeates the cognac only slowly.' The Troncais is not only tighter-grained than the Limousin, it also contains less tannin and more lignin than wood from its rival and so imparts a less woody flavour to the cognacs. So Limousin is not entirely suitable for the cheaper cognacs which are going to spend only a few years in wood; they are liable to absorb too much tannin and to become too woody. In the long run Limousin is more suitable for the same reason: it has so much tannin to impart that the cognac still has reserves to draw on after a decade or more in the wood.

Seventy per cent of the wood is cellulose, some of which is chemically inert. It is important mainly for the 'backbone', the mechanical strength, it gives the wood, although the spirit does absorb some of the sugars in the hemi-cellulose as the molecules shrink during the ageing process. But more important than either is the lignin, which forms about 23 per cent of the oak and hence has a much more important influence on the maturation process than the better-known tannins which form less than five per cent of the chemical make-up of the wood.

Already in 1743 the ever regulation-minded French administration had laid down rules for producing casks in the whole of the Saintonge. The trees used for Cognac's casks have to be at least fifty years old – most of them are centenarians. Moreover the process is very wasteful, using a mere tenth of the whole tree. Only the section of the trunk from just above the roots to the lowest branches can be used to ensure that the planks and their grain are straight and free from knots and faults. But not all even of this limited proportion is suitable: the heart itself is too knotty while the sappy wood under the bark is too rich in soluble organic essences which would pollute the brandy. The drying, too, is special. The staves are cut and then piled up in stacks in the open air. The trunks dry naturally and slowly at the rate of a year for every centimetre of thickness. Most of the planks are 5–6 centimetres thick, so reputable cooperages tend to dry their oak for considerably longer than the statutory minimum of three years – most of them use planks dried for five or six years.

The wood needs to mature, but the drying also has a chemical role to play. Lengthy exposure to the air and the rain washes away some of the more bitter tannins in the wood; others are broken down into more palatable tannins; and a mould develops that works on the lignins in the wood. Enzymes split the big (and tasteless) lignin molecule into four smaller ones, all of which taste of vanillin. The acid and the alcohol in the cognac dissolve the vanillin-lignins. These emerge with the vanilla aroma that is so essential in the finished cognac. The fuss about air-dried oak sounds absurd. It is not. With the help of the co-operative that markets the Prince de Polignac brand, the Station Viticole compared brandy stored in oven-dried oak with the same spirit stored in the air-dried equivalent. After a year in the oven-dried oak the spirit was bitter and astringent, fuller of acids and tannin than if

Cooperage: making casks is still a matter of skilled labour.

the air had been allowed to do its work unaided, while the compounds associated with the positive effects of maturation occur in greater quantities in air-dried oak

The cognac cask itself has always been special. Its shape was not unusual – the bulge in the middle, making it easier to roll, was a feature of other regions as well. Nevertheless, it was instantly recognisable by the hoops made of thin strips of lath laid around most of the sides of the cask, only the wood in the middle remaining visible, though the staves of today's casks are circled only sufficiently to enable them to be rolled more easily. The size of the cask is crucial, since it determines the extent to which the brandy will be exposed to the wood: the smaller the cask, the woodier the cognac and the faster it matures. As with the size of the alembic, balance has to be achieved. In the past the *barrique de cognac* held over 205 litres, although the brandy was housed in *tierçons* which held over 500 litres. But now virtually all distillers have standardised on smaller casks. By trial and error they have found that casks holding around 350 litres provide the correct balance even though, legally these can contain between 270 and 450 litres of spirit. When brandies are being assembled before blending, however, they are held in giant wooden *tuns*.

Not surprisingly, *la tonnellerie* (the craft of the cooper) has always been important. In his book Jean Taransaud, the late head of a firm founded in 1743, proudly styles himself *maître tonnellier de Cognac* – and one little affected by modern production techniques.[25] Because they are such substantial users of casks, the major firms became involved with some of the biggest *tonnelleries* in France. Hennessy took over the Taransaud family business in the 1950s. For a long time Rémy Martin owned Seguin Moreau, but it, like Taransaud was sold off in the 1990s. Today only Martell owns its own cooperage.

25 *Le Livre de la tonnellerie* (Paris, 1976).

The firms' previous self-reliance was explained by the horror stories they all have to tell of the leaks that developed in casks bought from outside, defects that ruined the quality as well as reducing the quantity of the spirit. As one grower put it: 'when you buy an old cask you have to know where it came from'. The slightest flaw in the cask can mean that the precious contents drain or become infected. In the words of Charles Walter Berry, the wine merchant who was the leading expert on cognac in London between the two World Wars: 'a split stave will cause a woody taste'.[26] Despite the size of the workshops, the casks are still made in the traditional way; the wood has to be cleaved along the line of the grain, not sawn across. Although some of the staves can be relatively mass-produced, the actual fabrication of the casks remains the task of individual craftsmen, each with his own rhythm of work.

Even though the wood is so dense, the casks so carefully made and the bungs so tight, there is inevitably some evaporation when cognac is stored in wood. Indeed the art of the cooper and the distiller is to ensure that the evaporation is controlled, so that the necessary reactions between wood, air and brandy can proceed at the appropriate pace. The spirit evaporates at very different rates depending on the humidity of the *chai*, resulting in a steady loss described by the locals as *la part des anges*, the 'angels' share'. Strictly speaking, a *chai* ought to be partly underground, as it is in Bordeaux. In Cognac the word is used to describe any warehouse used for storing spirit. Ageing is extremely expensive for two reasons: the cost of holding stock and above all evaporation which simply and inevitably reduces the amount of liquid over the years by between one and three per cent annually.

The ageing process is both physical and chemical. Robert Leauté divides the maturation process into five stages. In the first year the cognac loses its 'boiler taste' and takes on its first colouring, a pale yellow tint. In the next couple of years the spirit starts to absorb some woodiness –i.e. tannins and lignin – and ceases to be merely a raw spirit. In the two subsequent stages covering the next seven or eight years the woodiness should diminish, the cognac mellows, a hint of vanilla starts to creep in. As soon as a cognac is distilled you can tell something about its aging potential, if only from the richness, the oiliness, the sheer concentration of the spirit. But, according to Yann Fillioux, its fifth birthday is the first defining moment for a cognac with any pretensions to real quality. By then the spirit and the wood have started to blend and in his words 'one can start to talk of a cognac rather than a child'.

Brandies from the Grand Champagne – and, to a much lesser extent from the Petite Champagne and the Borderies – take much longer to mature than those from lesser regions simply because they are so concentrated and harder when young. Unfortunately, some of the producers in the Grande Champagne feel that they have to offer a VS to satisfy their agents even though they're not used to producing cognacs which are going to be sold young – more generally it is difficult to make cognacs suitable for selling young without adding sugar. From around their twelfth birthday the cognacs from the better

---

26 *In Search of Wine* (London, 1935). At the time he was one of the few English wine merchants who actually visited French vineyards.

crus steadily get more complex and harmonious. More prosaically, the spirit also gets progressively weaker, at the rate of up to one percentage point a year in the first ten years in cask but much more slowly after that – a brandy with fifty years in cask behind it will still be about 46 per cent alcohol. The balance is a delicate one: if the *chai* is especially humid, then the loss of alcoholic strength will be much greater, whereas an unusually dry warehouse induces unnaturally fast evaporation of what remains a strong spirit. The late Maurice Fillioux of Hennessy reckoned that a cognac left for twenty years in an especially dry *chai* will retain the youthfulness of a ten-year-old. The same period of time spent by brandy in an unusually damp *chai* will add five years to its physical age.

Many of the brandies sipped by the British aristocracy were shipped to England immediately after distillation and then stored near the docks. This produced the classic taste of what were erroneously called 'Early-landed, Late-bottled' cognacs. The two are not the same, since virtually all cognacs are late-bottled, in the sense that they are bottled only just before they are sold. According to Bernard Hine the cellars near the docks in London and Bristol where they were matured were colder and damper than those in Cognac. This is why the brandies are lighter and mature more quickly than those which remain at home – indeed they are smooth, elegant and delicious after a mere twenty years. This was much to the taste of old-style English connoisseurs. One of their breed, Maurice Healy, described such a cognac as 'of almost unearthly pallor and a corresponding ethereal bouquet and flavour'. By contrast they were – and are – not overly highly rated by many French blenders, who find them flabby and many of them are not sturdy enough to last more than twenty or thirty years.

Scientists now perceive the controlled evaporation involved in the maturation process as a continuation, albeit at a much slower rate, of the processes begun in the alembic. The evaporation is only part of the most important reaction involved – that of the oxygen in the air outside the cask and the wood of the cask itself. The wood allows the oxygen to seep steadily through to the spirit, and its metallic elements act as catalysts. This slow oxidation ensures that the aromatic elements in the spirits are preserved, although they would be lost in a speedier chemical reaction. The wood itself is profoundly affected by the spirit and gradually drained of the elements which enrich the cognac – inevitably, the longer the cask has been used, the more neutral its wood and the less important the role it plays in the chemical changes to the cognac as it ages.

The tannins and the lignins dissolve at different rates, so after five years only 10 per cent of the lignin in the cask has been absorbed but 20 per cent of the tannins; after ten years only 60 per cent of the tannin is left but 80 per cent of the lignin. The conventional wisdom that cognac takes up to fifty years to absorb all the tannin in the wood is challenged by Michel Caumeil, who reckons that after twenty or thirty years virtually all the tannin has been absorbed, so that the only role of the wood is a physical one – it continues to allow air through for oxidation. The tannins play an important role, as they do with maturing wines: they bring colour to the spirit, which is colourless when it emerges from the alembic, and at first they increase its bitterness. But, after a few years the molecules are enlarged and the flavour has mellowed. The lignin brings with it

CLASSIC OLDER VINTAGES

The quality of older vintages is largely a matter of chance – and, of course, the reputability of the producer or merchant. Charles Walter Berry reckoned that 1865, 1870, 1878, 1893, 1900, 1904, 1906 (still delicious), 1914, 1928 and 1929 were all exceptional. By contrast he declared that 1887, 1888, 1891, 1894, 1897, 1902 – with a few exceptions – and 1907 were all disasters. And as for the myth of extreme age he reckoned that a 1777 was 'much more interesting from the point of view of its age than for any other reason'.

an aroma of balsa wood and, when it breaks down, results in the vanilla and cinnamon overtones detectable in some cognacs. These processes are slow. Tannic matter really starts to build up only after eight years in cask, and while the aldehydes reach their peak after a mere thirty years (they have absorbed one of them, vanillin, within five), the volatile acids build up over the fifty years a truly old cognac spends in cask before it is transferred to *bonbonnes* or *damejeannes*.

These glass jars hold around 25 litres of brandy and in theory should protect their contents from the oxygen in the air and thus from further development. As a result, the oldest cognacs are essentially frozen in time. Unfortunately the Cognacais had a tradition of sealing them with sacks wrapped round a stopper, supposedly to 'let the brandy breathe'. This had – and in some cases still has – disastrous results, spoiling the contents of large numbers of precious *bonbonnes*. The Fillioux believe that cognacs should generally be left a mere thirty-five years in wood – others think it could be up to sixty years. In fact it all depends on the age and cleanliness of the wood, to ensure that the final brandy will not be too woody. Indeed, some blenders believe that even fifty years is probably too old. Yann Fillioux agrees: 'virtually all cognacs reach their peak when they're forty years old after that sheer age starts to dominate their other characteristics'. But all agree: 'a bad young cognac matures into a bad old cognac'.

Age does not automatically bring quality with it. After fifteen or twenty years some cognacs – not all by any means – become maderised and the fatty acids in the cognac are oxidised. But after twenty or so years the best acquire the very particular *rancio charentais* which develops in different stages, ending with overtones of leather and cedary cigar boxes. 'Once the *rancio* has started to develop,' the late Maurice Fillioux of Hennessy once told me, 'the cognac has reached its final form.'

Rancio derives from the French word *rance* meaning 'rankness', but in relation to cognac it means, above all, greater concentration, length and depth. It is widely misunderstood. Charles Walter Berry (who did not like it) described *rancio* as 'a special character of illness and fatness in some Brandies'. The richness it implies reminds some tasters of Roquefort cheese; indeed there is a sort of mild cheesiness in the nose, a sense of hidden depths, far removed from the foxy *goût de terroir* of young, inferior brandies but nevertheless a reminder of the earthiness of the spirit's origins. For me *rancio* is much more exciting, infinitely appetising, exactly like the essence of a fine fruit or Christmas cake, which combines a certain nuttiness with the richness of dried and candied fruits.

Chemically, *rancio charentais* derives from the oxidation of the fatty acids in the spirit, producing the ketones that feel so rich and fat on the palate. But this is only one of many such reactions. The scientists are still busy analysing the chemical reactions and their results on the palate. One team, under Dr Heide, detected 334 ingredients in cognac: twenty-four acetals (ethylates of aldehyde and alcohol), twenty-seven acids, sixty-three alcohols, thirty-four aldehydes, twenty-five ketones, seventy-seven esters, nineteen ethers, three lactones, eight phenols and forty-four 'diverse substances'. The scientists have separated and analysed only seventy of these, either because they form an important part of the mix or because they strongly influence the taste. The two are not the same: with Michel Caumeil I sniffed some totally neutral ingredients present in some quantity, and others – like some ethyl compounds – whose smallest whiff is strongly reminiscent of rotten fruit. But these considerations are for the perfectionists. The vast majority of cognacs are sold before their fifth birthday, before they have time to develop any of the complexities of a great cognac. The decision as to what is worth keeping and what is good merely for immediate sale is largely in the hands of the blenders in a few major firms. In Cognac the market reaches right into the cask.

Anne Cocher

4

THE PERSONALITY
OF COGNAC

Between the distiller and the drinker comes the blender. Most of the blends will be unremarkable, and most of the merchants – there are still over two hundred of them – resemble their eighteenth-century predecessors: they are largely brokers, intermediaries between the growers and buyers. Their stocks are largely 'tactical', held for a few years, relying on growers – and wholesalers like the Tesserons – for most of the older brandies they require. Only a handful are big enough to hold a balanced stock extending back through the decades.

Nevertheless, like great craftsmen the world over, the blenders – called *chef de caves* or *maîtres de chai* – have a clear idea in their heads and in the sample of old bottles in their tasting rooms, rather than on paper, of the essential qualities historically associated with their name. For the role of the blender is so key that it became an hereditary occupation. Until very recently generations of Fillioux were distillers to the Hennessys, a tradition established in the early nineteenth century, and until the 1980s the Chapeau family fulfilled the same role at Martell.

Continuity at Rémy: three generations of cellar masters

41

THE BIG FOUR

A mere four people are responsible for producing around 150 million bottles of cognac a year. They are the *chef de caves* or *maîtres de chai* for the four firms which account for the vast majority of cognacs sold in the world.

Yann Fillioux, the seventh generation of the family in charge of Hennessy's cognacs

Their job is even more complex than that facing their only real brethren, the people responsible for producing Scotch and other whiskies. Both groups have to produce millions of bottles in a range of ages and qualities in quantities which can fluctuate widely from year to year – and even more so from decade to decade. But the Cognacais have a unique complication: they are not buying their raw material wholesale from a handful of grain merchants but in relatively small quantities from several thousand small farmers who may provide grapes, or wine, or cognac which is usually newly distilled but may have been aged. So they have to add diplomacy to their other essential qualities – such as expert taster and blender to name but two.

Pierrette Trichet, Cognac's first female large-scale maître de chai, *in the vines*

Yann Fillioux, the veteran blender for Hennessy, far and away the biggest firm in Cognac, is in some ways a godfather figure to the whole community. Indeed, he is the seventh member of the family to have blended cognac for the Hennessy family and since he succeeded his uncle Maurice twenty years ago has had to double production and introduce a number of new cognacs while not diluting the style or quality of the final product. He has managed to discipline the growers into increasing the quality of their brandies and, for the first time, to bother about the quality of the wines from which they are distilled.

In the past other dynasties – notably at Martell – have performed the same role and blenders were invariably chosen from the cognac community, generally from the same firm. But today the situation is very different. Thirty years ago André Hériard-Dubreuil, as so often an innovator, recruited Georges Clot, a young chemist from Toulouse to blend Rémy Martin's cognacs. With Clot came a young chemist, Pierrette Trichet, who became fascinated by the product and its complexities and who went on to succeeded him, showing herself perfectly capable of introducing successful new blends. On her retirement in 2014 Trichet passed on the role to her protégé Baptiste Loiseau who, at just 34, is one of the youngest ever cellar masters.

The other two members of the Big Four have equally unusual backgrounds. Patrice Pinet of Courvoisier hails from the Vendée north of Cognac. He was educated as an oenologist at Bordeaux's famous faculty, became fascinated by brandies and found a job with Jean-Marc Olivier, who was rescuing Courvoisier's cognac from mediocrity, and after a twenty years' apprenticeship succeeded him several years ago. Because the firm's owners, Jim Beam, treat Courvoisier's premises at Jarnac as a production unit rather than the firm's headquarters, both Olivier and Pinet manage the 'factory' as well as blending the cognacs, a combination which has worked rather well and has not prevented them, too, from introducing successful new brandies. But the most outside outsider is Benoit Fil at Martell. He comes from a wine background, his father loved wine and his grandfather made it. As a student at Ecole Nationale Supérieure Agricole, France's leading agricultural school, he specialised in viticulture and soon after graduating was hired by Pernod-Ricard to oversee the winemaking at the group's subsidiary in far-off Georgia, subsequently running the whole business. He was then whisked back to Cognac where, he says, he realised that he needed to learn from his two key associates who were responsible respectively for the buying and the distilling for, contrary to traditional wisdom, the magic of cognac can be learnt by outsiders.

Patrice Pinet: at Courvoisier the man who blends also manages

Benoit Fil: from Georgia to Cognac

The major Cognac merchants have to rely on growers and distillers for the bulk of their raw material. Three of the biggest merchants, Martell, Hennessy and Rémy Martin, have vineyards of their own, but these account for an insignificant percentage of their requirements. Not only are none of the major firms remotely integrated, none of them buys grapes, they all buy wine and most of their brandy, generally immediately after distillation. They also have to buy in parcels of old cognacs when they are mixing their finest blends, for not even Hennessy or Martell can guarantee an adequate supply of every one of the hundreds of cognacs they require for their premium products. Obviously, all the 'serious' firms keep a tight control over the brandies they buy, mostly through contracts, usually unwritten, informal ones, with hundreds of supposedly 'independent', but closely supervised, growers. Some of them, like Hine, Courvoisier and Delamain, do not distil any of their own cognac but rely entirely on growers from whom they buy young cognacs.

The blenders clearly have an immense palette from which to work. Typically, Hennessy has 700 growers under contract. Rémy Martin buys from 500 individual growers who provide particular qualities to add to the basic cognacs bought from twenty *bouilleurs de profession* (professional distillers) who themselves buy wines from 1,200 growers. All of them have been trained, often over several generations, to distil their brandies in the specific fashion best suited to the house's requirements. At least once every year (twice at Hennessy) the blenders taste the thousands of individual casks they have in stock. Historic contracts with the growers offer the immense advantage of records indicating just how cognacs from a particular holding have developed in the past, making it easier to know which are capable of further improvement.

Since the late 1970s an increasing number of grower-distillers have begun to sell their own cognacs. In many cases this is because they can no longer rely on selling their brandies to the Big Four firms – Hennessy, Rémy, Martell and Courvoisier – which account for over three-quarters of total sales and who have reneged on their verbal 'gentlemen's agreements' as sales have varied so widely recently. But some are simply looking for independence. The classic case is Frapin, with its 315-hectare estate in the heart of the Grande Champagne which sold its cognacs to Rémy Martin until the 1980s and since then has had an increasing success with its own production.

The blending is the key, and very private it is too – for decades Maurice Fillioux never allowed any of the directors of Hennessy to attend his tastings. 'The problem,' he says, 'is to be able to guarantee the style and constant quality in the quantities demanded' – and this inevitably limits the possibilities. For the object is not so much to isolate a single star but to find cognacs which will mix to provide the firm with the constant blend which is the overriding object of the exercise.

Choices are made every year when the blenders taste every cask in their *chais*. Many will have been destined for the house's VS from the time they emerged from the still, the destiny of others is decided at the age of five when the casks are marked with elementary signs. At Hennessy they range from BB – perfect brandies 20/20 – down to a mere 12 which means simply 'correct'. The analysis can be pretty brutal: I noticed that two brandies from the Petite Champagne were dismissed as 'grape jam' and 'tisane' – herb tea!

All the blenders are juggling a number of variables: the type of oak they are using; the age of the casks; the length of time for which they mature their different levels of cognacs; and, crucially, the region from which they buy their cognac. At least three merchants, Rémy Martin, Hine and Delamain, sell only brandies from the Champagnes, as of course do the increasing number of grower-distillers who sell their own brandies from the region. For their VS (formerly Three-Star), VSOP and, in many cases, their Napoleons and XOs, all the other merchants inevitably rely on brandies from the Bois and the Borderies. But over recent decades they have become much choosier as to which corners of the Fins Bois they use. None buy from the west of Cognac, and they buy very little, if any, from the Bons Bois. Recently three firms – Leyrat, Léopold Gourmel, and Château de Beaulon – have headed the fight to prove that fine, elegant, floral, long-lived cognacs can be made from chosen spots in the Fins Bois. Beaulon is on a special patch of chalk on the Gironde estuary while Leyrat and Gourmel rely on estates in what used to be called *Les Petites Champagnes de Blanzac* – a small town in the south east of the Fins Bois.

A number of the bigger and more serious houses have a secret weapon: using brandies from the Borderies which are very special, 'nutty', intense and capable of ageing for

BOISÉ: COGNAC'S SECRET INGREDIENT

No one talks much, if at all, about *boisé* yet it is employed by many, if not most, producers. It is made by boiling chips of oak for as long and as often as is required to produce a thick, brown liquid which can add woodiness to the brandy and increase its apparent age. It thus provides a shortcut for those wanting to add a touch of new wood to their cognacs – and an alternative to buying new casks which now cost up to £500 each, which equates to over a pound per bottle of cognac.

several decades. 'They are well-rounded after fifteen years,' says Pierre Frugier, formerly the chief blender at Martell, which uses a great deal of the brandy in its Cordon Bleu. 'We pay the same for cognac from the Borderies as we do from the Petite Champagne,' said Maurice Fillioux. 'I can always distinguish a cognac from the Borderies – there's that little something. To talk about violets, as some people do, is a little poetical; to me the essence is of nut kernels.' This nuttiness so characteristic of the Borderies forms an essential part of the better VSs and VSOPs. Indeed, the brandies from the Borderies are tailor-made for VSOPs which include brandies of between five and ten years of age. Some purists claim that the whole idea of VSOP is unnatural, that the age range is too old for brandies from the Bois, too young for those from the Champagnes (though Rémy Martin has found fame and fortune by refuting this particular old wives' tale).

In theory, brandies from the Grande Champagne and even from the Petite Champagne are so intense as to be almost undrinkable before they are ten or more years old although Rémy Martin disagrees with the need for special treatment. 'They don't mature more slowly. They are simply more complex, and therefore it is more interesting to age them longer,' said Robert Leauté and indeed Rémy makes an excellent VS from the outer reaches of the Petite Champagne. Impressions of the aroma and taste of Champagne cognacs revert to the vine, to the flowers and twigs as well as the fruit of the grape, resulting in the preservation, in a uniquely concentrated form, of the natural qualities of the raw materials: nature transformed by man.

Not all cognacs, even from the Grande Champagne, have the capacity to age so vigorously and gracefully. Although the growers now all know how to distil good cognac, some of them are still careless. The Station Viticole imposes some form of discipline, since all the cognacs have to be sampled ('given the *agrément*') before they can be sold to the public, and this eliminates the worst brandies. Yet, broadly speaking, the buyer has very little legal protection. The producers are not allowed to give the exact age of their brandies and until 2016 the minimum age even for XO brandies is six after which they will have to be at least ten years old. Moreover, there are plenty of inferior, well-aged cognacs on sale, for any unscrupulous blender can fabricate a 'venerable' Grande Champagne cognac with some undrinkable, albeit genuinely aged, cognac plus generous doses of additives – sugar, caramel and the mysterious *boisé* (see box) – to increase the apparent age of the blend's taste. The reputation of the firm selling the cognac remains a better guarantee of quality than the legal description.

House style starts with the cognac itself, for there is a marked contrast between firms which rely primarily on the spirit and those, notably Martell and Delamain, which concentrate on the effects of the wood – Alain Braastad, the former chairman of Delamain says bluntly that the newly distilled cognac accounts for a mere 25 per cent of the quality of the final product. By contrast Laurent Robin of Louis Royer, 'not wanting to rely on the wood and the progress of ageing for the quality of the result,' is 'looking for the richest possible raw material'. However, this need not be related to the wine. When he was at Frapin, Olivier Paultes found that richer more aromatic wines did not necessarily produce richer and more complex brandies than more neutral ones.

Factors in their search for their own style inevitably include not only the source of the brandy but also the type of oak and the age of the casks. A high proportion of Rémy Martin's cognacs are destined for VSOP brandies, to be sold within six, or at the most ten, years of distillation, so it is looking for a type of wood which will speed the maturation process and, naturally, uses Limousin oak. Martell uses Troncais because it is looking for precisely the opposite qualities: the wood has less tannin and is denser and therefore less porous, so ageing is slower and less wood is imparted to the cognac. Indeed, the secret of the dry Martell style, originally destined for the British market, was that the cognac itself and the oak in which it was aged were both directed towards a target which is ascetic in theory, but in practice, fills the mouth with a balanced fullness.

The same considerations apply to the age of the casks. In theory, most firms keep their cognacs in new wood for up to a year to provide an initial 'attack' of tannin before transferring it to older casks to prevent them from becoming too woody. Like many distillers Yann Fillioux is wary of overly long contact with new oak, for him nine months is the maximum time, otherwise 'the cognacs are marked for life'. If the brandy is to be kept for fifty years or more it has to be kept in old oak from the start; this is the secret of Rémy's Louis XIII, the world's best-selling truly aged cognac. But, cask-wise, old age starts young, 'new' generally means a cask less than three years old and 'once it's twenty years old' says Yann Fillioux 'it is above all a neutral container.'

Some firms vary their use of new oak depending on the source of the grapes. Hine, for instance, uses old wood for Grande Champagne and new for Fins Bois to provide a shot of tannin. None of Delamain's cognacs, all of which come from the Grande Champagne, have ever touched any new wood, for the cognacs it buys have been lodged in wood which is at least seven years old and they keep the casks for at least sixty years. At the other extreme the equally reputable house of Frapin keeps its best cognacs in new oak for up to two and a half years, depending on the amount of colour (and hence, by inference, tannin) the spirit has absorbed. Both are exceptions: Delamain is seeking a light, almost ethereal style, while all Frapin's brandies come from a particularly favoured corner of the Grande Champagne, so they have enough basic strength to be capable of absorbing the tannins and other chemicals found in new wood.

All the houses are aiming at a standard product from grapes that inevitably vary every

A flat-bottomed gabarre, *the main means of transporting cognac before the twentieth century.*

year. If the year has been especially wet or the grapes are unusually ripe, the cognacs could be flabby, so Rémy Martin, for instance, stiffens their backbone with a longer stay in new wood. In very dry years the opposite applies. Some firms use old oak for Champagne cognacs and new wood for a third of those from the Bois. There is a regular routine as the brandies are gradually transferred to older and older casks. But the pace varies for, as Alain Braastad of Delamain says, 'Every cask has its own personality because of the very different qualities of the wood in which it is lodged.' All the blenders agree with him that while the brandy is above 40 per cent, the wood still contributes something to the final result.

So, of course, do the *chais* in which the brandies are housed. These are a cross between a commercial warehouse and, in the case of the fabled *paradis* housing the oldest cognacs, a living museum. Originally they were located on the banks of the Charente, so that the casks could be loaded on to the *gabares*. This was another lucky accident. Initially the Cognacais probably did not grasp the contribution made by the dampness of the riverside atmosphere to the quality of the cognac by reducing the strength rather than reducing the aromatic content. The maturing brandies must not be subject to draughts, while the newer *chais* away from the river are often air-conditioned to provide the right degree of humidity.

Today the north bank of the Charente in Cognac, and both banks at Jarnac, are still lined with handsome stone warehouses, inevitably blackened by generations of Torula compniacensis Richon,[27] the famous fungus that thrives (as who would not)

27 This special fungus was recognised in 1881 by Dr Richon, hence its name.

on the fumes from maturing cognac in the rich, damp air of warehouses full of casks of maturing brandy. It is so omnipresent that the local fraud squad allegedly uses helicopters to look for the tell-tale colour of the fungus on the roofs of buildings where illicit stocks of cognac are hidden.

The old sites had two problems, fire and flood, neither entirely conquered even today. In December 1982 when the Charente flooded, casks of brandy bobbed about like life rafts, and the dark stains left by the receding waters can still be seen half-way up the walls of Royer's *chais* by the river in Jarnac. The firms had been warned two days in advance but nevertheless even Rémy Martin was particularly badly affected because they ended up with casks half-full of old cognacs with loose bungs floating down the river. In the end the flood lasted a full month. Fire is an even more serious hazard. Vizetelly remarked that if Cognac 'were once to catch fire at any point, it would explode like a mountain of lucifer matches struck by lightning, and would blaze afterwards like an ever-burning omelette-au-rhum, intended to be gazed at but never eaten.' Rather more limited conflagrations are a regular occurrence. Yet when Hine built a new *chai* in 1973 everyone laughed when the firm installed sprinklers. After both Martell and Rémy suffered from blazes people stopped laughing. Despite the disadvantages of a riverside location, both Martell and Hennessy still retain their old sites, although both have also added new sites elsewhere. Rémy did not inherit any historic *chais* and now owns a number of rather unromantic sprawls in and around Cognac. In Jarnac Courvoisier dominates one bank of the river.

Of course there are many tricks to the trade when preparing cognacs for sale. For instance, they can be returned to new oak for a few months to give them a final boost of tannin and then put back into old casks to avoid too much hardness. Since the arrival of the appellation system the merchants are limited in the ability to tamper with their cognacs. They can add as much *boisé* as they like and 8 grams of sugar per litre but only one part of caramel. Unmentionable is the alleged use of artificial flavours imported by a handful of unscrupulous houses from Dutch fragrance manufacturers. Some merchants disguise the lack of any specific character in their cognacs with relatively heavy doses of caramel, but this can easily be detected from the rawness of the alcohol and the burning sensation it leaves on the palate. But because the sugars from the hemi-cellulose in the wood gradually infiltrate the cognac after twenty years, Hennessy for one, finds that it has to put only 2 grams of sugar, a quarter of the permitted level, into each litre – the Tesserons say that they have only 2 parts in 10,000 in their cognacs. The sugary syrup softens the young cognacs and 'rounds' them, while the caramel, neutral to the taste, merely standardises the colour. Nevertheless, the best accolade Charles Walter Berry could give to an 1830 cognac was that it was 'pure' and had 'never been touched or refreshed'.

Because the Chinese and the Japanese equate darkness with age, the blends sent to the Far East may well be darker than those sold in Europe or the United States. They also tend to be richer so that they can be diluted through mixing with ice without losing their flavour. The Japanese, for instance, were unhappy at the dry intensity of Martell's cognacs. And there's a new phenomenon – the many blends designed to be drunk when smoking cigars. To cut through the rough smokiness of the cigars these have inevitably to be heavy, rich, dull, caramelly and often unbalanced as well. I tend to agree – but then I'm not a smoker – with David Baker of Brandy Classics, the specialist importer, that 'you might just as well put cigar blends in your gravy browning'.

Purists often hanker after what they feel was a Golden Age, in general before 1914. In fact it was literally golden in character if not in quality, thanks to the far heavier doses of sugary syrup common in the past when the merchants enjoyed complete freedom as to the additives they could employ. Then they were particularly aware of the need to darken their brandies. Many British drinkers in particular were fond of rich brown brandies, partly because of a fond delusion that a dark brandy was an old brandy and partly because they were powerful enough to be diluted, then with soda, now with ice. In those not-so-far off Golden Days prune juice, sweet, dark and a trifle nutty, was a favourite additive, as it is even today with the brandy producers of Jerez, and if more nuttiness was required, almond could be added to le casks. Henry Vizetelly, the Victorian journalist, was shown a special locked storehouse and was offered a sample:

> *from an enormous cask of the burnt-sugar syrup, which 'brownifies' the brandy (English customers admiring a gypsy complexion), and which syrup is not nice at all; and also a glass of softening syrup, made of one-fourth sugar and three-fourths eau de vie, which sweetens and smooths the cordial for lickerish lips, and which is so delicious that you would not have the heart to reproach your bitterest enemy if you caught him indulging in a drop too much.*

Even the normally puritanical Tovey approved of such additions:

> *the old Cognac houses are very particular in the quality of their colouring, and prepare it with great lie; it is important, too, that it should be old, and it is made up with Old Brandy. Consequently good old colouring imparts a fulness and roundness to Brandy which is not to be met with in the coloured spirit, although the latter may merit the preference in character and finesse.*

Both 'dosage' and dilution are delicate operations. Only a few of the oldest cognacs, those of at least forty years old, are weak enough to be sold without dilution; the younger the blend, the stronger the basic spirit. To bring a three-year-old down from perhaps 60° to 40° is a delicate business. 'The dilution can never be too brutal,' says Michel Caumeil, who compares it with landing an aeroplane – after all, there are four hundred ingredients in the cognac which have to be blended with the water. Reducing strength is bound to be an important step which, if taken too quickly, can do severe damage to the cognac, for spirit and water do not mix naturally. When brandy is blended with water, molecules of fatty acids clash and the result is the sort of cheap, soapy cognacs found in all too many French supermarkets.

The decision is irreversible: 'once a cognac has been cut,' says Caumeil, 'it can never go into one of our best blends.' But even the meanest spirit cannot be brought down from its cruising altitude (or undiluted strength) in one go. The process occurs in several stages, each of them separated by a period of months – and, say some blenders, the last stage, reducing the strength from 45 to 40 per cent, is the most difficult. Many firms dilute brandies destined for sale in two or three years immediately after distillation to around 55–60 per cent. If you dilute immediately to below 55 per cent the cognac is too weak to attack the wood directly, it has to be stronger to extract the tannins. 'At Hennessy we prefer to keep the brandy's character,' said Maurice Fillioux, so they mix it a year before the brandy is to be sold. At Martell they taste even the distilled water. Obviously the slower the dilution the better. To slow the process some of the more scrupulous merchants use *petits eaux*. These are made by filling old casks half full of distilled water. Within six months the water has 'matured to reach around 20 per cent. But if the ages of the different elements in the final blend differ too widely – a blend, say of ten and hundred year old cognacs – then the contrast jars on the palate.

Following dilution the brandies are refrigerated to 15°F (-9°C) and filtered (generally centrifugally) to ensure that they do not throw any deposits even if they are left on tropical docksides or in icy Alaskan warehouses for weeks at a time. For a house style has to be capable not only of being applied on an industrial scale but also of surviving the many accidents that can happen between the Charente and the drinker. But whatever you do to it mature cognac remains the finest and most complex liquid distillation – in both senses of the term – of the heart of France. *La France profonde.*

PART II
THE STORY OF COGNAC

5

FROM SALT TO WINE TO COGNAC BRANDY

The town of Cognac itself dates back over two thousand years and was probably named after a pre-Roman chieftain called Comnos or Conos.[28] In Roman times Cognac was in a rich region and its capital, Mediolanum – Saintes' Roman name – was an important imperial city boasting 15,000 inhabitants. Nevertheless, for most of antiquity the region was relatively marginal for it was the Mediterranean which was the centre of Greco-Roman civilisation. But in later Roman times the European world became increasingly centred on the Atlantic coast from Southern Spain and Portugal up to the Low Countries, Britain and north-west Germany. This change ensured that the Charentes and the Gironde estuary were at the heart of the most important trade route in Europe.

The Charente was navigable as far as Cognac and its importance was recognised as early as the eleventh century, when the town was first fortified. The bridge next to the château was the first across the river inland from the sea and the town was also an important religious centre, but it was the Charente itself which was crucial.

The Cognac we know today started to emerge when northern sailors discovered the quality of the region's salt which they found very *conservatif*, that is, especially well suited to preserving fish and meat. Indeed, its qualities became famous throughout northern Europe as the Flemish, the Scandinavians and the Germans from the Hanseatic ports all spread its fame. Cognac flourished because it was on a tidal river at the limit of sea-going navigation, so could help transport the salt inland from the coastal salt pans at the point at which larger boats had to trans-ship their cargoes to boats capable of navigating the shallower upper waters of the Charente. It was also an *étape fiscale*, the stopping point

---

28 The town was variously called Compniacum, Compinacum, Compnacum and Coniacum. More recent variants include Coingnac, Compniac, Cougnac, Congnac, Coegnac, and as late as the eighteenth century, when the town was already world-famous, Coignac, Cogniac or Coniack.

where taxes had to be paid on cargoes travelling between the provinces of Saintonge and Angoumois. It also enjoyed a *monopole saulnier* (the right to insist that every cargo of salt passing up-river had to be trans-shipped in the town) granted by King John in 1199; additionally, its merchants paid a lower tax on salt than their unhappy brethren in Saintonge and Aunis nearer the coast.

In the second half of the twelfth century salt started to give way to wine. In 1152 Eleanor of Aquitaine, heiress to the whole region, married Prince Henry of England, who mounted the English throne two years later as Henry II and ruled a vast Anglo-French Empire for the next thirty-four years leading to an enormous wine trade, above all between Bordeaux and Britain. Trade was encouraged by the development of a new type of ship, the cogue, able to carry ten times as much cargo as the much smaller vessels it replaced. The cogues could sail as far up-river as Tonnay-Charente, a mere twenty miles from Cognac, described as a 'maritime town on a river', a port for sea-going ships, where they were loaded with wine, and later with brandy and paper – by far the most important product in the region and the one most coveted by the Dutch.

Almost inevitably, these changes ensured that the pattern of feudal relationships normal throughout France was broken. In Robert Delamain's words:

> *These two products, salt and wine created in the rural mass of the Charentais basin a mentality adjusted to commercial practices, a mentality which was highly unusual at a time when the whole economy elsewhere was confined within the limits of the* seigneurie *in which lords and peasants alike were forced to find within the domaine the wherewithal to clothe and feed themselves.*

During the Middle Ages the Charente region was a major supplier of wines to the thirsty British market. As late as the sixteenth century, when the English had been chased from France for a century or more, we find the expression *vin de Cognac*. Vines were first planted around Cognac in place of the *bois* (woods), which had been partially cleared for growing grain, and then spread to the Champagnes – the chalky hillsides round Châteauneuf overlooking the Charente valley – which had continued to grow cereals throughout the Middle Ages. In the seventeenth century these slopes emerged as the source of the best wine for distillation. Nevertheless, as in the Champagne region of eastern France, grain was still grown on the plains and river banks as the vines climbed on the slopes above.

Cognac also owed a great deal to royal favour. The town had been granted its first charter early in the thirteenth century by the hapless King John (*Jean Sans Terre* to the French), and it remained important – it was a favourite home for the Black Prince, the heir to the English throne, in the second half of the thirteenth century. The rival town of Jarnac, a few miles further up-river and its main potential rival, did not get a royal charter at the same time as John awarded one to Cognac, the first indication of Cognac's growing relative importance.

Early in the fourteenth century Cognac was separated from the feudal lordships that still governed most of rural France, whereas until 1789 Jarnac was dominated by its feudal lords. This is another reason why Jarnac has generally played very much a secondary role in the story. For King John had inadvertently set off the train of events that ensured that the famous brandy would be called Cognac and not 'Jarnac'. In fact the finest brandies have always come not from round either of these two towns but from the slopes above the little town of Segonzac which rightly calls itself 'the capital of the Grande Champagne'.

It helped Cognac that above the town the Charente is a difficult river, low in summer, high enough in winter to create problems when navigating under some of the bridges.[29] So the *gabares* had to be special, above all flat-bottomed. Nevertheless, it was not unreasonable for the merchant and historian Alain Braastad to call it 'a liquid motorway' because it provided a far simpler, cheaper and quicker means of communication than the treacherous roads of the time.

For nearly a century the region suffered from a combination of the Black Death and the Hundred Year's War and only really started to recover after the British had finally been driven out of Aquitaine in 1453 after the Battle of Castillon. The Charente region was reconquered by the French far earlier than Bordeaux, the last redoubt of the English occupation. In the short term this created problems for the locals, since they lost their most important market. Yet in the long run Cognac benefited from its stalwart loyalty to the Kings of France. The alternative buyers of the Charente's wines, who filled the gap left by the English, were from the same northern countries which had earlier taken their salt from the region, above all from the Netherlands. They provided a far greater continuity than had the English.

By the end of the fifteenth century paper, a staple of the local economy for several centuries, was being produced in increasing quantities thanks to the purity of the waters of the upper Charente. Three centuries after King John, a lucky accident ensured that Cognac was again singled out for royal favour. Francis I, the very model of a Renaissance monarch, was born in the town in 1492 and naturally showed his gratitude to his birthplace. When he ascended the throne of France twenty-three years later, he immediately exempted the inhabitants of this loyal town from all of the many taxes, forced loans and other levies imposed on the rest of the county of Angoulême to sustain the French army in its numerous wars. In the last decade of the sixteenth century another king, Henry IV, stayed twice in Cognac and confirmed the privileges accorded by Francis I. Not surprisingly, the town's inhabitants retained their feeling of being special, part of a wider world, during the tumultuous century that followed his death. Nevertheless, it is extraordinary that cognac established itself during a century and a half which witnessed repeated outbreaks of civil war.

In 1544 there was a revolt, brutally suppressed by the royal forces, against the *gabelle*, the dreaded salt tax. The suppression did much to encourage the rise of Protestantism – John Calvin himself had lived in Angoulême for several years. The Angoumois became one of the heartlands of French Protestantism and thus, inevitably, a major battleground in the religious wars that dominated the last half of the sixteenth century, with Jarnac at its heart. One of the crucial battles of the religious wars was in Jarnac itself in 1569 though

29 I counted seventeen between Cognac and Jarnac.

both sides were probably more concerned by the 'Little Ice Age' of the 1570s – which may have made it difficult to ripen grapes thus boosting the switch to brandy which could cope with acid fruit – than by religious disputes. The Protestants and their work ethic took root and provided a further boost to the inhabitants' commercial-mindedness.

Nevertheless, tolerance had always had its limits, as is shown by the fate of the defiantly Protestant stronghold of La Rochelle in 1622. Twelve years after Louis XIII had succeeded the tolerant Henry IV he started a brutal siege of the Protestant 'exception' which ended in the town's surrender in 1628 after unavailing efforts by the British to intervene. Inevitably, the fall of La Rochelle was a major boost to its smaller rival Cognac. The upheavals continued during the first half of the seventeenth century, culminating in the Fronde, the Civil War between the feudal barons and the young King Louis XIV, who had acceded to the throne as a mere baby, in 1643. Again Cognac was involved. As had already happened so often before, it gained from holding out on behalf of the king against the assaults of one of the leading 'Frondeurs', the Duc de Rochefoucauld, and was duly rewarded for its loyalty. The mayor was ennobled; the inhabitants were exempted from taxes for twenty years and were granted the right to hold four fairs a year, each to last three days. These provided an unequalled meeting place for the local farmers and merchants. As the century wore on, the fair-goers began increasingly to bargain, not over wine but over a new product, eau de vie.

Distillation for medical purposes had long been widespread in both Spain and southern France, a legacy of the long occupation by the Moors, then the experts in this as in so many other arts and sciences. The first distillers to sell their wares commercially, and not merely for medical purposes, were probably from Armagnac, a couple of hundred miles to the south-west of Cognac. Unfortunately for them the Armagnacais lacked Cognac's long commercial tradition and thus the merchant class required to act as middle-men between the local growers and distillers (who later combined the two functions) and the foreign buyers. It was this long commercial tradition which proved crucial in establishing Cognac's brandies on the European market.

The first record we have of brandy from the Cognac region entering international trade comes from 1517 when a *barrique d'eau ardente* was shipped from Bordeaux, but the first records of sales of eau de vie come from La Rochelle. In 1549 '*quatre barriques d'eau-de-vie bonne et marchande*' ('four *barriques* of eau de vie, wholesome and fit for sale') were traded, and in 1571 a certain Jehan Serazin was described as a '*marchand et faizeur d'eau de vie*' ('merchant and producer of eau de vie'). By the end of the century the trade was important enough to be considered suitable for the grant of a monopoly, a favourite means for impecunious French monarchs to raise money throughout the ages. In 1604, according to Pierre Martin-Civat one Isaac Bernard paid an unknown sum for a monopoly of the distillation and sale of all the eaux de vie made in the provinces of Tours, Poitou, Languedoc and Guyenne: effectively the whole of western France.[30]

Inevitably, this extremely wide grant was largely ignored by the Flemish as well as by native merchants, who dodged it by carrying brandies by road as well as by sea.

---

30 'La monopole des eaux-de-vie sous Henri IV', I00 Congrès Nationale des Sociétés Savantes (Paris, 1975).

Nevertheless, the monopoly was confirmed four years later, and it was not until 1610 that Bernard had to surrender it. This was largely because of the opposition of the powerful merchants of Nantes, although the list of merchants who had broken the monopoly was a long one, showing just how widely the trade had already spread. From then on the Cognac community was not hampered by any of the monopolies that restricted so many other French businesses.

Within fifteen years the brandies involved had been transformed into a unique spirit: cognac or, as it was more usually termed in Britain 'Coniack brandy'. It was largely a matter of horses for courses. The wines were not bad – it was simply that distillation was more profitable. Just as vines had formerly been concentrated on the uplands rather than the river valleys, so wines suitable for drinking continued to be produced wherever they could command a premium price, as they could in the Borderies whose sweet white wines, produced since the fourteenth century, were much prized by the Dutch, who paid up to three times as much for them as for the more acid products from the Champagnes largely because the sweeter wine was more suitable for transporting long distances. But after an appalling frost in 1766 they lost their market to competitors from Sauternes and switched to producing wines for distillation. With that – tiny – exception by the end of the seventeenth century, brandy was triumphant. Robert Delamain quotes a letter written by the *intendant* – the governor – of the province to Louis XIV in 1698:

> *Wine is the major product of the Angoumois, but the most important vineyards are in the Cognac district. The red wines find an outlet in Poitou and the Limousin. Very little is sold to foreigners who do not find them stout enough to stand the journey. But when the white wines are converted into brandy, which is their normal fate, the English and Danish fleets come to look for them, in peacetime anyway, at the ports of the Charente and drink them up, to the great advantage of the province.*

Cognac shared the advantages enjoyed by La Rochelle and above all Bordeaux, of a good trading position and easy access to the Bay of Biscay and thus to foreign markets. The virtues of Cognac's brandies had been noted as early as 1617, when a bill of sale at La Rochelle mentioned brandy that was guaranteed to be from Cognac. Five years later we find brandies from Cognac paying 9 livres in tax as against 8½ for those from Bordeaux and between 7 and 7½ for those from Spain or the South of France. In 1678 'Coniack brandy' was first mentioned in the *London Gazette*, the official English journal. The wars between Britain and France that occupied much of the next thirty years did not prevent cognac's rise to fame and fortune. They simply led to a greatly increased demand for brandy from the participants. And, as with claret at the same time, the scarcity bred of wartime difficulties seems merely to have enhanced the drink's attractions for a fashion-conscious market.

The success of 'Coniack brandy' was largely due to two very different foreign influences, the Dutch and the aristocratic drinkers of Restoration London. In 1581 the Dutch finally gained their independence from Spain, a triumph which triggered their subsequent dominance of maritime trade. They needed the spirit to compensate for the impurities in the water carried by their sailors during long spells at sea. A distilled spirit, eight or nine times more concentrated than wine, was obviously far cheaper to ship and could simply be cut with water by the buyer to provide the equivalent amount of liquid to quench the sailors' thirst.

The original trade involved the shipment of wine, not brandy, to the Netherlands as raw material for some of the many distilleries built there in the late sixteenth century. These were originally called *wijnbranders* (literally, 'wine burners') and the product therefore *brandywijn* or *brandvin* ('burnt wine'). These 'burners', the French called them *brûleries*, used a wide variety of raw materials, but wine was officially favoured: the Dutch government discouraged the use of the obvious alternative, grain, a concern that formed a recurring theme in the story of brandy. They found that the wines from the Charente provided a cheap as well as suitable raw material – as well as the wood to fuel the *brûleries* and oak for the casks required. Their supremacy lasted for over a century and affected every supplier who came into contact with them. Inevitably the Charentais had to follow the demands for the new product, brandy. They – followed by the British – were the first to produce spirits, largely gin, on an 'industrial' scale. They imported copper from Sweden, built the stills, and when the Cognacais began to distil their wines themselves they used the same Swedish copper as the Dutch and copper remained a major cost for the distillers since their stills lasted a mere twenty years. In 1624 an agreement is recorded between two Dutchmen living in the Charente to build a distillery at Tonnay-Charente. Strikingly, at the end of the seventeenth century stills imported from the Netherlands were 20 per cent more expensive than their locally made equivalents.

The Dutch influence was also boosted by the marriage, in 1643, of Philippe Augier, probably the most important Cognac merchant of his time, to a member of the Dutch Janssen paper-making family, for at least until the revolution of 1789, 'Holland paper' was a far more important product than cognac. Augier's father-in-law persuaded his son-in-law to move from Châteauneuf to Cognac and, probably, helped him with distillation.

As late as the 1720s the Dutch still took over half of the brandy exported from the district round La Rochelle. But cognac's emergence as the superior form of a routine drink would have been impossible without the existence of a market sufficiently rich and fashion-conscious to pay the premium price inevitable for a drink which was far more expensive to produce than comparable spirits made from grain. Fortunately for Cognac, after the Restoration of the dissolute King Charles II in 1660, the drinkers of London café society developed a marked taste for new types of luxury beverages. These included sherry, port, claret aged in wood and the first bottles of sparkling champagne. The first decade of the eighteenth century saw the full emergence of 'Coniack brandy'. In the words of Warner Allen, 'The British discovered that spirits from an unclean wine tasted vile.'

In January 1706 an advertisement in the *London Gazette* proclaimed that thirty-four 'Pieces of Old Coniack Brandy' were available for sale at the port of Southampton.[31] Clearly, this was no ordinary brandy, it was 'Old Cogneac, fit for drams', implying that

---

31 Britain was still employing the old calendar under which the year started on 25 March. By our reckoning it was January 1707.

it could be drunk neat. This was the first sign of the recognition that 'Coniack Brandy' was superior to its two great rivals, those from Bordeaux and Nantes, and indeed sold at a considerable premium to them. The original brandies which made Cognac famous came from the Champagne areas to the south and south-east of Cognac itself and from the Fins Bois de Jarnac north of the town. This intense localisation, which applied also to the other drinks made fashionable in London at the time was a major novelty in what one can only call a 'Restoration revolution', which placed a premium on drinks from a region where the soil or the climate was particularly suitable.

During the eighteenth and much of the nineteenth century the British tended not to drink their cognac neat. Their basic after-dinner drinks were largely port or Madeira, though they usually ended the evening with a brandy and soda. As Cyril Ray puts it, 'Until the turn of the [twentieth] century cognac was taken as a cordial – more an *apéritif* than as a *digestif* – or else as an ingredient for punches, neguses and toddies, hot or cold, to spend the evening over after leaving the port in the dining-room and then go to bed on. During the day it was taken as a long drink with soda – the celebrated B & S of Victorian literature and life.'[32]

The distillation of 'Coniack brandy' is still a contentious subject. For a start it has led to one of Cognac's most enduring, most widespread and most misleading legends: that the secret of the double distillation which resulted in cognac was merely a happy accident, the product of the musings of a local soldier-poet, the Chevalier de la Croix Marron. He had written a long poem called 'La Muse Catholique', which ran into two editions, published in 1607 and 1614 respectively. In a preface to the first edition, dedicated, as usual, to a great local lady, he remarks how he has been distracted from his Muse by 'a thousand different notions on as many different subjects...I have distilled the springtime of my spirits' – the pun is the same in both English and French. He then proceeds to dilate a little on this conceit. Unbelievably, a whole school of thought has been erected on this idle notion, this short, allusive, whimsical play on words and the myth is even enshrined in the standard work on the legal definition of cognac.[33] This silly and misleading myth, that the chevalier discovered the secret of cognac, remains the officially authorised version. I find the continued existence of this canard ridiculous and demeaning to Cognac.

In reality, the key to Cognac's superiority was that the wines from the region were so acidic, and so suitable for distillation, that their inherent qualities did not have to be filtered out by repeated distillations. In the seventeenth century, lesser spirits were distilled not once (as the legend assumes) but several times. Only the grapes grown around Cognac were capable of producing a superior, drinkable spirit after only two passes through the still. Raw materials – not just grapes – from everywhere else in France had to be distilled again and again to remove their noxious impurities. In the process, of course, they became nearly 'rectified': they lost the qualities inherent in the raw material. Only the grapes from Cognac produced spirit which, because it had been distilled no more than twice, retained the flavour of the original grape.

---

32 *Christie's Wine Review* (1979).
33 Marguerite Landrau, *Le Cognac devant la loi* (Cognac, 1981).

Using a mere two *chauffes* to produce a spirit which would be agreeable to drink was clearly a delicate matter. Their situation was summed up by one highly influential authority, Jean François Demachy, by training a pharmacist, who became director of the central dispensary of the French army. Demachy's work, his three-part *L'Art du distillateur d'eaux fortes* (which was even translated into German), provides a unique, encyclopaedic view of the problems facing distillers in the eighteenth century. Demachy was firmly convinced that only the best would do. Some chemists, he said scornfully, believed that if you rectified second-grade brandy, you got as good a result as with a double-distilled, first-rate eau de vie. It might be as dry, he said, but 'connoisseurs do not make the same mistake'. The distillers themselves agreed. They too understood that only the first quality 'combines an exquisite bouquet with all the lightness and dryness it is possible to imagine'. This is a contrast because in Demachy's time many second-rate spirits could not be used even for chemical purposes, let alone drinking, but were suitable only for use in varnishes because of their disagreeable smell.

By the middle of the eighteenth century the conditions for producing the very best cognac had been precisely defined, though the basic strength was a few degrees below the present day level of 70°. The key to the quality, then as now, was the separation of the *coeur*, the heart of the distillate, *eau de vie bonne et forte* as it was termed, from the richer, lower strength and generally second-rate, *secondes*. Indeed, 'double brandy' – double tax not double distillation – was undiluted with *secondes*. The Cognacais immediately realised and exploited their advantages though none of them advanced contemporary understanding of the chemistry of the distillation process. Reasonably enough, the Cognacais have never felt the need to change the formula which made them rich and famous, so the distillation of cognac, by and large, remains just as it was in the eighteenth century.

Although accurate measurement of the strength of a spirit became possible only through the work of Gay-Lussac in the nineteenth century, the first practical hydrometer to provide some indication of strength was invented in 1725 and by the 1760s most distillers – and the crucial London trade – had proper alcometers measuring the exact strength of the brouillis. Until then the strength had been a matter of guesswork. The result was that a mix of brouillis and wine was distilled into 'eau de vie de Cognac', normally to a mere 48 per cent, although brandies destined for the London market were 10 per cent stronger. Only when an 'alcohometer' was in regular use could the raw material consist purely of brouillis at 30 per cent, and the final spirit today's level of around 70 per cent.

As so often in French history the biggest problem for the cognac producers was the burden of taxes, a problem which also darkened the scene in the last twenty years of the twentieth century. As early as 1640 a special royal tax was imposed on brandies, and twenty years later eau de vie was taxed as an ordinary drink. By the eighteenth century the whole Cognac community had to pay taxes. The peasantry were hardest-hit, but the nobility and clergy, who were normally exempt, naturally protested most loudly. In 1713, at the instigation of the arch-priest of the small town of Bouteville, the parish priests of the Grande Champagne launched a bitter complaint. In 1744 a group of aristocrats joined in. They complained that their major source of income was in the form of wines suitable only for distillation, so they were hit by an anti-fraud tax dating back to 1687, which supposedly affected only merchants. The 'tax farmers'[34] argued that it applied also to the landowners, since brandy was not a natural agricultural product but resulted from art and industry and was therefore liable to the taxes levied on manufactured articles. The producers had to pay even on the large quantities of wine destined for their own consumption and were victims of their own success, for their vines were productive, and taxes on wines were based on the quantity produced. The specific 'farm' that hit the locals hardest was that of the *courtiers-jaugeurs*, licensed intermediaries who took a fixed percentage on every transaction within the area.

The problem extended even to the British market. In Britain French brandy had been a tempting target since Elizabethan times, and in wartime brandy was always among the first items to be prohibited. An attempt at a commercial treaty in 1713 merely exposed the depth of the opposition, backed by the politically powerful rum lobby. To the British taxman 'brandy' became 'spirit' above 66°, and the duty doubled (even higher duties were imposed in the 1750s). In France duty doubled above 60° (when the spirit became an eau de vie *double* instead of *simple*) and tripled for *esprit de vin* of above 86°. The reduced-strength spirit had then to be strengthened to just below 66° with some *esprit de vin* for sale to Britain. When the spirit reached London the importers would add six veltes of the stronger *esprit de vin* – and when a New York merchant was buying he asked for 'brandy fortified to the London standard'.

The tax system as a whole struck especially hard at a largely commercial community like Cognac. A cask of wine or brandy paid up to ten times its value in internal duties on a journey through France to Paris. Royal greed extended even to Cognac's vital – and officially encouraged – export business. The town's brandies had to pay a substantial tax when they passed through the ports to leave the kingdom. These dues trebled during the eighteenth century, and they were increased further in 1782, with the Cognacais paying double the amount levied on the Rochellais, a bias which led to a major protest.

Foreign countries were already exploiting the revenue-producing potential of these luxury imports. Even a free-trade city like Hamburg levied heavy import duties on wines and brandies. Despite all these complications the Cognacais enjoyed increasing success as they steadily reduced their dependence on Holland and on Ireland, both highly price-conscious markets. Nevertheless, the Irish were bigger buyers than the English, although the brandies they bought were described as 'best cognac', i.e. one down from that required by Londoners, but still better than those sold on other markets. In the eighteenth century Ireland had almost as many inhabitants as England and lacked the – albeit irregular – surpluses of grain which enabled the English to produce rival spirits, normally gin, as well as the regular trade with the Caribbean which provided another competitor, rum, for the English market.

By then the products of the region were divided into three levels, headed by 'Champagne brandy'. Judging by the buying books of the merchant Jacques Augier their production was confined to the Champagnes and the Fins Bois north of Jarnac – indeed maps of the time show this region as 'Champagne'. Then came 'Fine Cognac' from the west near Pons and the north round Saint Jean d'Angély which was said to be 'inferior to Cognac

---

34 Notorious entrepreneurs who had bought rights to levy taxes from France's invariably impecunious monarchs.

by 10–15 per cent in strength and flavour.' By the time of the French revolution the buyers had gone further, asking for 'pale', 'perfectly without colour as white as water' or 'not too high coloured'. Others preferred brandies which were 'capital and full of rich flavour.' Sometimes the richness was somewhat artificial. In the early nineteenth century Auguste Hennessy worried that Martell's cognacs were richer than Hennessy's because of the 'syrups' they used, which he guessed came from prune-juice. By 1789 some of the brandies were being sold when they were more mature. After the 1760s brandy for London was usually described as 'old', i.e. three or four years old. In 1768 James Delamain advised a London importer that 'what we usually ship for said market is from three to ten years old'. By the 1770s double distillation had been introduced, previously a single distillation had produced an inevitably less concentrated spirit of around 45 per cent.

The brandies destined for the London market – and to a much lesser extent to be sold to drinkers in the rest of England and in Edinburgh, always an important market – were inevitably the best. Heavier duties than those imposed in Ireland increased the pressure, but the Londoners knew what they wanted. As James Delamain wrote in 1788, 'the great connoisseurs are in London and do not have their equal anywhere else'. There were over sixty London importers and the existence of the City's financial markets helped the always cash-strapped Cognac merchants. By the 1770s London was the largest single outlet for the best 'champaign brandy'. But the importers were a canny lot, objecting to the dominance exerted by Martell during much of the second half of the century and encouraging newcomers to compete.

During the eighteenth century the merchants based in Cognac who supplied the English and Irish markets were using, not La Rochelle, but Tonnay-Charente, half way between Cognac and the Bay of Biscay, where sea-going ships could load brandies not only from Cognac but also those from Saint Jean d'Angély which had been carried down the Boutonne, a tributary of the Charente, as well as brandies from Pons carried along another tributary, the Seudre. During the eighteenth century more locks were built on the Charente itself, and the river became navigable up to Angoulême. During the eighteenth century Tonnay took a great deal of trade from La Rochelle, and unlike La Rochelle it was within the Saintonge region so was not liable to the duties levied in transit further west to the Aunis. For, unless the brandy was made locally, i.e. within the same province, it had to pay three duties.

Brandy shipped through La Rochelle and produced from the inferior vines grown near the coast got a bad name. In Flanders until quite recently second quality brandy was called 'Rochelle' with the name cognac reserved for the best brandies. The third grade included the brandies destined for northern France which came from the west of the region especially the islands off the coast. At Tonnay the merchants could do their own shipping without using expensive middlemen and they were free of duties if they were held in an *entrepôt* for export. Not surprisingly, by 1789 Tonnay dominated the region's foreign trade.

In the eighteenth century Paris provided at least as large a market as the export market, and was sometimes much more profitable and thus larger, even though Louis XIV's ever-increasing debts led him to triple the taxes on wines and brandies at the end of the seventeenth century. As Louis Cullen put it: 'you have an unstable Paris demand, a small but stable London market, and a totally fickle market in Ireland, which can at times be the largest single market but other times when prices are too high virtually disappears.'[35] During the late seventeenth century Nantes was a bigger supplier of brandy than the cognac region, largely because it was closer to Paris, but later even the second grade brandies of the Cognac region were more successful in Paris. This even though cognac, unlike the wines of Burgundy and Champagne which could be transported to Paris directly by river, had to be transported overland to Chatellrault in carts hauled by six oxen which could carry a mere six *barriques*. At Chatellrault they could be loaded onto barges on the Vienne and Loire rivers to Orleans, the *entrepôt* for Paris.

These cognacs came from the east and north of the cognac region and were sold by merchants based either in Jarnac – where Ranson & Delamain was already a major force – or the *Aigriers* – merchants based at Aigres in the very north of the region. The brandies were basically weaker than those destined for export so had to be beefed up with rectified spirit, which of course reduced transport costs. In Paris there were two markets: the biggest was workers, often on their way to work, indulging in the traditional *café cognac*, a market which persisted until well after World War II; the smaller buyers were richer Parisians – financiers and those round the court – who would order 'champagne brandies' of up to eleven or twelve years of age. According to Savary, by the 1740s Cognac supplied two-fifths of the brandy from the region and Saint Jean d'Angély 25 per cent, the same percentage as La Rochelle and the islands.

La Rochelle fought back, albeit unavailingly. In 1751 the town's merchants tried unsuccessfully to reduce the strength of the eaux de vie coming from up-country to the level of their own (inferior) products. But the Rochellais were not the only competitors. Thirty years later the Cognac merchants complained that they had lost their markets in the Baltic to rivals from Spain and other parts of France who sold inferior brandies which were often mixed with the 'real stuff' and passed off as pure cognac. The opening of the Canal du Midi in 1681 between the Garonne river – and thus Bordeaux – and the south of France made it much easier for unscrupulous merchants to substitute cheaper and inferior products from Languedoc where most of the region's ever-increasing harvest of grapes was distilled before the railway provided a viable means of transporting wine to Paris in the mid-nineteenth century. The tax system did not help. According to Demachy, merchants would try to smuggle *esprit de vin* from Montpellier into Paris disguised as *esprits odorants* – perfumes – which paid a lower rate of duty. They would add a drop or two of essential oil, or even rub the cork with it, in an attempt to convince the officials. Some fraudsters did not bother to distil a second time but disguised the basic liquor with lavender oil and water.

Many of the buyers were smugglers, for the heavy British duties inevitably led to a lively smuggling traffic throughout the century. In Rudyard Kipling's words, 'Brandy for the Parson' (together with that other highly taxed item 'Baccy for the Clerk') was a staple of the smugglers' cargoes. In the late eighteenth century Adam Smith concluded

---

35 *The Brandy Trade under the Ancien Regime* (Cambridge, 1998); *The Irish Brandy Houses of Eighteenth-Century France* (Lilliput, 2000).

that smugglers were the biggest importers of French goods into Britain (and vice versa), for by then the traffic had been institutionalised. 'Like drugs today' writes Professor Cullen, smuggling 'seemed to offer an apparently easy method back to riches and success' – especially as the Irish authorities were not overly keen to prosecute the guilty parties. In 1774 one Dublin brandy dealer explained to Richard Hennessy that 'the private traders have hurted [sic] our trade here very much'.

Despite all the folklore connected with the smugglers, they were probably not an important element in the trade for cognacs, but rather for inferior brandies. The smugglers naturally needed the sort of swift turn around available only in Nantes and above all Bordeaux, which also offered immediate delivery of large quantities of – necessarily inferior – brandies. The two major centres for brandies being shipped irregularly were Guernsey and Dunkirk, indeed in the early eighteenth century after the long wars between France and Britain the Guernsey dealers were the only group with any real knowledge of the brandy trade in Britain. But these were not necessarily 'cognac' for 43 per cent of the brandy listed as 'prizes of war' in the London press in the first decade of the eighteenth century was described as 'Spanish brandies'.

Smugglers were only one of many variables in a trade which fluctuated widely. The collapse of the complicated schemes put forward by the Scottish financier Law led to a temporary withdrawal by the Dutch and the bankruptcy of Augier in 1722, though the firm, and the market, recovered a few years later when the French currency fell in value. Other complications included the tax situation abroad as well as in France, while harvests varied wildly in both quality and quantity, and the buyers were quite happy to switch to competitive spirits. A number of wars throughout the century interrupted trade or forced sales to a neutral port like Dunkirk, Ostend, Hamburg or Rotterdam, sometimes getting there overland via Paris. Prices rose after the outbreak of war in the 1740s, the 1750s and 1770s. Nevertheless, the effects were sometimes surprising. The outbreak of the Seven Years' War in 1756 provided Jean Martell with enough of a boost to enable him to give up dealing in beef and tallow – he recorded that consumption of brandy in London and Dublin had tripled during the war.

An even more important factor was the availability of alternative spirits. In Ireland during the late 1750s bad harvests (and thus reduced supplies of grain for distillation into whiskey) were enough to send the price of cognac soaring, though any shortage of rum also provided an opportunity for the Cognacais – the shortage of grain lasted well into the late 1760s.

Right up to the French revolution Cognac was in many ways subordinate to Bordeaux, and a junior partner in the sales of luxury wines and spirits. During the century Bordeaux had emerged as France's leading port, thanks to its trading links with France's Caribbean colonies. As a result, most Cognac merchants had links or partnerships with the larger city. Bordeaux brandies could never compete in any market which demanded quality. In any case, for the Bordelais brandy was always a secondary product compared with wine, useful mainly for using wine which had, quite literally, passed its sell-by date. Nevertheless, many clients – especially the Dutch – were buying purely on price. So by the 1640s Bordeaux was exporting sizeable quantities of brandy. In any case the city was enormously important as a source of credit and as an *entrepôt*. Bordeaux was also the *entrepôt* for the – much smaller but better – quantities of brandy from the Armagnac region to the south.

Despite Bordeaux's importance in Cognac, and to a lesser extent in other 'brandy towns' like Jarnac there was a distinct 'agro-industrial' community that grew the grapes, made the wine and distilled and sold the brandy. In a relatively prosperous century grapes were a far more profitable product than grain – and the regular prohibitions on planting vines had little or no effect. From a number of contemporary sources we get the picture of an astonishingly modern capitalist society hampered by few of the feudal restrictions normal in pre-Revolutionary France. Indeed, the industry was so successful that 'the aristocracy of the counting house' aroused jealous feelings among professionals like lawyers and priests.

However the region's success was bedevilled by religious persecution. In 1661 Louis XIV had taken personal power and began to erode the rights of the 100,000 Protestants in the region, many of whom left even before1685 when the Revocation of the Edict of Nantes forced much of the Protestant community to scatter. Many of them went abroad to join the 'Huguenot Mafia', which provided local merchants with a network of contacts throughout Europe, above all in Britain and Holland. These included Europe's leading bankers, who were always prepared to lend money to their co-religionists. Those who remained were forced to abandon the many official and professional positions they had held and to rely on trade for their living. This change, boosted by their connections outside France, was enormously helpful for the region, as well as ensuring their continuing dominance of the trade. Inevitably Jarnac, Cognac's major local rival, slipped in importance but the town remained the refuge for such Protestant firms as Ranson and Delamain.

But even the Martells, staunchest of Protestants, had to go through symbolic Catholic marriage ceremonies to ensure that their children would be recognised as legitimate. Nevertheless, throughout two generations of active persecution the Protestants defiantly held secret services in lonely country barns or under trees like the ironically named 'Louis oak' which became a legend. The local inhabitants remained sympathetic, and the soldiers sent in pursuit of the preachers at the behest of the Catholic clergy often found it impossible to arrest them, though their whereabouts were known to hundreds of the local peasantry. For the Church, like the aristocracy, had a far weaker hold on the region than on most of rural France. The only memorials to their previous sufferings were the solitary cypress trees on the family estates, each marking the tomb of one of the faithful.

Despite the persecutions, the majority of merchant families remained intact during the terrible years but even then Catholics sympathised with, and often helped the Protestants who were soon building *granges*, barns, in which to worship. Effectively persecution ended around 1750 in Jarnac and a bit later in Cognac. Yet the Protestants' ambiguous position could still be exploited. As late as 1767 the dowager Countess of Jarnac, who had the monopoly of baking in the town, wrote a ferocious letter from her Paris home to M. Delamain, Jarnac's leading merchant, who had dared to encourage the locals to build their own bread oven. They were related by marriage, but the breach of her rights so infuriated the countess that she exploded: 'Remember your religion is that of neither the State nor of the king.'

By 1787 the Protestants had had their rights restored by an increasingly harassed monarch. They dealt mainly in cognac but, to earn a living, often traded in other products, notably paper, the region's most important product, and in both cases they acted as what we would call 'freight forwarders' assembling small lots to be transported in bulk. Right up to the revolution they were usually merely intermediaries for their richer brethren in La Rochelle. In return they sold imported implements and Dutch stills. Typically, Jean Martell did not deal exclusively in cognac, far from it, but also in leather, goat- and sheepskins, wheat, tallow, butter, coal, indigo, wood, flower bulbs and wool stockings; and in 1750, Guy Gauthier sold almost the same quantity of tanned hides, walnuts and clover seeds as he did brandy.

The three-cornered relationship born of the earlier Dutch dominance persisted, with the ultimate buyers located in London, Dublin, Hamburg or, most often, Ostend, where Richard Hennessy learnt the business. In terms of quantity the Dutch remained the biggest buyers, accounting for over twice as much as the British, with the Hanseatic ports along the Baltic also major clients. But as always, because the British were prepared to pay far more than the Dutch, they were far more important clients.

Some firms, like Ranson or Lallemand are known today for their later emergence under other names, a few, notably Augier, survived into the late twentieth century but most of the others like Prévot, Robicquet, Rouhaud, Pelluchon, Riget, Brunet, Marie-Séraphin and Riget have disappeared. These 'real' merchants described themselves as those from Cognac, Jamac and Pons, for Cognac, in the words of Etienne Munier, was emerging as 'the major township and trading centre of these provinces' (Saintonge and the Angoumois).[36] By this time *preuve de Cognac* had replaced *preuve d'Hollande* as a measure of a spirit's strength just as the name of cognac had become the standard by which all other brandies were judged. It was still a small town, with only about 2,000 inhabitants, but was increasingly recognised as important. It even enjoyed a superb postal service: there were four services a week to Paris, and letters took a mere four days to get there. Those to England took just ten days, even in wartime. Only a handful of merchants were actually based in Cognac, but a lot of business was done there. The *Dictionnaire Universel* describes how 'on Saturday each week a brandy market was held in Cognac. All the merchants and distillers meet to buy and sell.'

The families were already international. Guy Gauthier, although a Protestant, acted as a spokesman for the people of Cognac in Paris, and settled his son in the City of London after an apprenticeship in Holland. His brother worked in Barcelona and two other members of the family at Port-au-Prince in Haiti. The market was a big one; every year Cognac produced 200,000 *barriques de vins propres à brûler* (casks of wines suitable for distilling) from which emerged 13,400 pipes (each of three *barriques* or about 600

---

36 *Essai sur l'Angoumois à la fin de l'Ancien Régime* (Paris, 1977).

litres), adding up to eight million litres of eau de vie. In bad years the yield was somewhat less, since then it took six, rather than five *barriques* of wine to make one of eau de vie.

During the century a handful of merchants managed to acquire sufficient capital to mature their brandies before shipping them, though most brandy – except that destined for London – was shipped within the year following distillation and only the best 'Champagne' brandies were kept back for over two years. Nevertheless, as early as 1718 Augier shipped two *pièces* of cognac between eight and ten years old. By the second half of the century they were often stocking their brandies and not necessarily selling at the first opportunity. But whereas in Bordeaux it was the merchants who held the stocks, in Cognac the landowners made the running. As Munier noted in 1779, 'When the brandy has been distilled, the rich landowners often store it until they can get a high price for it. I have seen some who have converted into brandy and hoarded in their cellars the several years' vintages which they have sold in one fell swoop at the right moment, making 12,000 to 15,000 livres on the transaction.' Yet these were still relatively young brandies. In the 1780s Richard Hennessy noted that shrewd operators with enough capital had bought up most of one year's production and were not prepared to sell until they saw whether the next vintage would be good or not. They did not have to keep them for long. Brandy was called 'old' once it had spent a year in cask, and the oldest Hennessy brandies shipped were generally no more than four years old (although he occasionally sold brandies ten or even eighteen years old).

Prices were set by geographical origin as well as by age, for during the century brandy from the Champagne region grew in value by comparison with less blessed vineyards nearer the coast. By then too customers' tastes had started to vary. The northerners like the Dutch and Germans wanted colourless brandies while British buyers tended to want coloured, brown brandy. Molasses or caramelised or burnt sugar was used, not for colour but for sweetness but the buyers were not fooled. As James Turner wrote to his partner James Hennessy, 'your house I think overloads them with syrop [sic] and know that this will ever assist to cover a foul spirit.'

The three most prominent firms were Augier, the oldest, Martell and Delamain.

Jean Martell provided an early example of a theme which recurs in the history, making his way by marrying the daughter of a powerful local figure. *Il se fait gendre* – 'he made himself a son-in-law' – is the local way of putting such a union, the nearest Anglo-Saxon equivalent is probably the old Hollywood wisecrack 'the son-in-law also rises'. But such in-breeding – the sister of Martell's first wife had married an Augier – was inevitable in a small community conscious of its foreign origins, its different religious allegiances and one very separate from the native aristocracy and gentry. The same factors led to a similar pattern which prevailed among the Chartonnais of Bordeaux, the merchants who dominated the claret trade for two centuries.

Martell was not the first son-in-law in the Cognac business – that honour should probably go to Phillipe Augier, who in 1643 founded the oldest Cognac firm and got his start in life by marrying the daughter of a rich banker and paper merchant from Angoulême. In the 1720s Augier was in trouble and Martell took – temporary – advantage

JEAN MARTELL

Jean Martell, who founded the firm, was a member of a leading commercial family in Jersey, a major centre for smuggled goods. So it was natural for him to seek his fortune in Cognac, arriving in 1715. He started as a broker, buying casks of cognac and wines from the Borderies for buyers mainly in the Channel Islands, but also in Normandy, Picardy and Holland. He made an unpromising start. His arrival coincided with the short-lived boom engendered by Law's economic policies. The price of wines and spirits soared and then, inevitably, slumped. Martell was caught in the boom-and-bust and was forced to liquidate his first partnership. But he repaid his debts and enjoyed considerable success when he started up again, greatly helped by successive marriages to the daughters of two major Cognac merchants.

Jean Martell: founder of an empire – helped by two profitable marriages!

He married first Jeanne Brunet and then, after her death, her cousin, Jeanne-Rachel Lallemand, a direct descendent of Jacques Roux, a pioneering seventeenth-century Cognac merchant.

She provided the young hopeful with a secure position within the merchant hierarchy of the town. So there is an uninterrupted line from Jacques Roux to Jean Martell's direct descendants, the Firino-Martells, who owned one of Cognac's largest businesses until 1988.

of the trade he was conducting through Guernsey (it did not help that he was from the rival neighbouring island of Jersey) but by the end of the decade the London merchants were buying direct from Cognac, with a disastrous effect on Martell's business, and his failure to establish himself in the domestic business did not help. So the dominance of the firm through the following two hundred and fifty years owes more to his brother-in-law Louis Gabriel than to the founding figure. Gabriel transformed the business into a major local firm. He was a ruthless businessman who took over on Martell's death in 1753, stamping it with what Cullen calls the family's 'overbearing and narrow influence…the future of the Martell business was secured not because it was a Martell house but because it was a Lallemand one'.

The other major force was Delamain, the result of another son-in-law, for Marie Ranson, the descendant of another Protestant, married James Delamain in 1763. He was a Dublin-born Protestant and got his job because of his Irish contacts – a position naturally reinforced by his marriage. He was one of the rare outsiders in the cognac business but a man of authority who used his position as a freemason to come into contact with the leading lights of the region. By the 1760s his was probably the biggest firm with twelve stills and a leading position in the Irish trade, dominated by him and Martell. He was also in some ways a genuine original – the first man to introduce potatoes to south-western France.

But the merchant classes were not the only ones to benefit from the lack of feudal overlordship, for the peasant land-holders shared in the general prosperity. Many of the feudal rights had been transformed into fixed-money rents, so the peasants could pocket most of the profits resulting from any increased sales. The most burdensome feudal relic was the *Ban des Vendanges*, the *seigneurs'* right to decide the date of the harvest, a right that forced the peasants to harvest the nobles' grapes before their own.

Historically, the region's prosperous situation has been concealed because so much of the evidence left to us is in the form of complaints, directed mostly at the taxmen, which give the impression of grinding poverty. Indeed, in 1789 the peasants directed their complaints against the tax collectors rather than the nobility. Even Etienne Munier, himself a royal official, was misled. He grossly underestimated the yields and hence the profit available. Other witnesses were equally gloomy. In a naturally anonymous publication, *A Sad Picture of Rustic Folk*, published in 1786, the author explains that those who could not afford to distil their wines were forced to drink them, 'thus giving their children bad habits from an early age; and as it was natural to serve up worthless wines which would otherwise have been lost, they naturally took advantage of the excess'. Modern sociologists would call the result a cycle of rural deprivation, of which the legacy was a great many widows, deformed children and other signs of misery. It would be fairer to say that there were still large pockets of poverty and misery in what was, by eighteenth-century French standards, a prosperous and socially cohesive area.

For centuries everyone in the Cognac area had known that grapes were their most valuable crop, if only because the soil was often reckoned to be too impoverished for any other. As a result the clergy and the nobility, as well as humbler tenants, farmed the land themselves and did not follow the usual habit of leasing it to share croppers. Jean Gervais remarked: 'Formerly only the rich bourgeois and the better-off cultivated their own vines; nowadays virtually every peasant and simple rustic fellow has planted them for himself, which keeps them busy and means they give up working for others, so that the remaining day labourers, sought by everyone, prefer to work for those who can pay them to excess.'[37] For the peasants were fully alert to commercial opportunities, even at the expense of farming techniques. As Munier put it: 'In the Angoumois the peasants do not form a class apart, since they apply themselves indiscriminately to every type of cultivation. This over-extensive appetite is perhaps the cause of the bad farming methods in the Angoumois.'

Of course life was not always easy. The growers had to endure worries like the plagues of noxious worms, insects and other pests which periodically afflicted them and the growing shortage of the wood required as fuel for the stills. One author, Father Arcère, recommended the use of coal, which provided a more uniform and reliable source of

---

37 Gervais, *Memoire sur l'Angoumois*, 1725; reproduced in the *Bulletin of the Société Archéologique et Historique de la Charente* (1864).

heat and could be imported from England (in peacetime anyway). One merchant even imported coal as ballast when ships were returning from England, but the Charentais were conservative and remained faithful to the cheaper, local wood for another hundred years or more.

Many of the peasants had their own stills, although there were also precursors of today's *bouilleurs de profession* (professional distillers), some of whom had mobile stills. Throughout the century the more important distillers also speculated on the future price of cognacs. Old brandies had been worth more than new since the 1720s and speculation became even more profitable after the end of the American War of Independence in 1783, for the decade was a good one for the region. Tax increases imposed in 1782 were rescinded two years later, and a Free Trade Treaty with England, which came into operation in 1786, provided a new impetus for the cognac trade. Exports (and prices) rose rapidly. But that did not stop the inhabitants grumbling. The woes of generations exploded in the famous 'Doléances' of 1789, the endless pages of complaints that provided such a dense background to the Revolution. Typically, the citizens of la Valette, a small town near Angoulême, had hoped that:

> *having paid their* Tailles, *their poll taxes, taxes on utensils and equipment, forced labour, subsidies for waifs and strays, personal dues, the first, second and third portions of the 'twentieth', having paid their labourers, the priest and the landlord, and after we have endured bad weather, like hail, frost, rot and drought, we had hoped that what remained of our crops could be gathered into our barns and cellars. But far from it. Our friends the tax collectors are beating at our doors demanding that we pay over three livres for every* barrique *of wine we produce.*[38]

---

38 'Doléances de la Sénéchaussée d'Angoulême pour les Etats Généraux de 1789'.

6

REVOLUTIONS ON THE ROAD TO DAYS OF GLORY

Curiously the revolutionary period between 1789 and 1815 freed Cognac from Bordeaux's dominance and Cognac developed into a truly independent commercial centre for the first time. The major firms were transformed from being merely brokers with some stocks to proper merchants, employing managers, accountants and *maîtres de chai* – cellarmasters – in charge of distilling, stocking and blending the brandies

In 1789 the Cognacais had worse things to worry about than a mere revolution. In the previous year terrifying hailstorms had devastated northern France and resulted in a shortage of grain, while the winter of 1788–1789 had been memorably harsh, indeed the worst since 1709. The wine had frozen in the cellars; stocks of grain had been almost exhausted by early summer; the harvest that year was a mere twentieth of the average level and famine was averted only by a timely loan from Messrs Augier and Martell. Nevertheless, business continued as usual until the Revolutionary Terror of 1793–94. In 1791 the leading merchants of the district, Augier, Veuve, Martell, Allemand, Arbouin & Zimmerman, Hennessy & Turner, Ranson & Delamain and Guerinet & Robin, reasserted their traditional stand when they swore to use only brandies from the Saintonge and the Angoumois and not to imitate their competitors by mixing the local produce with brandies from the south of France or from Spain. The most important fraudsters were middlemen, especially those in the major *entrepôt*, the free port of Dunkirk. In the stern words of one eighteenth-century patriarch to his son: 'you will not sell under your name anything other than cognac…you must not mix your cognac with any other product.'

During the early revolutionary years the cognac trade came to be regarded as a 'sheltered occupation' with the locals hesitating to attack the merchants. Nevertheless, they had to be adaptable. M. Augier had been elected a deputy in 1789 but, like so many others was left stranded by the increasing extremism of the revolutionary tide when Irishmen who could not prove that they had been naturalised were imprisoned

The *ancien régime* disappeared in more senses than one and some in the trade could not cope with the uncertainties. The revolutionary shocks were too difficult for a member of the older generation like James Delamain. He was already fifty-two-years-old in 1789 and had been caught short by the speed of revolutionary events – in 1792 his patron the Comte de Jarnac joined the emigrés and his business never recovered. This put an intolerable strain on his relationships with his children – in 1797 he is recorded as believing that his family had failed. He died in 1817 and in a story which was to remain a theme in the history of the trade he left ten children who went their own ways, though by 1824 the name had been resurrected by one of his sons in partnership with a member of the Roullet family.

Ironically, it was during the revolutionary period that Hennessy and Martell, already a major influence, particularly in London, emerged as the dominating forces in the business and part of the local establishment, a dominance they retained until 1945. Indeed the commercial history of Cognac in the century and a half after the Revolution consisted largely of successive challenges to their duopoly from newcomers who often seemed invincible at the time but have rarely lasted more than one generation. For, as the local novelist Jacques Chardonne pointed out, even the most important merchants owed very little to inheritance: 'wealth does not last long in this business'. The duopoly was founded on the commercial risks and opportunities they grasped between 1789 and 1815 which enabled them to build up the capital required to concentrate on brandy.

Not that they had a duopoly at the time: shipping documents show that in the mid-1790s the long-extinct firm of Laberge was as big as either and that, together, the two halves of the Delamain business were almost as big. Yet the business was continually concentrating; in the 1790s probably only ten of the fifty or so merchants were exporters, the others largely merely suppliers.

The Martells were largely untouched by the Revolution, Jean Martell and Jean Augier commanded the local national guard and Martell was well enough placed to defend one of his salesmen against the accusations of the local revolutionary committees. Moreover they benefited from the Revolutionary Wars, for wars benefit brandy, a product much needed by exhausted, frightened troops. In particular Theodore Martell was involved in large purchases of foodstuffs for the land armies. He was not alone, the Broussard family held the valuable monopoly to supply spirits to the Napoleonic navy.[39] This was not a new business. Throughout the nineteenth century the French army and navy were both considerable buyers; when Rochefort, down-river from Tonnay, was growing in importance as a naval base and arsenal, the ships provisioned there required large quantities of cognac to sustain the sailors and prevent scurvy.

More surprising was the sudden blossoming of Hennessy's firm. 'Citizen Richard Hennessy' was safe enough to be charged by the local revolutionary committee with the sale of brandy, but the key to the firm's success was a seven-year partnership between Richard's son James Hennessy and James Delamain's nephew Sam Turner. By 1796

---

39 They remained major brokers until 2009 when the octogenarian Jacques Broussard sold his amazing stocks of old cognac to Martell.

James had emerged with the biggest share in a three-sided partnership, with seven of the sixteen shares, James had five and the ageing Richard – he died in 1800 – the remaining four. As Cullen notes, 'James Hennessy and Sam Turner were quicker to do business with the revolutionary governments in the 1790s than any other house.'

James had learnt his trade in London, which he visited in 1789 as a twenty-four-year-old, building on the London connections of his father's former partner, John Saule. In Cullen's words Turner and James – who was a commander of the Garde Nationale – were 'not put off by the challenge of transforming their business from orthodox trading to government orders which was

James Hennessy, the real founder

their whole business'. Their first coup was to act for a year on behalf of the revolutionary government in exchanging their brandies against much-needed grain imported through their foreign business channels. By the late 1790s they were sufficiently successful for the socially ambitious Richard to worry about his son's Irish brogue.

Turner and Jean Martell both spent the years between 1796 and 1799 in Hamburg which had become the major *entrepôt* for shipments to England, by then at war with France – the rival firm of Otard admitted that virtually all its overseas trade was through the city. They all faced severe price competition from the cheaper brandies from elsewhere in France – Hennessy and Turner claimed to take the greatest possible care when blending their brandies. Turner also found it useful to be in Hamburg to avoid accusations of royalism but he stayed because it was crucial to the success of the business It was also, and not coincidentally, a major financial centre, essential at a time of fluctuating financial problems in France itself. In the last years of the nineteenth century the peasants were naturally deeply mistrustful of the *assignats* and other dubious notes issued by successive revolutionary governments. To buy their precious cognacs the merchants had to come up with gold or foreign currency. The partnership suffered badly when Hamburg's bankers collapsed from over-stretch in 1799. Two years later Hennessy and Turner were only saved by a timely loan from the Martells. They continued to have problems with their bankers in Paris and remained in hock to the Martells and their bankers until 1805. Nevertheless, by 1813 James felt strong enough to end the partnership with Turner.

In 1795 the two families had been united through the marriage of James Hennessy with Marthe Martell, daughter of Frédéric Gabriel Martell. In her husband's frequent absences she proved as able a businesswoman as Rachel, Jean's widow. The marriage was something of a comedown for a clan which dominated the trade and had become accustomed to marrying its female offspring to local notables. Nevertheless, it responded to the view of marriage normal in bourgeois France until relatively recently. As Auguste Hennessy put it, in the nineteenth century marriage 'rests on considerations of [financial] interest

RICHARD HENNESSY

Richard Hennessy, founder of what is today the region's biggest firm, whose portrait still dominates the company's publicity, was not an effective fellow. Misleadingly, he is portrayed in military uniform, though he served for only a few years and left the French army in early 1753 after a five years' wait for a commission. His length of service was doubled by one of his Irish connections when he left the army, and the exaggerated figure was later exploited by his son James to prove that he was not a mere foreigner but the son of a man who had served in the French army for ten years.

In reality Richard was a small-time wheeler-dealer who entered the trade only at the relatively late age of forty-one, prone to fits of depression and relying for his livelihood on a series of fluctuating partnerships. Nevertheless, he was

Richard Hennessy: a soldier, but not for long

much loved: 'few men' wrote the generally disapproving Cullen, 'can have been loved as much as Richard...he was warm and kind also able simultaneously to retain the friendship of his contemporaries and of young people.' He was described as 'a younger son in trade with little resources' and was lucky to be the only survivor of a number of young Irishmen who settled in the region in the late 1760s and early 1770s. As one of the Irishmen who formed the link between Cognac and Bordeaux - the firm of Exshaw was the last relic of the Dublin–Bordeaux nexus - his major asset was not his business capacities but his connections with influential families in Ireland.

His 'career' was typical of many of those involved in the cognac trade, he drifted from Ostend to Bordeaux and then in 1765 to Cognac, stating bluntly, 'It was the only town in the province with a market dealing in brandy.' In 1776 he returned to Bordeaux and during the 1780s enjoyed the profits from a major distilling business in Bordeaux in partnership with an energetic Irish go-getter, George Boyd. His major contribution was to bring with him a distiller from Cognac during a period marred by the death of his beloved wife Nelly and two of his sons, both from scarlet fever (characteristically, he was defrauded by the woman he employed to look after his remaining offspring). Unfortunately, after some years their distillery was undercut by smaller competitors and Boyd's arrogance and 'hazy bookkeeping sense' (in Cullen's words) led to disaster and left a financial mess on his death in September 1788.

OTARD – OR O'TARD – AND DUPUY

The Revolution provided an opportunity for Messrs Otard-Dupuy, a partnership of two growers who had accumulated comfortable stocks before 1789 and one of the earliest examples of growers-turned-merchants, though Jean-Baptiste Otard had social pretensions. O'tard as he styled himself, claimed descent from an old Scottish family which, like the Hennessys, had settled in France for religious reasons, for it was useful to pretend to have connections with Scottish Jacobite gentry. Otard, who was based in Bordeaux, was sentenced to death by the revolutionaries and escaped only through the timely intervention of his loyal friends. Jean Dupuy was a local, who brought a new market to the partnership they established in 1794 for his uncle, Leon Dupuy, had pioneered sales to the newly independent United States.

At the revolution they had managed to buy up the finest corner site in all Cognac, the Château des Valois on the river guarding the bridge across the Charente, a fortress which had been reduced to acting as a rather dilapidated prison and had naturally become vacant with the fall of the French monarchy. Otard, an engineer by training, discovered that the damp cellars of the château offered the perfect conditions for maturing cognac. Ever since then it has provided an ideal warehouse – and a magnificent shop window for the firm's products. By the early nineteenth century they were on a par with Martell and Hennessy and were able to build lavish mansions. The town's first museum, for example, is housed in a mansion built by Jules Dupuy in front of the Town Hall, itself originally the town house of his partner, Léon Otard.

rather than happiness'. In a second link James's daughter Lucie married her cousin Jean-Gabriel Martell in 1816. Though the mutual interests of Martell and Hennessy became stronger and stronger they never hesitated to go their own way commercially. They even sold to New York; moreover, to one Jacob Schieffelin, the ancestor of the family which remained Hennessy's agents for nearly two hundred years. The American connection became valuable, not only because of the direct sales but also because the Americans were neutral, so in wartime their ships could be used to ship brandy to an equally neutral port for trans-shipment to England.

All the merchants benefited from the availability of cheap property confiscated from their previous aristocratic or religious owners. Martell and Hennessy established themselves in the former Couvent des Cordeliers just above the river, which they bought through third parties. Important newcomers included Otard-Dupuy and Thomas Hine, the descendant of a Dorset family who had originally gone to France to complete his education – a link arranged through the 'Huguenot Mafia'. He settled in Jarnac, went to work for Ranson & Delamain and soon married a daughter of his employer, James Delamain.

The Revolution had other important effects. It relieved the peasant landowners of their burden of feudal dues and institutionalised the tolerance unofficially granted to the region's Protestants under the Bourbon monarchy. More crucially, it removed the restrictions and taxes which had impeded the circulation of wines and spirits, and thus, for the first time, enabled the Cognacais to blend brandies from different distilleries. The ability to blend meant that individual merchants could establish their own style of spirit, although this development was slow to emerge.

The Napoleonic years were not a real disaster. Sales to Britain had been boosted by the Free Trade treaty of 1786 from below 50,000 hectolitres to over 60,000. When war broke out in 1793 sales slumped, but only to between 30,000 and 40,000 hectolitres. Exports and prices recovered somewhat, for even the new-style Revolutionary War did not mean the end of all trade with the enemy. Some elements of the former pattern of trade remained. An old-style shortage of grain in 1795–6 had its usual effect of increasing demand, and the Peace of Amiens in 1802 brought the usual result of an, albeit short-lived, slump, which led to the bankruptcy of Casimir Martini, one of Cognac's leading merchants.

Even the period of blockade and counter-blockade which followed the outbreak of 'total' war in 1804 included elements of sheer farce. Sales dropped, but because of excessive British tariffs, not on account of war – and even the licensing system merely complicated the traffic. The blockade which followed the British 'Orders in Council' of 1807 banning purchases of French wines and spirits for the British armed forces, and later the total ban on French imports, should have put a stop to the traffic but far from it: imports soared, partly because prices in France had dropped sufficiently to provide bargains for the British, who declined to deprive themselves of their habitual luxuries. In 1808 Sir John Nicholl, a British MP, recognised that 'we need a little wine and French brandy to rejoice and comfort ourselves'.

A system of import licences ensured that the British kept some control over the situation while still slaking their thirsts. As Jean Martell put it: 'We only want freedom to get out, and the blockade will not stop us, above all if we have good letters of credit.' Nevertheless, he had needed political protection at a high level in Paris to obtain the necessary export licences. The ban itself had been inspired not by patriotic fervour but by pressure from the 'West Indian interest', the traditional lobby of rum merchants whose sales had been badly hurt by the success of French brandies. Imports soared in 1809 in anticipation of the ban, which caused a temporary slump lasting less than two years until counter-pressure from the rest of the commercial community forced a relaxation. In 1812 things began to return to normal, a process that took nearly a decade.

It was not surprising then that, in 1815, as Frédéric Martell put it, 'It was with feelings of the greatest relief that the citizens of Cognac greeted the news of Napoleon's deposition.' But the region still had to cope with climatic problems. The previous decade had been uniformly cold, while ash from the cataclysmic eruption in April that year of the Tambora Volcano in Indonesia, the most powerful in recorded history, turned 1816 into a year without a summer throughout Europe, and it was not until 1820 that the weather returned to relative normality. The Restoration not only restored the status quo ante bellum it also reinforced the London connection. All three of James Hennessy's sons, James, Auguste and Frédéric, were automatically sent there to learn the business and Hennessy rapidly gained momentum, above all when Auguste took over. By 1815 Hennessy and Martell had emerged as real merchants, with proper accounting systems, even travel expenses, an important item, were properly checked, while Auguste talked of buying casks in their thousands. But even Hennessy had relatively little brandy over three years old and always relied greatly on purchases from what we would now call the spot market.

Economically the pattern established before the Revolution continued, with hundreds of small farmers, few large holdings (except those being accumulated by the merchants themselves) and even fewer labourers – a situation that produced the usual crop of complaints. One authority estimated that there were 1,500 growers with holdings large enough to produce a dozen *barriques* of wine. Most of them distilled their production themselves in small stills which held only a single *barrique* of wine and cost a mere 500 francs.

The period had left its scars. As one of Martell's colleagues put it: 'it is much to be feared that people will lose the taste for them [our brandies], and it is very difficult for a trade which has been thus disturbed to get back on to its former tracks.' Peace brought a short-lived boom in prices and a steady increase in sales from an average of 30,000 hectolitres during the war to over 80,000 in the late 1820s and over 100,000 in the following decade. British customs duties continued to rise, and at their post-war worst amounted to six times the value of the cognac itself, far higher than those payable on rival spirits like rum. So-called 'British brandy' enjoyed a considerable vogue, largely because it involved one-third of the duties imposed on the French equivalent.

The Cognacais, like their colleagues in Bordeaux, were almost totally dependent on sales to the British market, which took over four-fifths of their exports, so both communities were early campaigners for free trade. As one 1838 petition put it:

If the French government does not get a reduction of the exorbitant duties which disrupt our brandy trade, they will cease to be drunk at all which will force the wine growers to pull up their vines. This does not mean to say that they can plant other crops...the soil is too dry...the government should not forget that it is a question of 200 million francs and the ruin of 4,000 families...what distinguishes the Cognac trade from that of other spirits is that no merchant here bothers with distillation: the owners of the vineyards, in both the departments of the Charente, are at the same time farmers and distillers.

The signatories to the petition emphasised that although their traditional methods of distillation were both slow and extravagant, they were essential to retain the natural qualities of the grape and justify the price of cognac: 'These methods are the only ones that can be employed without damaging these qualities.' Distillers making lesser spirits from grain could use larger, quicker, more modern stills, the continuous stills invented around 1830 by one Cooley, an Irish customs officer. Cognac makers alleged that these produced inferior brandy. But at the back of the Gauthiers' house in the Rue Saulnier is the brick tower which used to house a steam continuous distillation apparatus. According to Guy Gauthier-Auriol, it provided a much smoother product than any other type. Some of the Cognacais did experiment with a new-style apparatus, using a second still by the side of the first, so that the distillation process could be more or less continuous with the second still being emptied only once a week to rid it of the accumulated lees.

Throughout most of the century the growers continued to hold the bulk of the region's stocks of older brandies, and the richer among them could choose whether to sell their brandy new, speculate by holding it for a few months in case the next harvest was bad, or age it themselves. In the early post-war years prices were still set in the traditional way. Every Saturday, wrote J-P Quénot,

> the day of the brandy market in the town of Cognac, the growers who wish to sell, the middle men who are buying to sell on, and the merchants from the whole region...repair to a small square in Cognac called Le Canton where most of the buying is done on the simple presentation of a flask in which the seller has put a small sample of the spirit which he agrees to deliver. The price at which most transactions have been concluded becomes the official market price, which the merchants use when calculating their selling price.[40]

The tradition provided the merchants with a chance to increase their profits. The official price was for brandies from *la Champagne*, defined as the whole of the arrondissement of Cognac lying on the south bank of the Charente (as well as some from the neighbouring department). As in the eighteenth century those from the north bank were worth less, and those from the outlying regions to the west formed a third division. The less scrupulous merchants, said Quénot, 'blend the different brandies and make their foreign buyers pay in relation to the full market price. To this considerable advantage they added the price of the cask, which they also make their suppliers pay, without allowing the amount when dealing with the growers.'

But there was one group that did not accept the existing order of things. In 1838 one Pierre Antoine de Salignac rallied some hundreds of the region's wine growers into the United Vineyard Proprietors Company, the Société de Proprietaires Vinicoles de Cognac. He launched the new co-operative as a direct challenge to the 'Big Three' houses – Martell, Hennessy and Otard-Dupuy – who, he claimed, monopolised the purchase of the growers' brandies (according to Quénot, six or eight houses controlled the trade). Salignac claimed, reasonably enough, that cognac owed its world-wide fame to its quality, and that this was provided not by the trademarks burned into the casks by the three firms but by the growers and distillers themselves. Their fight against the Big Three was soon so successful that within a few years the United Vintners' brandy, with Salignac's own name prominent on the label, joined the Big Three.

In Dickens' magazine *Household Words* his friend Henry Vizetelly gave a lyrical description of the relationship of the growers with Salignac as he witnessed it during a visit in 1855:

> When a peasant proprietor out in the country has burnt his wine into eau de vie, if the markets put on an inviting aspect, he loads the chariot before his door with precious tubs, he then washes his face and hands, puts on a clean shirt and blouse, and takes his Sunday broad-

---

40 in *Statistique du Departement de la Charente* (1818).

brimmed hat out of the closet. He proceeds slowly on his way with stately step, and enters the narrow crooked passages which Cognac dignifies with the name of streets, announcing his arrival by a long succession of what you might take for pistol-shots, but which are no more than harmless cracks of the whip. He stops at the gate of the establishment, say of Messrs R. & Co. his cargo is set down, taken in, rolled up an inclined plane, and measured at once by transfusion into a cylindrical vessel which has outside it a glass tube, to which a graduated scale is attached, communicating with the interior, and therefore showing exactly how full the measure is. That settled he walks off with the empty casks, goes on his way rejoicing, leaving the rustic eau de vie to be converted into gentlemanly cognac brandy.[41]

Salignac, too, had his imitators. Jules Duret and the founder of the firm of Barriasson used their position as managers of growers' co-operatives to launch themselves as merchants. Salignac himself had the strikingly modern idea that cognacs, like the wines of Bordeaux, ought to be graded by their age and quality, arguing that cognac's principal clientele, the better-off classes in Britain, could afford higher prices. He was also the only merchant who actually welcomed visitors. More traditional houses, in the words of Charles Tovey, 'would like the English consumer especially to retain the delusion that a special name branded upon the exterior of a cask has everything to do with the quality of its contents. They would not wish the world to know that any merchant in Cognac who has cash to go to market with can purchase from the farmers as good Brandy as another.' In an understandable effort to retain their aura of mystery they did not even reply to Tovey's letters.

Salignac did not confine his ideas to the market place, they had an additional, political, dimension. In his election propaganda he accused the Big Three of exploiting the growers and making monstrous profits at their expense. He mocked their claim that they had opened new markets: they still depended, he said, almost entirely on British buyers and even used British ships, to the great detriment of the French merchant navy. He finished with a splendid flourish: 'Stop giving yourself an importance which you lack. Your only claim to fame is to have profiteered at the expense of the growers…and the region has never forgotten the fact!!!!!'

His success in Britain – he increased sales by a half during the late 1840s – alarmed the older-established firms but Hennessy at least, managed to leap ahead through replacing its agents, Sandeman, with Twiss and Browning (who remained their importers for over a century). In Britain all the firms were pitching at two very distinct markets, the traditional aristocratic drinkers and a new class of much humbler buyers who drank brandy and water as a precaution, to nullify the impurities in London's water. As Auguste Hennessy remarked in 1849: 'The fact is that the public originally took to drinking brandy and water for medical reasons, and, having found it both pleasant and effective, they are likely to continue.'[42] Indeed brandy and water was a classic stimulant in Britain and – as *fine à l'eau* – in France as well. But drinking was largely concentrated in London which accounted for around three-fifths of total sales. Because many ordinary drinkers were

---

41 According to Charles Tovey, Dickens himself was the author, but Dickens never went near Cognac, and the style is unmistakably Vizetelly's.
42 Quoted in Charles Tovey, *British and Foreign Spirits* (London,1864).

looking for cheaper spirits they also took to 'British brandy' whose sales were roughly a third of those of cognac, which was also far more heavily taxed than native spirits, a problem which remained a theme in cognac's history throughout the twentieth century.

To Vizetelly, as to the Victorian middle classes as a whole, cognac was more than a drink: 'We are therefore...obliged to a district which supplies stores for our medicine chest as well as for our cellar,' he wrote. In the days before antibiotics brandy was widely prescribed: 'There are countless aged persons and invalids, whose stomachs cannot bear either wine or beer, to whom pure brandy, or brandy-and-water, is an indispensable sustenance.' The notion of 'medicinal brandy', the half-bottle kept in the corner cabinet of even the humblest British home, was firmly implanted by mid-Victorian times and was the foundation of Martell's long and profitable domination of the British market.

The Martells and the Hennessys were tempting targets, politically as well as commercially, for by 1815 they were what the French call *notables de Province*. Indeed when James Hennessy died he left a fortune as considerable as any of the group of aristocratic wine merchants living on the Quai de Chartrons in Bordeaux. The second quarter of the century saw a steady improvement in the region's fortunes. Judging by some 1846 tax returns, the Martells, the Hennessys, the Otards and the Dupuys were the richest, but the Commandons, the Planats, the Augiers, the Gauthiers and, in Jarnac, the Hines and the Bisquits all had substantial fortunes. In 1838 their growing financial needs led to the foundation of the town's first bank.

Both the Martells and the Hennessys provided Cognac with mayors and deputies and in 1824 James Hennessy had replaced Baron Otard as a deputy. Both families tended to be what Continental Europeans term 'liberals': they were secular, lukewarm or hostile to the Church's political pretensions; they naturally favoured Free Trade; and, in French terms, they sometimes strayed into a paternalist sort of radicalism. Auguste Hennessy, for instance, showed considerable courage in protesting against the seizure of power by the future emperor, Louis Napoleon at the end of 1851. Nevertheless, personalities, not policies, mattered most to what was still a highly restricted electorate. James Hennessy senior was extremely popular because he had been an early opponent of the reactionary King Charles X, whom he had helped to dethrone in 1830, so he was invariably elected. But when his son stood in his place he was defeated.

The political battle gradually became less stormy after Salignac's death in 1843, but his commercial ideas remained valid and the firm continued to prosper, first under Salignac's son and grandson, and then under the management and name of the Monnet family,[43] for the growers still felt the need for a manager of distinction who would lend his name to their product. Nevertheless the firm remained rather different: Jean Monnet remembered that some of the firm's more important 'shareholders' came to dinner every Saturday: 'well-off men, full of wisdom, close to the soil...the links between them and my father were closer than mere interest; there was also friendship and mutual trust'.

During the eighteen years of the 'July Monarchy' of Louis-Philippe, so abruptly terminated by the 1848 Revolution, many merchants moved away from their cramped

---

43 They later founded their own firm.

RUE SAULNIER

The Rue Saulnier (Street of the Salt Harbour) which leads down to the river in the heart of Cognac's old town is still cobbled, though recently, like so much of the old town, it has been cleaned up and 'gentrified'. Half-way up the street on the right is the Maison de la Gabelle, an imposing double-fronted structure, recognisable by the amiably battered and grotesque gargoyles on each side of the door named after a medieval tax on salt. It is key to Cognac's story, for the *gabelle* was an important element in the revenues of many impecunious monarchs.

Further up the street are the former offices of the cognac business owned by the Gauthiers; this is rather less imposing but is typical of the buildings that for hundreds of years were the homes and offices of such merchant families. Like its neighbour, it is double-fronted, the two halves separated by a covered corridor leading from the street to the yard behind the house. On the ground floor one side was devoted to work, in the front was a general office and a private office for the firm's partners. The dining room was on the other side of the corridor below the living room, the *grande chambre* and the bedrooms. The horses were stabled behind the house, and, despite its compactness, the other corner of the yard housed a still, which fell into disuse only after the First World War. The street, the Maison de la Gabelle, the Gauthiers' house, all emphasise the continuity in Cognac's story, the thread of international commercial awareness that marks this apparently sleepy little town, and thus makes it unlike the typical French town it appears at first sight.

Rue Saulnier, heart of Cognac's old town.

quarters in the Old Town. Some, like Auguste Martell, bought country houses and estates: by the end of the century some members of the leading families had become landed gentry, rather more interested in their estates than they were in their commercial affairs. But others remained within Cognac itself, for during the first half of the century the town expanded beyond the cramped alleys of the old town. In 1800 it still covered the same area, 226 hectares, as it had in medieval times and the population, a mere 4,000 in 1840, doubled in the twenty following years.

After a visit in 1845 the French author Aristide Guibert noted the narrowness of the streets and the lack of major public buildings, but underlined the fact that Cognac 'is probably the only spot in France which with so small a population is the *entrepôt* for so great a mass of value derived from the products of the soil' including new firms 'many founded by foreigners'.[44] As Vizetelly pointed out when he visited the town ten years later, 'twenty years ago Cognac was only a village; the same dull, steady-going place that it had been ever since the dawn of time. Now, not to speak of the merchants, the peasantry of the arrondissement of Cognac are the richest in France.' He contrasted the 'narrow side streets which look as if they were hewn out of the rock itself' covered with vines which 'seem to climb for the sake of reaching the summit of a natural cliff', with the many 'great houses in the town surrounded by that symptom of wealth, luxurious gardens'.

All this activity gave employment to an increasing number of local builders and architects, and, more directly, to 300 *tonnelliers* (coopers) in Cognac and Jarnac. As Vizetelly put it: 'Arthur Young's[45] test of a town's prosperity is manifestly visible; public and private buildings are being erected and restored on a liberal scale.' The town, like its principal product, was on its way.

It was the reign of Louis-Philippe's successor Emperor Napoleon III, between 1851 and 1870 which is remembered as a golden age for the Charentais, for they, together with the Bordelais, were amongst the biggest beneficiaries in France of the Emperor's unprecedented free trade policy. Not surprisingly the Cognacais remained loyal to their benefactor for a generation after his downfall, though they paid for their loyalty – the bill for the gigantic reparations imposed by the victorious Germans after the Franco-Prussian War of 1870 was met largely through a substantial increase in the taxes paid on spirits. At the beginning of Napoleon's reign British customs duties were still very severe. A first reduction in 1849 had only a limited effect because sales were hampered by the spread of oidium, a small fungoid growth that devastated all the vineyards of the south-west in the early 1850s. It was soon found that dusting the vines with sulphur provided an effective remedy, and by the end of the decade the vineyards were back to normal. Although the price of new cognac more than doubled, an enormous harvest in 1858 restored stocks to their historic levels.

The Cognacais had shown their marketing skills by sending £1000 worth of brandy to British soldiers in the front line during the Crimean war five years earlier 'to keep the cold out of our poor soldiers' stomachs' as Vizetelly put it. So they were well prepared for the expansion that followed the signature of the free trade treaty between Britain and France in 1860. In Britain, before the treaty, cognac had cost eight times the sixteen francs it fetched on the local market: afterwards it cost a quarter of the previous figure, putting the French product on equal terms with its British competitors. Before the onslaught of oidium sales had risen to nearly 200,000 hectolitres. By 1849 the share of French brandy in the British market had doubled to one in twelve bottles. They dropped to a mere 110,000 in the 1850s and by 1860 had recovered only to 150,000 hectolitres. Within ten years they had soared to 450,000. Not surprisingly, Cognac is the only town in France to boast a Rue Richard Cobden, named after one of the men who had preached the gospel of free trade so effectively – the French negotiator, one M. Chevalier, lacks this mark of honour.

---

44 *Histoire des villes de France* (Paris, 1845).
45 A much-quoted eighteenth-century British traveller.

The prosperity spread to the owners of the vineyards and most of the stills – the merchants usually bought rather than distilled the brandies they sold. In the words of François Pairault, an historian at the University of Limoges 'You could make back 25–30 per cent of your investment in land in just one year...Small winegrowers with just a couple of hectares could make a good living.' Nevertheless, although a number of new firms were formed, the trade remained highly concentrated. Between 1852 and 1870 the top dozen firms were responsible for over 70 per cent of the exports – sales in France were relatively unimportant. Hennessy alone accounted for nearly one quarter of the total, and Martell just over one fifth. The growers assembled under the Salignac banner supplied 9 per cent and Otard-Dupuy 5.6 per cent while Salignac and Bisquit-Dubouché had nearly 5 per cent each.

Nevertheless even the biggest firms were not big businesses; their stocks were not enormous. In the 1870s the venerable house of Augier reckoned that it had the second biggest stock of cognacs, although this amounted to the equivalent of only about a million bottles of normal-strength brandy. Much of the region's production was exported immediately to be aged in wood in Britain while the growers still held most of the older brandies – and thus remained in a strong position to bargain with their customers. In the late 1840s two-thirds of Hennessy's stocks were less than two years old, and only one-ninth more than five years old, a proportion that did not change dramatically in the following quarter of a century. The evidence is obvious to every visitor: the older cognac warehouses are not large.

In some ways the trade remained set in its traditional ways. The railway line from Angoulême through Cognac to the coast was completed in 1867, but brandies continued to be shipped by barge to Tonnay-Charente – the river route was only abandoned after 1926, when the government stopped spending money to ensure that it remained navigable. By that time a number of firms had established their cellars nearer the railway line than the river. However, one relationship was totally transformed in the third quarter of the century: that between the Cognac firms and their customers. The Cognacais started selling their product in bottles under their own name and not, as previously, in anonymous casks whose contents were to be bottled and labelled with the name of the London merchants. These all-powerful middlemen also controlled other markets in the British colonies (especially India, an increasingly important outlet).

The revolution was a dramatic one, though as early as 1847 Denis Mounié's accounts record a shipment of a hundred cases of 'Old Pale Cognac Brandy' to London, until the late 1850s the merchants had been relatively helpless. Unscrupulous foreigners could – and did – import inferior brandies and have them stamped as of French origin because they had passed through a French port. All this was stopped by the French law of 23 June 1857, by which trademarks could be registered and thus protected against interlopers. Within a few years every house in Cognac had registered several brands. The Tribunal of the Chamber of Commerce in Cognac, which started registering marks in 1858, is a rich repository of brand names. There are 16,000 in all, although only 3,000 are still legally valid because they have to be re-registered every ten years.

The locals were anxious to establish trademarks because they could then personalise their products even further by putting them into bottles, not surprisingly Litho Bru, still the region's major producer of labels, was founded in 1865. Martell owns what is probably the earliest bottle of cognac dating from 1848. This also is unsurprising. When it came to register its brand name in Britain the firm claimed that the name had been in use for eighty years. Two relatively new firms, Jules Robin and Jeanne-Antoine Renault, also seized the chance early to make their name by bottling their cognacs. By 1855 the practice was widespread: at Salignac's 'establishment' Vizetelly saw a man making thirty or forty cases (or, as he playfully called them, 'volumes') a day. The Act of 1857 provided a further boost. Between 1860 and 1875 the Martells were transporting a quarter of their sales in cases of a dozen bottles. In the 1870s the trade as a whole matched this proportion but by that time half of Hennessy's sales were of bottles.

The next step was to identify the contents of the new-fangled bottles according to age. According to family legend, it was Auguste Hennessy who systematised the idea. Noticing a star engraved on a window in one of the firm's offices, he devised a system by which one star meant a two-year-old brandy, two stars a four-year-old, and three stars a six-year-old. The term 'old' meant more than six years old. Had the Hennessys registered the star system, they could have protected the idea, but they did not. But then the Hennessys were always rather careless in registering their ideas. A generation later Maurice Hennessy came up with the idea of using the letters XO to indicate an Extra Old cognac and failed to register the name.

The legislation allowed the less scrupulous members of the trade to display an impressive ingenuity. In 1870 Messrs J. L. Martel registered a splendid spoof label, virtually the same as that of the two-l Martell's, boasting, truthfully enough, that their maison was *fondée en 1870*, a dig at the real Martells, so proud that their venerable firm had been founded in 1715. Many labels boasted of their suppliers' successes at exhibitions. But the Big Two could afford to be above such gimmicks. In the words of its official history, Martell never even 'submitted its products to any of the exhibitions, large or small, which have multiplied everywhere and which give rise to a veritable avalanche of awards sought by houses of the second rank'.

During the golden years Hennessy was clearly in the lead in the century-old two-horse race. The Martells were in the middle of a transition between the Martells themselves and the Firinos, who had married into the family, for the tradition of sons-in-law taking over continued as strongly as ever. Alexander Bisquit's son-in-law, Adrien Dubouché, himself had a son-in-law, Maurice Laporte, who duly added his grandfather's name to his own.

The dominance of Martell and Hennessy forced lesser houses to find some distinctive mark to help in specific markets. Typically Bonniot registered a 'Fine Vieux Cognac' under the pseudonym 'Paul Dupont' (the French equivalent of 'John Smith') that was 'expressly bottled for India'. Many other firms employed more than one name: P. A. Maurain had used 'John Bellot', with a label, clearly aimed at Far Western thirsts, of a cowboy (or could it be a gaucho, for the Latin American market was growing rapidly?) lassoing a buffalo. But my personal favourite was registered by Charles Rousseau, 'Imperial Brandy

Proprietors', it showed a dishevelled young lady, clearly the worse for wear, hanging on to some wreaths, in which she was entwined, as though they were life jackets.

Commercial pressure also led to the first attempts to define the different sections of the Cognac vineyard. For at least a century the inferiority of the cognacs from near the sea had been acknowledged by the lower price paid for them. But in the boom years what had hitherto been a rather rough-and-ready regional classification was defined more precisely. The initiative was taken by the Salignacs, who felt that their members were being cheated because the big houses used brandies from outside the choicest slopes. So, as Tovey put it: 'Salignac bound them to ship only the Brandy grown in a defined district (of which a map is prepared) well known to produce all the finest qualities.'[46] This was the first indication of a battle which remains central to the whole business: the dislike of the major firms to labelling the precise geographical origin of their brandies, preferring to rely on their own names and not to reduce their dominance over the growers in a particular sub-region. As Hennessy put it in 1885: 'everywhere in the world where we send our products they are known under the name of Cognac or eau de vie Hennessy, but we have never mentioned the term "fine champagne" on our invoices...the different qualities of our brandies are the result of blends of different vintages.' For only the merchant knew the proportions of the vintages and origins of the brandies in the blend.

The first map of the Cognac district had been prepared in 1854 by the Co-operative at Saintes and naturally took the town as the beating heart of Cognac. As we saw in Chapter 1 Salignac's response was to commission a well-known geologist, M. Coquand, to carry out the first proper survey of the area in order to pinpoint the superiority of the Champagnes, a classification which remains broadly followed even today. Some years later the merchants of Angoulême followed suit but their map was so biased that Segonzac, the historic heart of the Grande Champagne, was placed firmly in the Bois. By the late 1860s a *Dictionnaire de Crus* and a series of maps, drawn up by an engineer called Lacroix, had been published, which defined and redefined the boundaries between the different *crus*. Unfortunately, he set a precedent by being too tidy-minded to cope with the fragmented geology and geography of the Cognac region.

The principal effect of the mania for classification was a proliferation of names for the enormous area covered by the Bois. At the summit were the Premiers Fin Bois de Jarnac. Charles Walter Berry, the leading English connoisseur of fine cognac, tasted and approved of a *fine* Fin Bois. But these cognacs were merely top of a hierarchy, which naturally included Deuxièmes Bois, followed by Fins Bois, Bons Bois, Bois Ordinaires, Bois Communs, Bois à Terroir and so on. Tovey listed 'Champagne fine and common, Champagne de Bois and Eau de Vie de Bois, as well as that of Annis (Aunis) produced from the vines on the banks of the river'. Robert Delamain claimed that some London buyers divided the region into no fewer than sixteen different *crus*. The distinctions made were commercially important, since a Champagne cognac could be worth 40 per cent more than a mere Bois. Not surprisingly, the distinctions gave rise to all sorts of frauds. The growers naturally blamed the merchants, but everyone was at it. In 1858 a report by the Sous-Préfet of Barbezieux firmly blamed: 'an enormous number of the smaller

---

46 *British and Foreign Spirits,* op. cit.

distillers [who] buy a little wine and distil it at home. It is these fellows…who have given the local brandy trade a bad reputation. For most of them mix the local product with raw alcohols from the Nord and spirits from Languedoc,' where two-thirds of the ever-increasing production of wine was being distilled. 'Unfortunately it is almost impossible to convict them of the frauds of which they are undoubtedly guilty.'

He was being a little unfair to the authorities' efforts. Tovey noted that in 1857–8 a number of growers had been convicted of fraud and received long sentences which 'had a very salutary effect, and contributed in a great degree to stop all adulteration and sophistication'. But some merchants were forced to stress on their labels that the contents were 'real' or 'pure' Cognac and one firm boasted that all its cognacs had been produced in its own distilleries. In Tovey's time these fraudsters could plead a lack of local grapes caused by the oidium. But the frauds continued in the 1860s and early 1870s, when the area growing grapes for conversion to cognac started to expand even faster than the market. Indeed, by the mid-1870s it formed the largest single vineyard in France. Thirty per cent of the arrondissement of Cognac was already planted with vines. So growth was concentrated in the woods to the north and west, in the Deux-Sèvres and more especially in the Charente-Inférieure, (now known as Charente-Maritime) where nearly 60,000 additional hectares were planted with vines in the third quarter of the century, all adding to the acreage of *bois*. In the peak year of 1875 the vineyard had grown to 116,000 hectares in the Charente, 116,000 in the Charente-Maritime and several thousand more in the adjacent department, more than doubling the 1850 figure.

Not surprisingly, production far outstripped sales. One estimate, based on the figures given in Berrault's annual survey of Cognac, is that between 1861 and 1876 the region produced nearly eleven million hectolitres of cognac but exported under 4.5 million. The remaining 6.5 million represented no less than twenty-four times the exports shipped annually at the height of the Napoleonic boom. Although the town only counted 13,000 inhabitants the boom had attracted every type of business, ranging from six cork merchants to forty-nine insurance companies. It was even worth the while of Le Grand Bazar de la Ville de Paris, a pioneering department store, to establish a branch in the town. And English visitors could be lodged at the Hôtel de Londres (today the Hôtel François 1er).

The vines' productivity was minimal, a maximum of 50 hectolitres of wine for every hectare – less than a third of today's level. Vizetelly had remarked how 'the culture of vines for making eau de vie differs considerably from the management of mere wine-making vines. It is also more careless or slovenly in appearance'. A contemporary piece of agricultural research had commented on how loosely the rows of vines were planted, with enough room between them for an ox team to plough. The slovenliness of the vineyards, and of their owners disguised their general prosperity. In the late 1850s Tovey shrewdly remarked how:

Anyone who observed these people congregated together at the Cognac or Jarnac market or fair, would at once recognise them from their appearance as a class of men who, having had a difficulty in getting what wealth they possess, are determined to keep it, and are earnest in their endeavours to increase it. Although in their best apparel, they are ill-dressed and shabby-looking; the clothes they wear might at some time or other have been genteel. Some appear in dress coats, with outrageously large coloured silk handkerchiefs round their necks. The ill-fitted clothes show that the present wearers are not the original proprietors…one keen and subtle-looking man, whose clothes would not have fetched five shillings, was pointed out to us as a man worth eighty thousand pounds.

His observations were echoed by a later visitor, Charles Albert d'Arnaux, a well-known illustrator who signed himself 'Bertall'. In 1878, at the suggestion of Honoré de Balzac, whose novels he had illustrated, he published *La Vigne*, an entertaining account of a visit to the Charente – although it was inevitably rather patronising, he being Parisian and they provincials and therefore, by definition, simpletons.[47] Bertall had arrived from Bordeaux, where the vines were grown in fastidiously tended rows, and the contrast was startling, given the proximity of the two regions – even today Bordeaux and Cognac, both dependent on the export of a luxury product derived from the vine, remain worlds apart. In Cognac, he noted, 'The vines seem to grow haphazardly, like cabbages or beets in a field. Their branches wander at whim, without stakes, laths or ties, and the general impression of a vineyard is of a vast carpet of greenery, which is not dulled, as it is elsewhere, by the powdery grey tints of the stakes or posts intended to support the vine and its fruit.' This neglect extended to the wine making. The growers did not even bother to de-stalk the bunches of grapes, which were crushed either mechanically or by the peasants' feet. It was all rather casual. But it did not matter much. As he pointed out, the wine was merely an intermediate product. What mattered was the cognac, especially the older stuff, and he was lucky enough to meet an owner of some of the best.

M. Curlier, a partner of M. Courvoisier, who was becoming a major force in the market, introduced Bertall to a grower, M. Saunier, rich and sage like those who dined with the Monnets every Saturday. 'A small, grizzled man, completely tanned, baked and baked again by the sun; his face was wrinkled as a dried grape. His slim face, sharp and fine like a fox's muzzle, like some Norman countenances, is illuminated by small clear grey eyes, shining with intelligence and good-will.' He was modestly dressed, and even his precious pressoir and still were 'old, covered with a sheen resulting from long years of use'. M. Saunier was not a superficially worldly man. He suspected Paris: he had only been there once and regarded it merely as the refuge for local ne'er-do-wells one of whom had been shot as a communard; another had been transported for his part in the same revolutionary uprising. This provincial outlook and modest exterior concealed a fortune (estimated by Bertall at two million francs) in old cognac, which M. Saunier was in no mood to sell. 'Keep your money, I'm keeping my casks,' he told M. Curlier.

He was not alone in his wealth. Twenty years earlier Vizetelly had noted that 'the peasantry of the arrondissement of Cognac are the richest in all France. Some few are worth as much as sixty thousand pounds sterling'. In the words of the novelist Jacques Chardonne 'their character, formed by continuous relationship with nature, its constancy

---

47 This was republished by Bruno Sepulchre and quoted in: *Le Livre du Cognac: trois Siècles d'Histoire Paris* (1983).

and its caprices, remains unchanging...the Champagnauds [the inhabitants of the Grande Champagne] remain amongst their vines. They remain peasants, because that's what they want. But they are rich, and know it better than anyone. They send their sons to a grammar school and their daughters to the convent; they will become mothers, fine and discreet, capable of running a house they will scarcely ever leave.'[48]

Tragically this general prosperity was about to be destroyed by the phylloxera louse which had probably been brought from the United States when some American vines had arrived after the oidium epidemic of the 1860s. In 1872 the Charente was officially declared 'affected' and that year it first got a grip on the grapes in the Champagnes. The dry summers of 1873 and 1875 encouraged the spread of a bug which hated water, and indeed, could be exterminated by flooding the vineyards. At first some officials blamed the scourge on the way the growers had overproduced but by the next year it had spread to the Charente-Inférieure. Once established, the pace of its spread was frightening. On 7 July 1874 the Sous-Préfet of Jonzac declared that all was well. Ten days later he reported the first outbreak; by September a number of villages had been hit; and by the next year 1,250 hectares had been ravaged. The relatively wet summers of 1876 and 1877 came too late to save most of the region's vines. Ironically, the louse was almost welcomed at first, because by the 1870s stocks were running dangerously high. Within little more than a decade the situation had been completely reversed. As table 1 in Appendix II shows, the size of the vineyard, which had reached a peak in 1878 at over 285,000 hectares, dropped by over three-quarters in the following seven years. Late frosts in 1880 and 1881 which destroyed three-quarters of the crop completed the region's ruin and by the 1890s the vineyard had shrunk to an average of 47,000 hectares, a mere seventh of its maximum extent.

When Bertall visited M. Saunier the magnitude of the disaster had become all too clearly apparent. Even in untouched areas he noticed the tell-tale signs that the 'little louse' had begun its destructive work: 'Here and there, unhappily, a few stains, yellow or earth-coloured, had appeared and darkened the carpet of greenery.' Once the louse had taken hold the damage was appalling: 'We easily pulled up a stump whose roots, frayed, blistered, destroyed, had retained neither their strength nor their life.' These were not isolated outbreaks. On both sides of the road between Cognac and Jarnac they saw 'a stretch five miles long and two miles wide, where the devastation was so complete that the roots were fit only to burn, and the harvest did not produce a single grape'. Within a decade the stocks of growers like M. Saunier had been exhausted. For eighty long years thousands of growers like him would not regain the prosperity they had enjoyed in the imperial years of the 1860s. Moreover, their misery was compounded by a simultaneous, and decisive, switch in power from them to the merchants.

---

48 *Chronique Privée de l'an 1940* (Paris, 1941).

7

DISASTER, RECOVERY, OCCUPATION

There are regions where the collective memory stops short at the war of 1914–18; others, like the Vendée, stop at the Revolutionary wars; phylloxera serves as a full stop in the collective memory of the Charentais. There is before and after; before implies halcyon days, the Golden Age; after implies the hard grind of daily reality. For many years after the crisis, the word 'phylloxera' remained the ultimate threat hurled at naughty children, while many growers preserved a row of old vines 'out of friendship', in the same way that you keep a family souvenir.[49]

Julien-Labruyère knew what he was talking about for as he described in another book his own family was affected.[50] His great-grandfather was a notary who committed suicide because of his financial problems. For eighty years some growers ostracised the family because they had lost the money they had deposited with him – in the absence of a proper rural banking system the notaries acted as bankers as well as lawyers. One simple statistic is enough to show the effect of phylloxera. It took until 1970 for sales to reach their pre-phylloxera peak. At its low point the vineyard was a mere fifth of its pre-phylloxera total and even in 1976 at the height of its post-war expansion it was less than a half the size it had been before the plague. Inevitably, sales of imported spirits dropped considerably in Britain, Cognac's biggest market, in the quarter of a century after phylloxera, a fall compounded by the arrival of cheap and heavily publicised blended Scotch whisky.

The growers lost not only their new-found prosperity but their independence as well. Phylloxera completely upset the long-established balance of power between the merchants and the growers, who were forced to sell their precious stocks in order to survive. The

---

49 François Julien-Labruyère, *Paysans Charentais* (La Rochelle,1982).
50 *A la Recherche de la Saintonge maritime Versailles* (1974).

crisis taught them a lesson which has lasted to this day for it had a permanent effect in making them reluctant to sell their older brandies. Many of the older generation still feel that the longer they keep them, the more valuable they become. 'We can wait' was, and remains, their slogan.

Many tried to sell their land but, not surprisingly, found that during the first years after the onset of the plague its value had dropped by nine-tenths. Some looked for jobs in other parts of France, for there were precious few available in Cognac at a time when the whole socio-economic structure had been disrupted. In 1873 2,000 coopers had been employed in 200 workshops in the town; ten years later there were 93 workshops employing a mere 321 workers. The growers could live off their stocks for a few years but had no financial reserves left to pay the costs of replanting, so most of them had to sell their precious stills and market the produce of their grapes as wine, not as cognac. The mobile stills they were forced to use could not be guaranteed to make spirits of the delicacy and quality required by the buyers. Not surprisingly the population of the Grande Champagne fell by a quarter in the last years of the century.

In general the merchants were better off, though not by much. Hennessy's profits fell to nothing and it took the rest of the century to recover to the levels of the 1870s while Boutelleau, the family firm of the novelist Jacques Chardonne was saved only by the removal of his father as manager and the support of its bankers. Boutelleau was based in Barbezieux and indeed bankruptcies were concentrated in other outlying towns like Niort, Angoulême and Saint Jean d'Angély. Not surprisingly, the old fear that once customers lost the habit of buying a specific drink they would not easily be recaptured proved true, partly because phylloxera sent the price of cognac soaring and made it, for the first time, purely a luxury beverage.

The Cognacais, like the Bordelais, tend to pin all the blame on the pest. Preoccupied with their own troubles, they ignored a world slump which afflicted other luxury industries at the same time. A wave of protectionism, set off by the tariffs imposed by the French government in 1892 – and which particularly affected sales to the United States – undid all the good work done by the free trade treaty thirty years earlier and effectively helped to prolong the slump until after World War II, just as it did in Bordeaux.

Phylloxera transformed the shape as well as the size of the Cognac vineyard, for it was simply not worth replanting the outer areas, which in any case had never produced very good cognac. This land soon found its true vocation as dairy farms. By the end of the century the number of cows in the region had trebled and Charentais butter had become renowned through the efforts of a number of pioneering agricultural co-operatives. The rest of the region had to struggle to return to the only product it knew, but progress was slow.

Replanting in the very special conditions of the Charente was a painful and costly process. Elsewhere in France the growers rapidly took to vines grafted on to American rootstock immune to the louse. But these grafts did not suit the chalky soil of the Charentes and the deeper the chalk the greater the difficulties – the Champagnes with the most dense chalky soils of all had problems with chlorosis. As a result, a stubborn lobby fought for more than a decade to avoid this solution, pinning their faith on chemical remedies, notably the injection of sulphur-based compounds into the soil. These chemicals were both expensive and unsatisfactory, since they never completely eradicated the pest and the treatments were seemingly endless.

In 1877 a group of growers headed by André Verneuil of Segonzac, one of the region's most heroic figures, sent the first of a series of missions to the United States to discover rootstocks suitable for grafting on the Charente's chalk. But it took the talents of four distinguished scientists to find the solution.[51] By no coincidence three of the four were connected with the University of Montpellier, founded at the end of the twelfth century and thus the oldest in Northern Europe, which to this day occupies a pre-eminent position in the study of the vine.[52]

The first clue was provided by Pierre-Marie Millardet at the University of Bordeaux. Millardet was looking for a 'direct producer', an ungrafted vine not susceptible to phylloxera that could be used to replant the vineyard. He didn't find what he was looking for, but did find, in Texas, a species named Vitis Berlandieri Planchon. Unfortunately the graft proved difficult to take. Millardet then discovered that a hybrid rootstock combining Berlandieri with Chasselas, named '41B' would do the trick. History has rather neglected his contribution to solving the phylloxera problem. Publicly the credit went to Pierre Viala, a twenty-something professor at Montpellier, who had been sent to the United States as late as 1887 by a now-desperate Cognac community to find a suitable rootstock. After a six-month tour of the Eastern and Southern United States he too found Berlandieri being grown by an adventurous Texan nurseryman Thomas Volney Munson in the small town of Denison and returned in triumph. However, his triumph was marred because the rootstock he brought back was not a hybrid and had to be replaced with Millardet's 41B. Despite this Viala remained a hero, thanks to the book he published in 1889 relating his journey and, more legitimately, through his missionary efforts to demonstrate the virtues of 41B. The Cognacais were properly appreciative of Munson's efforts; the town is twinned with Denison and in 1988 a plaque was erected in the Station Viticole in Cognac dedicated to his memory.

Even then there was a lingering concern over the new vines and an inevitable delay before grapes from the new vines had been transformed into cognac – grafting was easier in Cognac because the quality of the wine was less important than in wine-making regions. There was very little cognac until 1893 and that was from the Fins Bois, while the Grande Champagne only started harvesting in 1895 because the plants were too young before then.

The growers soon found that they could not graft the plants themselves and had to buy their vines at the special nurseries which sprang up all over the region, many of which were run by dubious characters who sold inferior, albeit higher-yielding varieties. Fortunately, more reputable specialists soon took over, most of them based, now as then, at Nercillac north of Cognac where the humidity of the river valley provided particularly suitable conditions. In 1889, two years after the first grafted vines had been planted, the Cognacais set up a viticultural research station, the first in France, to help with the reconstruction.

---

51 The story of the solution to the phylloxera problem is well told in Kyle Jarrard's book Cognac (NJ, USA, 2005).
52 The vines which proved that Australia could produce decent wine came from Montpellier.

It was run by a young man, Louis Ravaz, a pioneer of scientific viticulture and a leading missionary for grafted vines, who was only twenty-six when he was appointed. He was the last of the tiny band of Samaritans who saved Cognac from the pest, developing further refinements of the rootstocks required to suit the varying chalkiness of the region's soils.

Nevertheless, in the long run the plague did help Cognac by eliminating the tens of thousands of hectares of marginal land from whose grapes decent brandy could not be made and greatly improved the cultivation of the remaining vineyards. For when the Charentais did come to replant, they did so in an unprecedentedly scientific fashion. Cultivation was rationalised. Where previously the vines had been planted higgledy-piggledy and often very close together (with only one metre between the rows), the new vineyards left enough room for a horse or ox-drawn plough. Before phylloxera, planting was simply a matter of bending a branch into the ground and letting it take root. This was clearly impossible with a grafted vine.

Unfortunately the bunches of Folle Blanche proved too compact, leading to the development of grey rot, but the Charentais soon found another variety, Ugni Blanc, which came to dominate the area as the Folle had done before the plague. Sadly, Ugni Blanc produces cognacs that are less floral, less aromatic, less characterful, than those distilled from the Folle Blanche. Moreover, the change widened the contrast in quality – and thus price – between brandies made in the Fins Bois and those from the Champagnes.

The government did not help. The French Revolution had done away with many dues and duties on the production and transportation of alcoholic drinks, but they were far too tempting a target to escape the taxman's attention for long. The first post-revolutionary retail tax on spirits had been introduced in 1824; it was sharply increased in 1860 from 60 to 90 francs per litre of pure alcohol and boosted again, to 156 francs. But the biggest blow came in 1900 when the tax was increased by a further 50 per cent. As a result, the total tax burden borne by a bottle of spirits, including the local taxes payable in major cities, amounted to six times its original value. Not surprisingly, throughout the twentieth century the Cognacais remained convinced that they were being unfairly discriminated against. In the bitter words of Jean Lys, in his thesis on the cognac business: 'Spirits are products that have to pay dearly for their right to be consumed.'[53]

When the Cognacais finally emerged from their ordeal with phylloxera they found that their markets had been largely usurped by a wave of 'industrial', mass-produced spirits made from grain, potatoes, and beetroot, some of which even dared to take the name of cognac. The effects were dire – and immediate. 'Cognac in large quantities now enters England which comes out of potatos and not out of grapes' noted the *Pall Mall Gazette* in 1882. 'Pure cognac can be secured...only through English holders of old stocks.'

There was brandy from everywhere, 'cognac du Cap' – Cape of Good Hope – 'cognac d'Australie' and many others. 'Fraud stalks the land, powerful and unashamed,' wrote a local author at the time, 'it sows confusion in the mind of the consumer and the inferior quality of its products depreciates the market value of genuine cognac.'[54] Many of these

---

53 Jean Lys, *Le Commerce de Cognac* (Université de Bordeaux, 1929).
54 Henri Boraud, *De l'Usage commercial du nom du Cognac* (Bordeaux, 1904).

spirits were so deadly that, for the first time, a strong temperance movement sprang up in France. In its 1907 catalogue the Army & Navy Stores, the biggest purveyor of cognac in Britain, was forced to state that 'the brandies bottled by the Society are guaranteed grape spirit from the Cognac district' – 'Champagne cognac' held pride of place, costing four times that asked for 'cooking brandy' which was 'French and pot still distillation but not entirely from the Cognac district'.

In the short term the fraudsters were of some benefit to Cognac, at least they ensured that the customer base for brandies alleged to have come from the region was not lost. Moreover, these imitations filled the gap in the years when there was not enough of the real stuff. But by the end of the century production was returning to normal: the frauds had outlived their usefulness and were damaging the market, not only because of their poor quality but also by their sheer quantity. In 1900 the world was probably buying fifteen times as much 'cognac' as the 5,500,000 cases actually being produced in the Cognac region itself.

The worst offenders were foreign, and therefore hard to prosecute. A local court condemned one German who set up under the name of 'Albert Buchholz, Cognac'. And Martell, together with Moët & Chandon, Benedictine and Grande Chartreuse managed to pursue one delinquent, whose premises in Barcelona were found to contain copies of their labels, 'bold and widespread forgeries, carried out with rare skill'. The fraudster, M. Rapau, fled to Bordeaux and was duly sent to prison for a year. But in most countries the Cognacais were helpless. The Germans were the worst offenders. As early as 1892 the Cognacais were complaining about brandies 'chemically fabricated in Germany, employing essences of every description including those most harmful to public health'. The German government actively encouraged imports of wine rather than brandy, which paid twenty-seven times the amount of duty levied on wine (fortified wines paid even less, half the duty on ordinary wines). So German merchants would send fortified wines (*vins vinés*) to Germany strengthened with industrial alcohol or even grape brandy. Once the product was over the frontier, the Germans promptly renamed it 'cognac', for the customs documents which accompanied it were clearly marked with the name of the area in which it was produced. In another widespread fraud, shiploads of industrial alcohol were sent from Hamburg, touched at a French port and returned duly baptised.

The Cognacais fought back, in the law courts at home and abroad, and in the field of international diplomacy; they even fought against the lexicographers. Not unreasonably, their own council protested against the definition of cognac in the great dictionary of M. Littré: 'A brandy from Cognac, and thus by derivation, an excellent brandy.' Although the Cognacais blamed foreigners for most of their troubles, unscrupulous merchants from all over France also set up post-boxes in Cognac with their names on them, arranged for someone to re-direct the letters addressed to them and thus established legal residence. By 1889 it was reckoned that 179 firms were operating that one type of fraud alone.

The growers and the merchants, either individually or through the Chamber of Commerce, hoped that the French courts would prove an adequate defence. Basing their case on a miscellany of laws the Cognacais hoped to follow the Champenois, who had exploited a law of 1824 by extending the protection it provided to the name of their region to its best-known product. But the judges let Cognac down. In 1886 a court in Bordeaux ruled that one M. Perpezat, a Bordeaux-based merchant, could label his offerings 'Old Brandy Perpezat et Cie Cognac'. The Cognac region, it said, extended to Bordeaux because merchants based in that city also sold it. But there was a limit. A court in Douai in Northern France ruled that cognac was a 'special spirit, whose qualities derived from the soil which produces it', condemning a local man on the grounds that the 'special soils' did not extend all the way to the Pas de Calais.

For a short time Cognac's problems resulted in the type of conflict between growers and merchants which affected most French wine-growing regions (including Champagne) in the years before World War I. In Cognac the growers even demanded an export tax combined with a state monopoly for the sale of spirits in France itself. The merchants were naturally wary of the tax on exports and the effective nationalisation of their domestic trade, an attitude the suspicious growers took as further proof that they benefited from the sale of fraudulent spirits. The merchants then brought up reinforcements: they recruited the thousands of workers involved in ancillary trades, from glass to cooperage, who depended on the cognac trade and organised their own mass demonstrations against the proposals.

The growers in Cognac, however, were far less radical than their equivalents elsewhere in France. They were not only farmers, they were also distillers, *bouilleurs de cru*. So, of course, were millions of other French farmers, who in other regions constituted the wine-growers' worst enemy, for they were using lesser raw materials, like pears, apples, grain, potatoes or beetroots, to produce rough raw hooch to be consumed at home or supplied illicitly to cafés throughout the country. By contrast even the humblest peasant in Cognac was distilling a noble (and expensive) spirit designed for a discerning, generally foreign, buyer. The growers even launched a magazine called significantly *Le Vrai Cognac*. So, in the long run, the Cognac growers were bound to break ranks with growers elsewhere and support the merchants.

All French producers, not only the Cognacais, quickly realised that domestic legislation could never provide adequate protection. It took until 1890 for a treaty called the Convention of Madrid to provide legal protection to 'regional trademarks for products derived from grapes' which included products manufactured from grapes like cognac and champagne. Unfortunately the two major empires of Germany and Austria-Hungary ignored the provisions of the treaty, and even the British played them false for a while. A judge ruled that the Convention did not apply in Britain because the Treaty had not yet been ratified by Parliament.

But the treaty could never have worked without proper protection at home. This was eventually provided through the application of an ancient tax, the *aides*, which imposed taxes on goods as they moved through France. So this enabled a cask of cognac to be provided with the official certificate – the *acquit* – that showed it had indeed been produced in the region, but only after battles to ensure that the certificate included the origin of the product. It took nearly half a century to surround Cognac with a complete protective system. The first effective legislation, in 1905, was designed to suppress frauds committed when describing any agricultural product. Adulteration was defined as adding alien substances or omitting essential ones. But the legislation was so general that it took thirty-five more years to complete the legal framework. The first loophole found by the region's less scrupulous merchants was that authorised warehouses or cellars could house brandies made from lesser grapes grown in nearby regions like the Vendée to the north or the Gironde to the south.

This gap was plugged by a new law which came into force in 1909. It was the result of a true partnership between the growers, headed by Albert Verneuil and the most important merchants, including Edouard Martell and above all James Hennessy, one of the heroes of the time, a deputy between 1906 and 1935 who had bought 600 hectares of vines, partly at least to help him with his election as deputy. It was this piece of legislation which, over 200 years after the superiority of 'Coniack brandy' had first become apparent, belatedly gave legal recognition to eau de vie de Cognac. This was enshrined in the famous Appellation d'Origine Contrôlée, the guarantee not of quality but of geographical provenance. In the end the region included the whole of the Charente-Maritime, most of the Charente and slivers – now more or less vine-free – of the Deux-Sèvres to the north-west and the Dordogne on the extreme east of the Cognac region.

In 1919 these Appellations d'Origine were provided with further protection by a law making it a criminal fraud to pretend that any imitation which did not meet the standards historically associated with the product, '*les usages locaux, loyaux et constants*' ('local, honest and habitual usage'), could be prosecuted. These were further refined a couple of years later when it was ruled that only caramel, oak shavings and 3.5 per cent of sugar could be added to the spirit. And in 1929 cognac's special status was recognised when it was allocated its very own *acquit jaune d'or*, its 'golden identity card', to distinguish it from lesser wines and spirits which accompanies even the smallest quantity of cognac when it moves on the public highway. Fraud at the vineyard itself was supposedly prevented by regulations forcing growers to declare the size of their holdings and, before every harvest, the quantity they were going to ferment and distil. A law passed in 1900 ensured that every still was registered and duly hall-marked.

It took the whole, miserable post-World War I period to refine the legal description of cognac. This was no mere technicality. In 1924 the Australians had protested against the only evidence the merchants could provide of the age of their brandies – a certificate signed by the mayor of Cognac. After the end of Prohibition the Americans queried the authenticity of brandies being sold as five, ten, twenty or even 100 years old, and in the 1930s a system was devised to ensure that the age of every lot of cognac was registered. Another major gap in the regulations was even more basic: double distillation. It was only in 1935 that a decree was issued confirming that 'real cognac' had to be distilled twice. Even when single distillation was outlawed the prohibition applied only to brandies distilled on the mainland. Distillers on the Iles de Ré and d'Oléron were allowed to distil once only; but they were permitted to call their result merely 'cognac'. They could not use any of the sub-appellations, not even Bons Bois, and recently, they too have been forced to distil all their cognac twice.

Double distillation was one instance where the law was merely providing backing for the historic norm. The same applied to the 1936 definition of the grape varieties which could go into a bottle of cognac. In 1927 high-yielding hybrid varieties had been banned, and nine years later the varieties were divided into those which could form the bulk of the production and 'supporting' varieties. To no one's surprise, only three principal varieties were allowed, Folle Blanche, Saint-Emilion and Colombard; five others, Sémillon, Sauvignon, Blanc Ramé, Jurançon Blanc and Montils, could only form 10 per cent of the total. The same decree distinguished between cognac, eau de vie des Charentes, and eau de vie de Cognac.

During the 1930s the Cognacais also defined their boundaries more precisely. A commission of inquiry was appointed which included such well-respected local figures as Robert Delamain and Gaston Briand. In contrast to other parts of France, where the process was accompanied by the most frightful squabbling, they soon agreed on boundaries between the sub-appellations, Grande and Petite Champagne,[55] Borderies, Fins Bois, Bons Bois and Bois Ordinaires, an agreement legalised by a decree dated 13th June 1938. But the resulting boundaries were over-generous, they followed the administrative boundaries rather than the more refined definitions established by Coquand or Ravaz. In theory, as Robert Delamain put it, all the legislation did was to 'purely and simply legalise the map of the different crus then in use'. Unfortunately the boundaries of the Grande Champagne covered the whole 'canton' of Cognac which included the rich soils of the Charente river valley.

Age posed another set of problems. In 1933 a group of merchants suffering from the effects of the slump passed off brandies from the 1930 and 1931 vintages as 'Grande Champagne 1811'. The locals took immediate action, but only on 4th July 1940 did the civil court at Saint Jean d'Angély confirm that age was an essential element in the legal description of cognac and that cheating would be subject to the same penalties as other frauds. Amazingly, this crucial judgement was handed down just after the Armistice, when the roads of France were choked with refugees and, supposedly, the whole of France's administrative mechanism had ground to a halt. The following year an historic injustice was overturned. When France was divided into eighty-three departments in 1790 the Cognac region was divided into two, Charentes and Charente-Inférieure. But in 1941 it was promoted to become Charente-Maritime.

Phylloxera had ruined most growers, but it also put enormous commercial and financial strains on the supposedly triumphant merchants. They needed to recapture the markets they had lost while only the bigger ones had access to the bank credit required to buy and hold the stocks formerly stored by the growers. Fortunately, banks flocked to Cognac in the last twenty years of the nineteenth century, led by the then privately owned Banque de France which established a branch in the town in 1882. The credit was vital. Before the plague Hennessy had held in stock only enough cognac to supply its customers

---

55 'Fine Champagne' was also defined, as a cognac containing at least 50 per cent spirit from Grande Champagne.

THE MARTELL FACTORY

In 1892 the *Revue Périodique Mensuelle* included a survey of the Martell establishment in its series on major industrial undertakings. The three-storey *chai au coupage* (blending hall) was dominated by fifty immense cylindrical tuns, each holding 175 hectolitres. On the top floor the line of thirty-six tuns could hold 6,300 hectolitres connected by 300 metres of piping. This gigantic hall was unique in Cognac. The *Revue* informed its readers that Martell's still-room was 50 metres long and that each of its four stills held 6 hectolitres – six times the previous average, for phylloxera seems to have heralded a major attempt to, replace 'domestic' scale stills with 'industrial' ones. Martell, said the article, had been forced to become distillers in their own right. They had to defend themselves against 'frauds on the part of unscrupulous growers; and that is why their purchasing service is so sophisticated and why Martell possesses a laboratory so well equipped with apparatus and instruments' (a far cry from the informality of Vizetelly's day less than forty years earlier).

By the 1890s Martell was important enough to feature in a business magazine.

for six months. After 1880 they held enough for up to six years' sales, though these of course had slumped.

The Big Two had enough capital to build, quite literally, round their stocks, erecting the town's first major industrial buildings. Martell and Hennessy found that they were able to fix the annual price for each year's vintage and expect it to become the norm, a duopoly broken as late as 1954. Given the price of the vines they could have bought up the whole vineyard, but they merely extended their estates, aiming only to be substantial country gentry. The principal reason, according to the late Maurice Hennessy, was that Cognac's leading families, though they obviously felt they had a leading role to play in the region, did not want to own or control it. Indeed they were aware of their responsibility to the electors on whom they depended (the Martells, for instance, were ardent defenders of the rights of the *bouilleurs de cru*, the growers who distilled their own cognac).

Martell was staging something of a come-back. It had bought stock so aggressively that sales were not reduced by phylloxera. Its new installations were also required to increase the proportion of its sales which were dispatched in bottles which already represented 90 per cent of its output, as against a mere half for Hennessy, and was also stealing a march at home. Martell painstakingly built up its distribution network throughout France and until the late twentieth century was a major force in the domestic market. Both at home and abroad the Firino-Martells were prepared to get down to the grinding hard work of selling: the late Jacques de Varenne of Augier remembered going around Liverpool with Michel Firino-Martell before World War II. Martell, he said, 'was quite prepared to knock on doors, and every evening we would go round the pubs to see if they sold his cognac'. In lean times the Martell's reputation for being rather dour and plodding, for acting as *l'épicier du coin* (the corner grocer's shop), served them well.

By contrast, during the golden years the Hennessys had acquired some rather grand metropolitan habits. 'James Hennessy thought it was really rather vulgar to bother with the French market,' as the late Alain de Pracomtal, his great-nephew and the former chairman of Hennessy put it to me. As a result the Hennessys were virtually unrepresented in their native country except in the smarter bars and restaurants.

In the later half of the nineteenth century both the Hennessys and the Martells moved from living 'over the shop' to country estates near the town. At the extreme, Jacques Hennessy, who owned nearly half the family firm, lived exclusively in Paris where he died in 1928, not having left the city for the previous twenty years. According to Janet Flanner (Genet of the New Yorker), 'For eighty-nine years he inhabited Paris as a bachelor and bon viveur...he never took any exercise, never walked if the effort took him away from carpets...His eyesight remained remarkable: he never wore spectacles, claiming to be able to distinguish naturally between a blonde and a brunette.'[56]

The merchants' attempts to impose their brands on the outside world were greatly helped by a revolution in bottle making. Until nearly the end of the nineteenth century bottles were hand-blown by men whose lungs and throats routinely suffered permanent damage from physically blowing thousands of bottles from molten glass. 'Beside every glassworks they build,' wrote Max de Nansouty in 1901, 'they had to lay out a cemetery which was never idle.' The hero of the revolution was one Claude Boucher, a Cognacais of humble origins, who invented a machine for blowing glass. Previously the only machine-made glass bottles seem to have been inferior, moulded varieties.

As Jean Monnet remarked: 'Although he had literally revolutionised the glass industry, and thus the marketing of Cognac, in local society he always remained within the ranks of the suppliers.' Monnet knew what he was talking about. His grandfather had been a small grower – Maurice Hennessy remembered how well he played the fiddle at village weddings – and it had been his father who had climbed into the ranks of the merchant class. And climb it was: 'Cognac society was divided into two very distinct classes: on one side there was the merchant class, and on the other everyone else, which in practice meant mostly suppliers.'

Boucher's invention provided a colossal boost to the merchants' efforts to impose their brand names on the world. They were benefiting from a world-wide trend towards brand names which, in the 1880s, established the major brands of Scotch whisky and champagne

---

56 *Paris was Yesterday* (London, 1973).

as well as of cognac. This was symbolised by the confrontation in Britain between Martell and the Gilbey family, then far and away the dominant force in the market with 2,000 licensed agents throughout the country. At the end of the 1860s the Gilbeys tried to force Martell to supply cognac for their own 'Castle' brand. Martell refused, and for several years the Gilbeys contemplated his plight with some smugness. But by the 1880s they were forced to stock his cognac, not under their name but under his even though in the meantime Sir Walter Gilbey's favourite daughter had married into the Hine family.

Nevertheless, Scotch had made considerable inroads. It was while serving with the Malakand Field Force on the North West Frontier in 1898 that the young Winston Churchill first 'overcame his repugnance to the taste of whisky'.[57] As he pointed out: 'all this whisky business was quite a new departure in fashionable England. My father for instance could never have drunk whisky except when shooting on a moor or in some very dull chilly place. He lived in the age of the brandy and soda.' Michael Broadbent points out, that 'it was not until the last decade or so of the century that "liqueur" brandy became generally accepted as a great post-prandial digestif'. The threat from blended Scotch whisky, containing as it does so high a proportion of cheaper industrial grain whisky was naturally perceived as serious, leading even the lordly Hennessys to advertise their wares for the first time – the firm also had to sell in lots of a mere ten cases, a far smaller quantity than the minimum quantities on which it had previously insisted.

But there was another, parallel trade in bulk brandies: at least one firm boasted that it had installed special equipment for creating and designing brands in buyers' own names – a practice which foreshadowed the 'buyers' own brands' now sold by retail chains the world over. These were sold largely on price, whereas before the introduction of bottles 'own brands' were those sold by the smarter wine merchants, who were emphatically not competing on price.

Business generally remained poor, and the Cognacais had to search for markets all over the world – Berrault's *Annual* provided exchange rates for dozens of currencies from Turkey to Uruguay. Hennessy was already established in China and was the first firm to set up in Japan as early as 1868, a mere three years after the country began to open up to the outside world. Most youngsters from Cognac families spent their youth tramping round the world. Jean Monnet, the future 'founder of Europe' found it perfectly natural to be sent to London at the age of sixteen for a two-year apprenticeship before embarking on a prolonged tour of Canada when barely out of his teens. Monnet had already learned to think of the world as a string of clients to be visited: 'If that took us to Singapore or New York that was scarcely felt as a privilege attached to our profession because it was our primary responsibility.' It was a good education for a statesman; in addition there was the training in languages and modern politics absorbed at the family table:

> *I went to Egypt where I learned other forms of persuasion. I would accompany our Greek agent from village to village. We visited the wholesalers, who bade us sit down, we drank coffee while they busied themselves with their own business. We learned that you had to wait for the appropriate moment. At a certain point Chamah, the Greek, decided that*

---

57 Quoted by Michael Broadbent in *Christie's Wine Review* (1979).

we must bring the matter to a head. At that point he would write in his notebook the quantity which he considered it reasonable for our customer to take, a figure which was never discussed. He had simply respected local customs. Later, in the East, I rediscovered the importance of time, which made me wonder sometimes whether Cognac was not in fact closer to Shanghai than to New York. In China, you had to learn to wait. In the United States you had to learn to persist. Two forms of patience to which Cognac, itself the result of a certain length of time, predisposes you so well.

Before World War I a number of countries – Belgium, Holland, Sweden, Denmark, Canada, India, Argentina and, to a lesser extent, the United States, Russia, Norway and Egypt – had all become substantial customers. But the bulk of the exports went to two contrasting outlets, France's numerous colonies, which took nearly 15 per cent of the total, and Britain, which took 40 per cent in volume but provided 55 per cent of Cognac's total export receipts. For the colonials bought cheaply in cask, while the British imported virtually all their brandy in bottle. Half-bottles of Martell Three-Star could be found in millions of humble British medicine chests, while the cognacs of Hennessy, like those of Hine and Delamain, were largely consumed by the aristocracy.

The recovery was not helped by the prevailing confusion over labelling. The 1907 catalogue of the Army and Navy Stores in London lists eight cognacs from Martell alone: X, XX, XXX, VO, VSO, VSOP, ESOP ('guaranteed over forty years in cask') and Extra ('guaranteed over fifty years in cask'). Variety went further. In the museum in Cognac there are bottles of every shape with dozens of trademarks involving various combinations of Grande, Fine and Champagne brandies, as well as a rash of dire-sounding mixtures, like Le Coup de Jarnac, described as *'Liqueur hygiénique à base de Fine Champagne'*. More logical was Brandy Bark, a 'tonic elixir containing as chief ingredients genuine champaign brandy and royal yellow bark'. This was almost certainly the new wonder drug, quinine, so Brandy Bark was probably the prototype of that modern fad, brandy and tonic.

Other companies looked for specific markets: labels were registered for a cognac to be sold in railway buffets, a *Cognac des dames* and 'pocket bottles' (each containing 'Five glasses of excellent Cognac'). Other brands were topical. In 1876 Bellot's National French Brandy Company had commemorated the centenary of an independent United States and in 1889 the anniversary of the French Revolution and the construction of the Eiffel Tower were duly acknowledged.

But one of their most powerful marketing tools and one of the most surprising, was the name of Napoleon. The region remained faithful to both Napoleons – his supporters had cheered Bonaparte on his way when he was travelling through the province on his way to Rochefort – and Saint Helena elected a Bonapartist deputy for forty years after Napoleon III had been dethroned. The name started to spread in the first decade of the century, when the trade was still convalescent. The successful identification of the drink with the emperor is rather puzzling: for a century Napoleon remained an arch-villain in Britain, and it would have been natural to use the name of the ruler associated with Cognac's Golden Years, and not that of his uncle. Yet the connection was made with the first emperor, and it served its purpose.

The weapon was used at three levels. The name was freely attached to any dusty old bottle of brandy. Even today the London sale-rooms still offer bottles of so-called 'Napoleon' brandy. These are often labelled 1811, the Year of the Comet, which remains embedded in the subconscious of the world of cognac. By now the cognacs are naturally rather awful. One was described to me as like 'the water you've washed your leather boots in'. The Napoleonic magic was sufficiently powerful to cover bottles labelled with the names of his first wife (*Impératrice Joséphine*), his house (*Maison de l'Empereur*), his tragic son (*Le Roi de Rome*) and even events associated with the Emperor. One rather tactless label even celebrated *La Grande Armée*, the army he led to its frozen fate in the Russian winter of 1811–12. Needless to say these Napoleonic bottles were almost invariably phoney.

More permanently the name of Napoleon was, and is, attached to a particular quality between VSOP and XO, providing a particular benefit to Courvoisier, which for nearly a hundred years has exploited the name and the picture of the emperor in a brilliant and sustained piece of image-building. To be fair, this was perfectly reasonable, for Courvoisier did have a genuine Napoleonic connection. Emmanuel Courvoisier, the firm's founder, was a native of the Jura, near the Swiss frontier. He had based himself in Paris, cultivating the business available at Napoleon's Imperial court, and even supplying the emperor himself.[58]

Courvoisier's partner, Louis Gallois, was the builder of one of the first warehouses for wines and spirits which transformed Bercy, a dreary suburb on the eastern outskirts of Paris into the centre of the French trade in basic wines (*la grosse cavalerie*: figuratively 'plonk', literally 'the heavy mob'). Their sons transferred the brandy business to Jarnac, and in the 1840s Courvoisier's son bought out his friend and partner, retaining the Napoleonic connection by supplying spirits to the court of Napoleon III. The business passed to his nephews, the Curlier Brothers (it was a M. Curlier who had shown the Parisian artist Bertall around in 1877) passing to the Simons, Anglo-French wine merchants in 1909; by introducing the Napoleonic image a few years later they greatly boosted the firm's fortunes.

The Simons were the exception, the first and only outsiders in a narrow, introverted world which had many parallels with the Chartronnais of Bordeaux, another largely Protestant merchant oligarchy living surrounded by Catholic peasants in a major centre of Anglo-French trade. Life for a well-established merchant family could be temptingly easy. According to Gerald de Ramefort, whose family bought the business in 1930, by then the Otards were 'more interested in public and social life than business, living like lords in the beautiful châteaux they bought around Cognac or in their Paris apartments, and of course, they used to spend a lot of money'. The biggest spenders were probably the family of Jules Robin, a firm that was as big as Martell and Hennessy in the late nineteenth century thanks to its virtual monopoly in the trade of cheaper cognacs with France's ever-growing empire. The older generation long remembered their gorgeous equipages and the state they kept.

---

58 Today Courvoisier exhibit a variety of Napoleonic memorabilia in its grandiose head office by the Charente in Jarnac.

THE GAUTHIERS

In the early 1980s the world of the Cognacais was recalled by Jean-Frédéric Gauthier-Auriol, sitting in his study in the family house in the rue Saulnier a few hundred yards from the river, in reminiscences recorded by Catherine Petit. He was talking of the 1920s but could just as well have been referring to pre-1914 Cognac:

> There were four employees in the office and one very important gentleman, the *maître du chai*. I remember well how the *gabares* were loaded: the workers from the warehouse loaded the cases on big wheelbarrows we called *twins*. They also loaded cases on to horse-drawn carts: they were branded wooden cases – cardboard packaging was a revolution...My grandmother had a ladies' maid who stayed with her for forty years and a manservant she kept for forty-three years. Our governess (*la miss*) came from England. At lunch we spoke English. If you spoke a word of French, they whisked the dessert past your nose...as I loathed caramel flan, when I saw it in the kitchen before lunch, I automatically spoke French! For me English was another native language...there wasn't a single merchant who hadn't spent a year's apprenticeship in England.

The Gauthiers' world was one large family (Gauthier's grandmother was a Mselle Delamain) firmly, exclusively Protestant:

> the Protestants were like a plate of macaroni cheese: if you pulled one strand you brought with it the whole plate...we adhered to certain principles in our house: we went to the chapel every Sunday...my uncle Guy remained a bachelor. He had a mistress whom we called 'the admiral' because she was the daughter of a Breton admiral; my grandmother never allowed him to marry her. For she was Catholic and, what is more, she did not come from the same class as us.[59]

---

59 Catherine Petit, *Les Charentes: Pays du Cognac* (Paris, 1984).

The First World War did not greatly affect the fortunes of Cognac. Apart from the absence of able-bodied men, many remembered on the endless lists of names on the *morts pour la patrie* in the tiniest of French hamlets, it did not change the pattern of Cognac's life – although Meukow, one of Cognac's most reputable concerns, was seized because it had been owned by the German Klaebisch family. By contrast, peace brought an avalanche of problems. In France itself sales were badly affected by a tax on luxuries first imposed in 1917. This started at 10 per cent but was raised to 30 per cent in 1924. The locals naturally complained: their drink was taxed at a higher rate than imported luxuries like furs and diamonds, which paid only 10 per cent. The only consolation was the article in the

Treaty of Versailles that obliged the Germans to officially recognise the status of Cognac. A number of countries, Greece, Spain, Italy and Portugal among them, protected their local wine and spirit makers with heavy import duties. As always the cognac community fought an uphill battle against the forces of protectionism, at home and abroad, with James Hennessy launching a petition in favour of free trade in 1927. Taxes were a crucial factor: exceptionally, the Egyptian market remained healthy because duties were low. But the habit of heavy import duties spread to Argentina, whose economy had, in any case, declined dramatically after the war. Indeed, the market in much of Latin America suffered from a similar combination of economic misfortune and increased duties in a pattern that was to recur half a century later. In a few markets, such as Holland, a reduction in sales volume did not involve too great a loss in cash terms because imports were increasingly in bottles rather than the casks used for the cheaper brandies.

Even the key British market suffered. In the years after the war British purchases were a mere sixth of the quantity they had been in the golden days of Napoleon III, and under half of the only slightly less glorious days of Edward VII, in the first decade of the twentieth century, largely due to the success of blended Scotch. The Cognacais were still effectively on a 'sterling standard', since many of their costs, like transport and insurance, were payable in pounds. After the war the franc was weak, which vastly increased their costs. Excise duties on all spirits had risen five-fold since 1914 and in 1920 the British Government suddenly imposed an additional 33 per cent duty on imported spirits. The effect on sales was so severe that revenue from customs' duties dropped by half and the increase was soon withdrawn. The recovery after the franc had been devalued in 1926 was sluggish.

Duties had always been a problem but Prohibition was a new terror. It virtually wiped out the American market (although substantial quantities were smuggled in from the tiny French-owned islands of St Pierre and Miquelon, south of Newfoundland). The wave of dramatic anti-liquor measures spread to Canada and the Scandinavian countries. If sales were not totally forbidden, then they were channelled through state-run liquor boards with little interest in increasing sales. Their influence can be felt to this day, although a small group of merchants – such as Tiffon and Larsen – have specialised successfully in supplying the Scandinavian liquor monopolies.

The mood in Cognac was naturally defensive. The most dramatic result was the agreement made in 1922 between Martell and Hennessy. They were already used to working together: since the mid-nineteenth century they had set an agreed price for the cognacs they bought from the growers. The families had, of course, been connected by marriage and friendship ever since Napoleonic times but fears that one side or the other would be dominant had prevented any formal business links. Fortunately Maurice Hennessy's father had spent most of his time in Paris, leaving his son alone in Cognac. As a result the Martells became a second family to him: 'I spent weekends with them in their house near Royan,' he told me. 'I had a room in their house. I remember leaving my gambling winnings in a drawer and finding them there untouched the following weekend. It was like home to me.' The dramatic drop in the British market altered all that. Maurice himself was in Bogota at the time. He returned post-haste and talked his idea over with his friend, Paul Firino-Martell, who convinced his father and uncle of its soundness.

In a formal agreement designed to last twenty-five years they set up two new companies named Martell and Hennessy in both of which the two families had substantial shareholdings – indeed they worked together so closely that the post was opened in the same room. They then divided up the world between them. Martell was granted a 'privileged situation' in Britain and indeed at one point enjoyed 80 per cent of the market. The Hennessys retained their traditional Irish connection and in the longer term benefited greatly from the running start they enjoyed after the war in the Far East and the United States – even during Prohibition they could sell some cognac since their agents, the Schieffelins, were a pharmaceutical company and so could sell limited quantities of 'medicinal brandy'. The partners did not actually prohibit sales in each other's territories – the Hennessys retained an agent in Britain. In China, traditionally a Hennessy fief, the local agents got together in the 1920s to agree on a common price structure. Between the wars both families had relinquished active management of their businesses. Maurice Fillioux's father, Raymond (who had worked for Jean Monnet for a time), was responsible for a great deal of the Hennessy business, while at Martell distant relations – MM. Castaing and Castillon – enjoyed a great deal of power.

The arrangement at least ensured the continuing supremacy of the two houses. Indeed, in the 1920s, according to one authority, there were only 'two cognac firms of the first rank'.[60] Most of the others had suffered from one or other of the region's many problems. Camus had relied too heavily on the Russian market, the Otards on Latin America. The last Otard, Marie-Thérèse, had married the aristocratic Comte de Castellane which didn't help. Gerald de Ramefort put it bluntly: 'when their competitors began to sell their brandies in bottles under their own names, they did not follow the trend. "We are not grocers," they said loftily.'

Less aristocratic houses also suffered. In the mid-1920s Jean Monnet was called back to Cognac from Geneva, where he had been one of the driving forces behind the fledgling League of Nations. As he wrote in his autobiography, 'At Cognac I found a situation which was financially bad and psychologically worse. No sooner had I arrived than I met a friend at the Café du Chalet. "I must talk to you," he whispered, "not here, but round the corner." I had forgotten that side of life in the provinces. "It seems that you are going into liquidation," he whispered.'[61] Monnet soon realised that the problem was simple and soluble: because Monnet's father believed in quality and loved good cognac, he had accumulated enormous stocks of old cognacs, which he could not sell at a time when the fashion was for young spirits. So sales and working capital were precariously low: 'You could go bankrupt in Cognac,' he wrote, 'despite having a good product and a well-respected brand name; it was enough to believe in what had always been, but was no longer true – the value of rarity and the danger of change. Many other firms were killed

60 Lys, *Le Commerce du Cognac Bordeaux* (1929).
61 *Mémoires* (Paris, 1976).

by their founders' obstinacy in preserving the practices that had earned them the esteem of a clientele that was both small and sophisticated.' Monnet, anxious above all to prevent his father from suffering the same fate, arranged to exchange some of his oldest cognacs for younger, more saleable spirits.

Like almost every other firm, his was on the defensive. They all retreated into their shells or like him, looked elsewhere for a career. Members of the Delamain family had already made names for themselves as scholars, scientists and amateur archaeologists investigating the region's numerous pre-historic remains. In the 1930s one brother, Jacques, made his name as an orchidologist (many small French orchids carry the family's name),[62] another, Maurice, founded the famous Parisian publishing house of Stock – with his brother-in-law, the writer Jacques Chardonne who was from Barbezieux as his partner. Robert wrote the classic history of Cognac – a brilliant essay which largely ignores the commercial side of the story in which his family had played such an important role.

The only market showing any signs of life was the Far East, particularly China and Japan. In his analysis of the exports of cognac Jean Lys attributed the increase to the fact that the local intelligentsia had returned from their education in France with a taste for the spirit and indeed the Cognacais seem to have penetrated to major cities far inland from their major markets in Peking and Shanghai. But quenching 'native' thirst was reinforced by the presence throughout the Far East of substantial groups of thirsty – and well-heeled – Europeans, either as colonial overlords or, especially in China, as commercial leaders. Despite competition from houses including Martell, Rémy, Adel Seward, Bisquit and Denis Mounié, Hennessy, which also had an agent in Japan, was the market leader. In 1921 Sincore & Co, the Harrods of Shanghai, was selling 500 cases a month. Louis Randon, Hennessy's agent in the Far East, including French Indo-China (a lucrative market) for nearly thirty years until his death in 1937 even adjusted his prices to ensure that Chinese restaurateurs could afford to put two bottles of cognac on a table seating six or eight diners (he also gave regular gifts to the best-known night club singers). Randon's correspondence, preserved in the Hennessy archives, shows the problems faced by the Cognacais. China was in a perpetual state of upheaval, often amounting to civil war, but the biggest problem was counterfeits of every brand of cognac.

The most significant event of the inter-war years was the arrival on the scene of André Renaud, who in 1924, took over the bankrupt firm of Rémy Martin. Founded in 1724 Rémy Martin had been profitably taken through the upheavals of the French revolution by the founder's grandson. Then, when Paul-Emile Rémy Martin inherited the family firm in 1875 he spent a great deal of his own money re-establishing the firm's vineyards, but much more on the lavish transformation of his mansion at Lignières, which had been badly damaged by a fire in 1869. As the cost of rebuilding mounted, the business declined. The banks started to press and new finance was injected, enabling Renaud to acquire an historic name on the cheap.

---

62 Nevertheless, family pressure ensured that, as the eldest son of the family, he became chairman of the firm.

RÉMY MARTIN AND ANDRÉ RENAUD

André Renaud was the very model of the ambitious son-in-law, the husband of Pierre Frapin's only daughter Marie, the single most marriageable girl in the whole region.

For the forty years after he took control of Rémy Martin in 1924 until his death at the age of eighty-two in 1965, Renaud dominated the firm. Renaud was a curious mixture, a peasant rooted to the soil, a man who loved to ride through his vines. But first and foremost, he was an intellectual with a doctorate in law. Throughout his life he read voraciously and he thoroughly enjoyed an intellectual argument. Physically he was not an imposing figure: rotund, with a small moustache, invariably wearing a trilby hat, summer and winter, indoors and out. In addition to his Cognac business Renaud was a remarkable stock market operator whose other investments included an

André Renaud, the business genius who created Rémy Martin

interest in the Pathé film company and the publisher Maurice Delamain.

In his business he was an autocrat, working his employees hard but looking after them when they were old or sick. For quite a time after the takeover it was a small business with only thirty employees, many of whom had worked for the firm's previous owners. Their day started at 7am – and God help late arrivals – and even when business was slack stopped a full twelve hours later. If orders poured in, then they stayed on, sometimes until 11pm. They worked a six-day week (sometimes extending into the Sabbath) with no thought of holidays, and, as the firm's history puts it: 'the firm was not well-known for the size of its wages'. Renaud believed that money spent on anything except increasing his stocks was wasted. Not surprisingly, he was never popular within the Cognac community.

He would have preferred to go into business with his father-in-law, Pierre Frapin, with whom he remained close throughout their lives, but Frapin never gave up hope that Albert, his tubercular son, would recover sufficiently to take over the business so would not let his son-in-law near it – although he allowed him to exploit his stocks.

It was natural for Renaud to concentrate on selling brandies labelled Fine Champagne largely from his father-in-law's extensive stocks , which he combined with the quality of VSOP, long recognised as that immediately above the basic level but never really promoted as such. In 1927 he created 'VSOP Fine Champagne' which has formed the basis of the firm's fame and fortune ever since. His challenge was fundamental, for the Big Two have always refused to define their brandies' precise origin. His initiative was typically arrogant, for Rémy was small, poor, and relatively unknown. Even in 1939, the firm was smaller than Frapin.

To sell his doubly-special product Renaud needed salesmen who would put up with his unappealing blend of stinginess, autocracy and ingratitude ('it's ok' was his highest compliment). Otto Quien was a key-figure - half Dutch, half-German, born in Shanghai and educated in Switzerland. The wine business Quien's father had set up in Bordeaux in the 1920s was ruined in the crash of 1929, so he had a wife and son to keep but no job. As a young man Quien had spent six months of every year in Indonesia (then the Dutch East Indies) working for an uncle who owned a major wine and spirits business with substantial sales throughout the Far East. The colony naturally housed a large and thirsty group of Dutchmen but Quien was the first person to exploit what later became a crucial market for the better cognacs - the generally affluent Chinese living outside their native country.

Quien preferred to work on commission rather than accept the pay offered by the stingy Renaud and agreed what amounted to a bet on his capacity to sell; he won his bet, and not only in the Far East. Once Prohibition had been repealed Quien turned his eyes to the US.

Within France itself most firms made do with what were called *agents multicartes*, sales representatives who sold a wide variety of alcoholic products and who would naturally concentrate their efforts on the best-selling products. But Renaud managed to recruit a real charmer, Pierre Rivière. In Paris his first point of call was the city's best restaurants, and one by one he converted them to the Rémy cause.

With the end of Prohibition and the economic slump, there was some improvement in the 1930s, but recovery was naturally aborted by the defeat of France in 1940. Even today the period of Occupation remains a largely no-go area. The histories of individual firms pass over the period in silence while a relatively recent illustrated history of the period[63] makes no mention of the cognac business, still less of individual firms or their bosses – though Kyle Jarrard[64] persuaded some typical locals to speak up and provide an excellent picture of Cognac during the occupation. As he put it: 'Here is where Cognac's often hermetic world becomes even more closed in.'

Like many other parts of France Cognac emerged from the war relatively unaffected physically and managed to distil cognacs despite the lack of such essential items as bottles and corks – the 1940 Hine remains a delight to the palate. As was common, even families were split during the war. The novelist Jacques Chardonne's sentimental attitude towards his own, idealised vision of traditional rural France led him to be a stout supporter of Marshal Pétain during the war, like many other traditionalist Frenchmen who could best

---

63 Christian & Louis Moreau, *Les deux Charentes sous l'Occupation et la Résistance* (Gemozac, 1987).
64 *Cognac* (Hoboken NJ, USA).

PIERRE FRAPIN

Virtually the only grower to be able to break free from the historic dependence on the merchants and exploit the superior quality of brandies from the Grande Champagne on a major scale was Pierre Frapin, the biggest land-owner in the heart of the region with a vineyard of over 300 hectares. He was no newcomer, his granddaughter Geneviève Cointreau has traced the family back to the thirteenth century, and found a direct relationship with the great fifteenth-century novelist Rabelais, as well as estates in the Champagnes dating back to the seventeenth century. It needed unusual personal qualities, including pride in his brandies and what his granddaughter calls a desire to 'valoriser ses propriétés' – add value, make the most of his land and the fine brandies it produced, largely

Pierre Frapin: the first grower to achieve world-wide renown

from Les Gabloteaux, which, with its neighbour Fontpinot, produced two of the few 'single estate' cognacs in the region. Nevertheless he did not put all his brandies into his own brand, he remained a friend and supplier to the Hennessys, and also sold to Courvoisier.

Frapin is remembered by his granddaughter as 'a man of natural authority'. But behind the mask of authority, was someone who enjoyed taking risks, a fearless horseman. And when motor cars arrived in the Charentes he soon became notorious for his fast and reckless driving – he used regularly to cover the twelve miles between his vineyards and Cognac in precisely twenty-two minutes.

From the start he multiplied the stakes by going out of his way to distinguish himself from *les Messieurs de Cognac*. His brochures, in excellent English, emphasised that 'The Frapins' vineyards are in the very heart of the Grande Champagne, the finest growth in the Cognac region.' Fortunately Frapin's stocks were sufficient for him to be able to advertise that his cognacs were *authentique, extra*. They were indeed: within five years of founding the business he had won a major prize at a fair in New Orleans. This was only one of two dozen awards lavished on his brandies. He was an early exemplar of a grower who bypassed the merchants' stranglehold on his fellows.

be described not as fascists but as premature anti-Communists. By contrast his son Gérard Boutelleau was a resister. He was one of a relatively small group, though there were many others who performed heroically in silence, like the secretary at Jarnac's town hall who kept from the authorities the many letters her office received denouncing local Jews.

Renaud was loyal to his German partners the Sichels. Though Jewish they had been allowed to remain in charge of their business throughout the 1930s because of the foreign exchange they brought in from the wines they exported. But in early 1940 they were forced to flee and spent the following winter as penniless refugees in the Pyrenees. It was Renaud who sent them regular monthly payments to keep them alive until they managed to procure passports (some of them false) and make their way to Spain and thus to the United States. Two members of the Hine family were actively involved in helping escaped British prisoners on their way south. Pierre Firino-Martell, as mayor of Cognac, had to adopt the two-faced attitude required of all such officials. In 1941 the eighty-five-year-old Pierre Frapin resigned as mayor of Segonzac, three years before his death, unwilling to tolerate the whims of the German occupier any longer. That same year, André Royer, the mayor of Jarnac, was replaced by an official more accommodating to the Germans, though he returned to the Town Hall after the Liberation.

The Hine business suffered from the requisition of the substantial stocks of cognac awaiting transport to Britain, the firm's biggest market, but the only firm in real trouble was Courvoisier, liable to confiscation as enemy property, for it had been an English-registered company since the Simon brothers had bought it. Two of the managers, George Hubert and Christian Braastad, calling themselves 'Hubert et Cie', bought the stocks and retained the name, using pre-dated documents. Unfortunately, eighteen months later the Germans found out and put in a sequestrator to run the company. By contrast Mark Foucauld sought a patent for a cognac called 'Swastika Brand'.[65]

At first the German forces – especially the Navy – confiscated any stocks they could lay their hands on, but order was soon restored with the arrival of a local commandant, Gustav Klaebisch. He and his brother Otto, who was appointed *Weinführer* in Champagne, probably owed their splendid jobs to von Ribbentrop, Hitler's foreign secretary, a former wine and spirit merchant, importer among other brands of Meukow cognac, owned by the Klaebisch family before it was requisitioned at the outbreak of World War I. Ribbentrop was in a good position to dictate the choice of *Weinführers* not only because of his previous business but because his closest political ally was Otto Abetz, the German Ambassador in Paris.

Klaebisch himself was a friend of many of the merchants, for he had been educated in the local lycée. He was no Nazi – he did not even requisition the family's former firm – and as early as October 1940 foresaw Germany's fate. 'The worst thing that can happen to a man,' he told Maurice Hennessy, 'is to see his country defeated twice within a generation.' This remarkable man seemingly took neither pleasure nor profit from his powers – and neither did his associate Gustav Schneider who, for instance, helped locals avoid forced labour in Germany by getting them sent to build the Atlantic Wall. Bernard Hine believes that the Germans' object was to protect stocks of cognac for post-war use because they, like most Germans, believed that it would be over within a few months.

---

65 In the 1970s his family's firm was bought by the Compagnie Commerciale de Guyenne. The Foucauld brand is still sold to the German supermarket group Metro.

The key official figure of the occupation was Maurice Hennessy. He had only one eye, yet had somehow managed to become a pilot in the French Air Force and could have stayed in Britain after the fall of France. However, he returned home with one simple object: 'to try to safeguard our productive capacity, in the form of our vineyards, and our working tool, our stocks of cognac'. His basic strategy, as he explained it to his fellow merchants in 1941, was equally simple: 'We should think ourselves lucky if after the war we are in a position to start again.' He ensured that most of the Cognacais regarded the increasing volume of cognac they were forced to deliver to the Germans as 'a tribute imposed by the occupying power on a number of named persons of the occupied country'. This definition of 'tribute' meant that the merchants were obliged to furnish supplies under a quota system measured as a proportion of their previous volume of business, while no such obligations were imposed on the growers.

The 'tribute' was enormous: 'In 1940,' said one observer, 'the Germans took two years' sales in four months.' The pace was sustained: over 8 million bottles in 1941, 6.5 million in 1942, nearly 8 million in 1943 and nearly 4 million in the few months of 1944 before Cognac was liberated, although the Cognacais now claim that much of the 'tribute' was paid not in true cognac but in alcohol made from beetroots. The French market had soared to nearly 30 million bottles in 1941, a far higher figure than the pre-war record of 22 million bottles in 1935. Obviously, ordinary exports, which had been running at just under 15 million bottles during the pre-war years, dropped to a mere couple of million by 1944 – but the region's financial and commercial structure remained intact, as the Germans paid handsomely for their purchases.

For Cognac, like so much of provincial France, the Occupation could have been worse, and indeed brought some advances, especially in bringing together both sides of the Cognac community. Maurice Hennessy had acted, nominally, as president of the town's Chamber of Commerce. He found a partner, Pierre Verneuil, among the growers. To preserve the region's stocks they devised two mechanisms: the Comités d'Organisation pour Produits Alimentaires, designed to share out scarce foodstuffs, and the Bureau de Repartition, established to organise sales to the Germans. As in Champagne and Bordeaux, wartime hardships produced a new communal spirit between growers and merchants, last seen in Cognac in the equally hard times that had followed the phylloxera (Hennessy's partner was the son of the grower who had done so much to re-establish the Cognac vineyards). Although some of the greedier, or more pro-German, merchants wanted to sell more than their quota, the mechanism worked smoothly enough.

Of course there were exceptions. As the local historian Gérard Jouhannet puts it many people 'put business before patriotism' when dealing with the Nazis. Bernard Hine describes a 'grey market' where some firms 'made a pile of money during the war by selling to anybody at very high prices', though he added, 'the more reputable houses didn't do that but smaller ones did and they disappeared within the next few years'. In Hennessy's words: 'Thanks to the prevailing spirit of mutual understanding, if the merchants' stocks suffered considerably, those in the hands of the growers expanded so much that at the end of the war the stock the region had at its disposal was bigger than that available in 1939.'

Before the occupation the merchants probably owned nine-tenths of the stocks but most of the growers decided not to declare their real stocks to protect them from requisition and in 1945 the firms found that they owned a mere 60 per cent.

Most of the region was liberated during the summer of 1944 though the Germans retained strongholds round the ports of La Rochelle and Royan until April 1945. Allied bombing had been light, though the important railway station at Angoulême was bombed, killing over a hundred civilians, and Cognac's airport at Châteaubernard on the outskirts of Cognac itself, used by German bombers looking for Allied shipping, also suffered.

After the liberation sixty men accused of collaboration went to jail, generally for only a short time. Among them, not surprisingly, was Chardonne and so, far less reasonably, were Renaud and Firino-Martell – though he was released by popular demand. As always Renaud's experience was unique, while he was helping the Sichels he was also exploiting his friendship with Gustav Schneider to the full, enlisting Schneider's help to smuggle what he said were a few hunting rifles to friends in the unoccupied zone. In the event these turned out to be a dozen superb shotguns and four thousand cartridges. Renaud also worked with the resistance network commanded by the former sub-prefect of Cognac.

After the war Klaebisch worked with his brother Otto, who became Martell's importer, while Schneider disappeared from the region in 1944, was imprisoned in the United States and after his return to Germany became a distributor for Rémy Martin. In Cognac itself there was even a proposal, not surprisingly unrealised, for a square named after Klaebisch himself.

8

THIRTY GOLDEN YEARS

To the French, the years from 1945 to the first oil crisis in 1973 are known as *les trente glorieuses* – the thirty glorious years. Cognac shared in the glory with sales reaching a record high of 140 million bottles in the early 1970s, more than at any time since the phylloxera crisis. Nevertheless, the day of Germany's surrender, 8th May 1945, had not been one of undiluted rejoicing. That night there was a disastrous and unprecedentedly late frost, which reduced that year's crop to a mere quarter of even the reduced wartime level and one-fifth of the pre-war average. Not surprisingly sales immediately jumped once the war was over: whereas only nine million bottles had been exported in 1945, 21 million bottles were sent abroad in 1946. But the great majority went to the United States, to Allied troops, mostly American, to Britain (and its still extensive empire), a couple of million to Belgium and the French Empire, leaving only eight million for the French themselves.

Inevitably the merchants had to draw on their stocks, which had already been greatly depleted by official German requisition. As a result, by the end of 1946 they held only 260,000 hectolitres, three-quarters of the level in 1939 when they held over four-fifths of the total, while in 1945 the growers, many of whom had managed to hide their stocks, held virtually the same amount as in 1939. The occupation had provided them with capital and hence confidence and for the first time since phylloxera struck, they were sufficiently well-off not to have to sell their brandy to the merchants as soon as it was distilled. This did not entirely suit Maurice Hennessy. As he wrote after the war: 'The risk [and, he implied, the profits] of stocking is one that is inherent in our trade.'

The growers' boldest move came in 1947 with the creation of the Prince Hubert de Polignac trademark. The Co-operative de Cognac had been set up in 1929 to resist the downward pressure on prices, and two years later the growers formed a business called Unicoop to sell cognacs directly to buyers at home and abroad. Traditionally, the co-operatives had been confined to the fringes of the Cognac region. In the nineteenth century the growers had relied on the names of their general managers, M. Salignac and then M. Monnet, to sell their cognacs, and inevitably their firms had moved away from the co-operative ideal. The use of the name of one of France's most distinguished families[66] was a declaration that they were now in the mainstream. Nevertheless the co-operatives have never enjoyed the success of their brothers in Champagne, for the power of the major firms was greater and the co-operatives have had to rely very largely on the unprofitable business of supplying 'buyers' own brands' for supermarkets.

The growers were also sufficiently confident to maintain their war-time co-operation with the merchants, a link symbolised by the foundation of the Bureau National Interprofessionel de Cognac. Like similar bodies in Champagne and Bordeaux, the BNIC grew out of the collaboration of an individual merchant working with the growers more systematically, more closely, and more personally during the Occupation than ever before. Like them the BNIC could trace its origins back to an earlier, voluntary body without much power or influence – in this case the Union de la Viticulture et du Commerce, founded in 1921. The Bureau National de Repartition had provided a much better model: it included two members each from the growers and the merchants and four nominated by the central government. For eighteen months at the end of the war the fledgling BNIC was directly controlled by the Ministry of Agriculture, but it gained a – relative – independence in July 1946. It is an unusual animal, for, unlike its brethren elsewhere in France, it has official powers normally vested in central government officials.

The final constitution gave the locals the real power: the central government's representatives have acted as observers rather than exercising the behind-the-scenes control usual in France. The Bureau was even endowed with its own source of finance, a one per cent levy on all sales. But the BNIC was always hampered by the influence of the major firms and finds it difficult to mount generic campaigns in France and abroad because they feel that this would also promote their smaller rivals.

The control over the price of wines and brandies held for so long by Martell and Hennessy ended in 1954, and two years later the BNIC stepped in to try to establish a generally agreed price structure. Years of squabbling ended only in 1960, when the Bureau was given wider powers. The result was a scale of *comptes* on permitted ages (see Appendix I) as well as the historic price gap of between 5 and 10 per cent between cognacs from the Grande Champagne, the Petite Champagne and the Borderies (normally priced together) and the different categories of Bois. In 1962 the Big Four (which now included Rémy as well as Courvoisier) ensured that single vintage cognacs could not be sold to the public. This placed cognac at a disadvantage compared with Armagnac, which could legally sell single-vintage bottles and, to make matters worse for the Cognacais without any effective control over their age claims.

Martell and Hennessy had split in 1947. Their corporate 'marriage' had always been personal, based on the mutual trust and affection binding one generation of both families. But Maurice Hennessy's closest friend, Maurice Firino-Martell, had died. Maurice Hennessy was not willing or able to impose his policies on his younger cousins, like Kilian Hennessy, let alone on his even younger nephews, Gerald de Geoffre and Alain de

---

66 At the time they owned Pommery champagne.

Pracomtal, who were to guide the company through to the 1990s. Of course, the division had never been absolute: just before the war Maurice packed off his cousin, Freddie, a thoroughly Anglicised member of the family, to Britain to organise a more aggressive sales policy. Freddie proved a worthy scion, shrewd and amiable, and his efforts were part of a process that ended Martell's dominance of what was still cognac's biggest single market.

Even after the firm's stocks had been reconstituted after the frosts of 1945–6, Maurice Hennessy believed that the outlook for the future was bleak. He believed that the immediate post-war surge in the demand for cognac came partly from the markets deprived of Scotch, which would return to their pre-war allegiance as soon as they could, indeed, in the 1950s it was Scotch, not cognac that took the fancy of the average American used to whisky.

Hennessy's pessimism proved unfounded but only after a decade or more. In France cognac suffered because rum, its biggest competitor, outselling cognac by five bottles to one, attracted a lower tax burden. The result was that many smaller growers remained heavily indebted to the Crédit Agricole. But during the 1950s cognac, like all French luxury goods, was greatly helped by successive devaluations of the French franc. Inevitably there were losers. Jules Robin collapsed with the loss of the firm's colonial markets where *fine à l'eau* had been the favourite *apéritif* of the hard-drinking colonials in French Indo-China, above all in Vietnam, lost by the French in 1954. A similar fate befell Chabanneau which had relied heavily on sales to what were then the Dutch East Indies. The newly-independent Indonesia inevitably banned cognac imports. Another venerable firm Exshaw, was crippled by its former dependence on another Imperial market, that of the British in India

In the first fifteen years after the war total sales doubled, but mostly in traditional markets like Britain where sales trebled. But there was clearly scope in non-traditional markets as Europeans could increasingly allow themselves small luxuries. In 1958–9 Denmark still took more than West Germany and Ireland (where cognac is often called simply Hennessy), Italy or the Netherlands. The increasing prosperity of Western Europe was reflected in increasing sales, while Jean Monnet as 'father of the Common Market' helped by ensuring that cognac was not classed as an agricultural product and so was not submitted to the disciplines and idiocies of the Common Agricultural Policy and shared in the reductions in duties granted to 'industrial' products.

The surge of economic growth throughout Europe combined with the reduction of duties which followed the Treaty of Rome establishing the Common Market in 1957. As a result, in the fifteen years ending in 1973 sales to the then West Germany multiplied ten-fold to around half those in France itself which had grown by less than a half in the same period. The Cognacais were also helped by the gradual suppression of the rights of the *bouilleurs de cru*. Until the 1950s millions of them had been allowed to distil up to 10 hectolitres of alcohol, ostensibly for their own use. In reality half their production – up to 40 million bottles annually – trickled out to their families, to friends and to small cafés throughout France, thus competing with the cheaper cognacs.

During the 1950s sales nearly doubled in the United States, which took 40 per cent of exports. The Cognacais hired a New York public relations outfit headed by Edward

Gottlieb in a pilot effort for the Cognac Bureaux, later established in other major markets. Gottlieb's efforts were both imaginative and far-reaching. He lobbied groups of potential buyers like the Physicians' Wine Appreciation Society – those were the days – he published three books on cooking in which cognac naturally featured prominently. He even produced an embarrassingly titled but indubitably effective promotional film *Fun at the Chafing Dish* and ensured that the film was frequently mentioned in the smarter magazines. In the long term the combination of price and his campaigns preserved cognac's up-market image.

The biggest beneficiary from the boom was Courvoisier under Christian Braastad. He was born in Jarnac of Norwegian parents, but they returned home soon afterwards. He naturally learnt the Scandinavian languages so was snapped up by the Simon brothers in the early 1930s to sell to his native markets and, as we saw, during the war was one of the two managers who tried to save the firm from sequestration. By then he had 'gone native' and married a Mselle Delamain – their son Alain ran his mother's family firm for many years. Christian was an even better organiser of salesmen than a salesman himself and in the fifteen years after the war provided Courvoisier with the industry's first example of competent, orthodox, non family-dominated management. Braastad continued to promote the firm's connection with Napoleon and introduced the same type of frosted bottle as Rémy had used for its VSOP, although Courvoisier's was more squat and business-like.

The key to Courvoisier's profitability was that Braastad did not hold much stock. He bought as and when required, often using brokers, the courtiers historically so important in Bordeaux but less crucial in Cognac because of the direct links between growers and merchants. Braastad's strategy worked brilliantly – for a time. But then the success not only of his firm but of the region as a whole caught up with him. In 1946 sales of cognac had represented six years' stocks. By the end of the 1950s they were down to less than four years' requirements.

In 1956–58 the harvests were exceptionally low and as a result by the early 1960s Courvoisier was caught with inadequate stocks even of younger brandies and desperately needed a substantial injection of capital to restore them. Typically, André Renaud had anticipated Braastad's difficulties. He had hidden his precious brandy stocks successfully from the Germans and naturally flourished after 1945 when demand, especially for older brandies, was increasing faster than the supply. He also sold cognacs to rival firms on generous credit terms, for, as so often, he had a hidden agenda. At the height of the crisis he swooped, demanding immediate payment for all the cognacs he had supplied to an individual house over a long period. He knew that the firm involved would be in deep trouble if it had too small a capital base – and most family firms are at their most vulnerable when sales are growing because of the need to finance ever-increasing stocks.

Two of the most vulnerable of Renaud's customers were Delamain and Courvoisier. Nevertheless, he failed in his attempts to take them over. In the case of Delamain the family managed to find the cash to pay up. He then presented his bill to Courvoisier in the full expectation that Braastad couldn't pay. He was right. His next step was a proposed take-over on terms which remain unknown to this day but were certainly not generous – the locals claim that the bid was made in cash. But he didn't succeed. For by the 1960s outsiders from the whole world of spirits were eager to participate in such a fast-growing a business sector especially through so successful a firm as Courvoisier. Within a few months Courvoisier had found what would now be called a 'white knight' in the person of Cliff Hatch of Hiram Walker, the major Canadian liquor company notable for Canadian Club. Person is the right word, for Hatch was married to Christian Braastad's daughter Sylvie.

Hiram Walker's arrival was a sign that Cognac was no longer a backwater but about to become one of the battlefields on which the world's liquor companies were increasingly competing in attempts to provide the widest possible range of spirits. The availability of capital from its new owners enabled Courvoisier to maintain its sales momentum and by the 1970s was almost as big as Martell in Britain, thanks to its links with two of Britain's biggest brewery groups, Whitbread and Allied Breweries. Many other firms welcomed these newcomers. Many, and not only the smallest, tended to be undercapitalised or, as so often in France, suffered from family squabbles – *indivision de famille*. French inheritance laws ensure that over the generations shares get into the hands of relations uninterested in the business and only too happy to sell. Bass, the British brewers, bought Otard and for a time tried to promote the brand in its pubs and off-licences. Jean Monnet's firm was bought by the German firm Scharlachberg; Berger, an *apéritif* firm, bought Gauthier; Benedictine bought Denis Mounié (which it subsequently resold); and the Spanish firm Domecq did the same with Lucien-Foucauld. None of these often-hurried investments were profitable or long-lasting.

But some of the newcomers made a bigger splash. In 1967 the heirs to Laporte-Dubouché sold Bisquit to Pernod-Ricard, which already owned Renault, producers of superior brandies much appreciated in Sweden. Ricard, who had built up his fame and fortune on pastis, indulged in the biggest capital investment since the Martells in the late nineteenth century, planting many hectares of new vines and building a major new distillery and bottling plant at Rouillac in the northern Fins Bois. He was confident that he could increase sales through his considerable sales force in France. Nevertheless, the competition was so stiff that both brands faded within a couple of decades.

By contrast Sam Bronfman, the former bootlegger who had built Seagram into the world's biggest spirits business, adopted a far more subtle approach. He had failed to buy Martell, Courvoisier and Bisquit so, aiming to repeat the success he had enjoyed with Chivas Regal, a deliberately superior – and thus expensive – Scotch, he bought Augier, the oldest firm in Cognac and asked its former owner Jacques de Varenne to buy enough old stock to launch the Cognac equivalent of Chivas. The partnership was an unlikely one, while 'Mr Sam' was a toughie, albeit a charming one Varenne, was a wry, aristocratic figure related to the Hennessys – indeed was Maurice Hennessy's closest friend. The idea could have had the same beneficial effect on the cognac industry as Chivas had enjoyed with Scotch, but sadly Mr Sam died in 1971 and the idea got lost in the following years with the Samless Seagram preferring to launch an – inevitably unsuccessful – cognac

Kilian Hennessy, architect of the merger with Moët et Chandon

under the name of Mumm, one of the group's brands of champagne.

But the fashion was catching and in 1971 Distillers Company (DCL), the world's biggest distillers of Scotch, bought Hine, owned by too many members of the Hine family to be safe from takeover. DCL left the brothers Jacques and Bernard Hine, in place and brought in a new chairman, Brian Thomson. He proved invaluable in ensuring the continuing independence of the firm, shielding it from interference, though he was unable to get much finance for investing in stocks of cognac. The takeovers inevitably forced Martell and Hennessy to think about their future. The Firino-Martell family decided that it could and should remain independent. But the shareholders within the Hennessy family were more numerous, more dispersed, and most were not involved in the business. As a result Kilian Hennessy, who had taken over from his cousin Maurice in 1969, looked for a partner. The natural one was Moët & Chandon, another luxury drinks business, still family-controlled although it was quoted on the Paris Bourse, and a gentlemanly merger was arranged in 1971 between Hennessy and Comte Robert-Jean de Vogüé, the dominant figure in the champagne region after the war.

Cognac was now firmly embodied in the upper reaches of the international spirits business, which itself was becoming increasingly polarised between a handful of international giants and a few highly respected specialists. This division ensured the survival of the Big Four – who started to set up their own foreign subsidiaries instead of relying on local agents – and helped a firm like Hine, which could rely on the agents who distributed other DCL brands like Johnny Walker world-wide.

Hiram Walker's timing had been excellent. By the end of the 1960s the five other members of the original Common Market[67] accounted for nearly half Cognac's exports, a 10 per cent increase in market share during a decade when sales throughout the world were also rising. Sales to Germany, a mere 2.3 million bottles in the late 1950s, jumped over three-fold in the decade and indeed by 1970 Germany had, albeit temporarily, replaced the United States as Cognac's single biggest market.

But the biggest surprise came in the Far East. Sales to Hong Kong rose five times in a decade; by 1970 the Chinese there had become by far the biggest consumers of cognac per head in the world. The 'overseas Chinese', those in countries like Singapore and Malaysia, and later in Thailand and Taiwan, as well as in Hong Kong, were also interested

---

67 Germany, Italy, Netherlands, Belgium, Luxembourg.

only in the best cognacs. They drank cognac, not in sips after meals but with their food in decent-sized glasses filled with ice. Rémy Martin had a head start because of Otto Quien's pioneering efforts but the others soon started to catch up. Typically, by 1970 cognac was France's biggest single export item to Singapore, the most sophisticated market of all.

As sales mounted those in bulk fell sharply from a third to a fifth of the total in the twenty years after 1950, mostly to the Scandinavian state liquor monopolies. A vicious price war for this trade was won by the co-operatives, thus squeezing houses like Hardy and Tiffon which had relied on the trade. As a result they increasingly started to sell under their own names, sometimes for the first time and obviously at a major disadvantage compared with the established brands. But the biggest customers were the Japanese. The Japanese government had imposed duties of over 200 per cent in an effort to keep cognac out to protect its native spirits industry; despite this burden Japan grew into almost as important a market as Hong Kong thanks to a major loophole. The Japanese were allowed to import three litres of spirit duty-free, an enormous saving on heavily-taxed domestic purchases. As a result, an increasing proportion of sales were made through duty-free shops at airports in the Far East. This provided a major opportunity for Camus' la Grande Marque, an old firm that had nearly gone out of business just after the war. Not surprisingly Michel Camus 'a gambler who was both lucky and clever' as one friend put it, was happy to sell to a new firm, Duty Free Shoppers. This had been founded by two young graduates from the well-regarded Cornell University Hotel School who acquired the duty-free rights for virtually every airport on the Pacific Rim, originally intending to attract American servicemen returning from tours of duty in the Pacific. Not surprisingly, the major houses refused them credit but Camus snapped up the opportunity. Both sides flourished as the number of Japanese tourists anxious to return home with presents continued to multiply.

Camus naturally devised special cognacs for the new market, notably Celebration, launched in 1963. This was composed of three- to ten-year-old cognacs from the Bois and was promoted as superior to the ordinary VS. He later added a Napoleon and even today Camus has a special offering aimed at 'office ladies' called Josephine, complete with a delicious picture of a Mucha lady. In time all the firms benefited from the duty-free market which eventually accounted for a tenth of world-wide sales. Other firms created new offerings for the market, like Martell's Cordon Noir and Exshaw's Age d'Or, purely for Hong Kong. Martell even had to produce a Napoleon especially for the market. These brandies were tailored to the taste of the new drinkers; they were generally rather dark-coloured brandies which could cope with the inevitable dilution with ice.

The apparently never-ending increase in sales naturally created pressure from all sides for increased plantings. Ineed it was assumed that up to a further 80,000 hectares would be needed to cope with the apparently insatiable demand. In France any additional acreage is inevitably a matter for prolonged argument, since the precious *droit de plantation* (right to plant) in AOC regions is strictly controlled and thus a valuable asset. Because cognac had been such an unprofitable product for several generations the area planted with vines between 1940 and 1959 had remained virtually the same, at just over 60,000 hectares (148,000 acres). In 1959 a mere 2,000 hectares (5,000 acres) were authorised, but during the 1960s the process speeded up so that by 1971 the total had risen to 80,000 hectares (198,000 acres), reaching a peak of over 110,000 hectares in 1976.

Production was bound to rise substantially, especially as yields also increased. Better clones of Ugni Blanc, better cultivation, more fertiliser, better insecticides, meant that yields rose from an average of a mere 20 hectolitres of wine a hectare in the late 1940s to 50 hectolitres ten years later and then continued to rise. Despite the generosity of the allocations the BNIC was under considerable pressure to help young growers, the *jeunes agriculteurs*. Unfortunately, the authorities were unable to change the structure of the vineyard. Holdings continued to be tiny – only 3,500 out of 30,000 were larger than five hectares. But the average quality was also improving, for growers in the lesser *crus* could transfer their rights to plant vines. Between 1965 and 1972 the Bons Bois and Bois Ordinaires transferred an extra 1,700 hectares (4,200 acres) to the nobler *crus* while the BNIC granted rights disproportionately to the better *crus* – with the Petite Champagne receiving a fifth of the total. Nevertheless, everyone was left dissatisfied for one reason or another.

The situation was also complicated by the fact that by 1970 over three-fifths of the cultivatable land within the Grande Champagne and the Borderies was planted with vines, some of them, inevitably, in unsuitable *terroirs*. In the Grande Champagne some were even planted in the alluvial plain of the Charente, soils which peasant wisdom had kept vine-free over the centuries. In the Petite Champagne some magnificent chestnut trees on stony clay soil were uprooted to make way for yet more vines.

The surge in production left many growers deeply in debt. They all wanted to distil the ever-growing quantity of wine they were producing – indeed the average capacity of the stills owned by the *bouilleurs de crus* jumped by a half between 1966 and 1973, though only to 13 hectolitres, half the permitted maximum – and they spent considerable sums on converting their stills to gas; almost as much was being spent on tractors, new stills, casks and other equipment. Yet all this expenditure seemed reasonable enough when the cash yield from a hectare of vines tripled between 1959 and 1973, with the Fins Bois doing nearly as well as the nobler *crus*.

With prosperity came greed. In the words of Gerald de Geoffre, who succeeded his uncle Maurice Hennessy as the merchants' chief representative on the BNIC, 'inevitably between 1965 and 1973 the growers got into the habit of assuming that everything they produced would go for distillation – and at ever-rising prices. Although production in those years never actually fell below consumption, prices were rising faster than the sums they were paying in interest to the Crédit Agricole (then as now the key financial institution in rural France), so they were naturally unwilling to sell to us.' According to the BNIC prices rose only about 10 per cent annually during the late 1960s, but a study by the Banque de France showed that cognacs kept to age during these crucial years could double or even treble in value. Stocks remained historically low, a mere year above the three-year level that had caused such a crisis in the early 1960s and increased the pressure for even more planting, for the BNIC's apparently sober forecasts showed no net improvement in stock through the 1970s.

The situation was complicated by the arrival of André Hériard-Dubreuil who had taken over at Rémy after Renaud's death in 1965. Despite family problems, in the thirty-five years after he took over he transformed what had been a relatively modest single-product firm into a major player in the world drinks industry, a unique achievement in cognac's long history. He was always obsessed with quality: 'you have to sell cognac expensively, you have to sell it well' he would say. In 1973 Hériard-Dubreuil hired the region's first technical director – his rivals depended purely on their *maîtres de chais*, their blenders, technicians rather than scientists. Moreover he chose Robert Leauté, a lecturer in science, whose role was 'to translate the ideas of the marketing people and tell them they're impossible'. He in turn supervised the work of a chemical laboratory in Toulouse, two of its staff, Georges Clot and Pierrette Trichet, then joined the firm and successively became *chefs de caves*. Against the less dynamic opposition the firm tripled its sales in the fifteen years after his father-in-law's death. By the time of his death in 2002 at the age of eighty-four he had elevated Rémy to second place in the Big Four and had boosted the sales of VSOP from the miserable 5 per cent of the market they had held in 1945. Today the proportion is far higher and Rémy is responsible for four in ten of all the bottles of VSOP sold in the world.

Hériard-Dubreuil was always looking at the long term, always anxious to expand his empire away from cognac. His first major financial coup came when he took over Nicolas, the venerable Parisian wine company, transferred the – gigantic – stock to new premises and sold the firm's old premises in Bercy in eastern Paris at an enormous profit. He made less of a success with the group of merchants he built up in Bordeaux. But Champagne was another story. In 1973 he bought Krug – which he subsequently resold at a handsome profit – adding Piper-Heidsieck and Charles Heidsieck, in the 1980s. He then allowed a wine-making genius, the late Daniel Thibault, the finance, and the seven or more years required, to transform the brands into model drinks. Unfortunately in 2010 financial pressures forced his daughter to sell both companies. Outside Europe he failed in two ventures, in Australia, where Otto Quien had spent the war protecting the firm's interests, with Château Rémy, and in California in a joint venture with Schramsberg, makers of the state's finest sparkling wines to make double-distilled 'alembic brandy'.

As by far the biggest buyer of brandies from the Champagnes he naturally pressed the case for the growers there to be allocated the largest share of new plantings – he also paid more for brandies from the Champagnes than Martell or Hennessy, historically always worried by any shift of power towards the growers. But Hériard-Dubreuil realised that the links between the merchants and the growers could no longer be left to handshakes over successive generations. So he created Champeco, the first ever institutionalised commercial partnership between the two sides, and introduced formal three-year written contracts between Rémy and the growers. The agreement also enabled Rémy to expand more quickly, reducing the cost of holding stock – by far the biggest item of capital expenditure in the business – by sharing the burden with the growers and Champeco itself. This helped him greatly since one of his biggest problems was with his bankers, often distraught at the level of his firm's borrowings.

In the 1960s Rémy became a cult drink, both in traditional markets and in the Far East, thanks to the pioneering efforts of Otto Quien and a later, equally legendary salesman,

FAMILY SPIRIT, THE RÉMY STORY

André Renaud had three children, a son who was killed in a riding accident while still in his teens as well as two daughters. It had been assumed that Max Cointreau, the son of Renaud's friend André, would marry Renaud's older daughter, Anne-Marie. But he preferred her younger sister Geneviève, a choice which was to lead much later to the most extraordinary family feud in the region's history. During the war new company legislation had forced Renaud to reorganise the shareholdings in Rémy, leaving a majority to Anne-Marie who at the time was the only daughter old enough to be entitled to own shares. The legacy thus gave her the right to control the company after her parents' deaths.

André Hériard Dubreuil, who transformed Rémy into a world-class empire

Personally Renaud preferred Cointreau to André Hériard-Dubreuil who had married Anne-Marie in 1941 and whom Renaud dismissed as a mere engineer. Nevertheless, he proved to be an even more far-sighted businessman than his father-in-law. Not that he was an outsider, his great uncle had been a partner of the last member of the Rémy Martin family, and his father had married a Mselle Gautier, owners of another family firm. André himself was well-enough educated – by the Jesuits – to be admitted to the Ecole Polytechnique, which had trained France's elite engineers since Napoleon's time, and then went on to another highly selective establishment the Ecole des Eaux et Forêts. He was thus the first graduate from such ultra-selective establishments to manage a cognac company. His first stay in Cognac had been brief since he soon had to flee to Paris to avoid being sent for forced labour in Germany, but as soon as he returned in 1944 he began to make his mark. Nevertheless, he claimed that if he hadn't met his future wife he would have embarked on another career 'anything but be a cognac merchant like my father' he would say.

The inevitable show-down between the two sons-in-law was made more abrupt because of the family problem. Max Cointreau's wife Geneviève had inherited just under half the capital in Rémy Martin, a minority holding which, under French law, gave her substantial rights, though Hériard-Dubreuil did not allow his in-laws any say in the running of the company. The Cointreaus refused to subscribe to any capital increases. So Rémy had to rely increasingly on expensive bank borrowings. The financial limits entailed by this reliance first showed up in late 1976, when the French government was desperate to find a French buyer for Château Margaux. Hériard-Dubreuil could not find the mere 7 million francs (£700,000) required.

Later in the decade his wife forced him to put his elder son Michel at the head of the firm. His managerial inadequacies led to the departure of Yves Blanchard, the firm's brilliant sales director, and the demotivation of the rest of the management team. A few years later, but after the damage had been done, Michel was removed – he was later ordained as a priest in the Orthodox church – and his father, still only in his late fifties, took back control. But his biggest problem was with M. et Madame Cointreau. The family battle began in 1973 when Max Cointreau presented himself as a candidate for mayor of Segonzac. He was opposed – unsuccessfully – by Roger Plassard, Rémy's chief buyer. The feud worsened after the death in 1978 of Madame Albert Frapin, 'tantine', the beloved aunt of both Anne-Marie and Geneviève, shortly after she had rewritten her will. In it she left control of Frapin to her younger niece, partly because Anne-Marie's husband controlled Rémy. Hériard-Dubreuil promptly stopped buying any cognac from Frapin, which virtually disappeared from the market until the late 1980s.

The result was an inconceivably bitter and complicated legal battle that lasted for over a decade which Hériard-Dubreuil tried to keep secret. Basically it concerned two points: whether 'tantine' was capable, mentally and physically – she was crippled by rheumatism – of altering her will and the high-handed way the minority had been treated. The battle went to the Cour de Cassation, France's highest legal tribunal, eight times, until the Cointreaus eventually allowed themselves to be bought out of Rémy at a handsome profit. A few years later Hériard-Dubreuil rounded off his empire by buying Cointreau, which was no longer run by Max's branch of the Cointreau family.

By the time the legal battles were over he had, nominally at least, handed over to his two other sons, Marc and François. But he found them much less able than his daughter Dominique and in the mid-1990s installed her as chairman instead of his sons. Until she resigned in early 2013 she combined running the group to general applause with a number of high-profile roles, most obviously as chairman of the Comité Colbert, which brings together thirty of France's proudest purveyors of luxury products. Today the group remains independent, a powerful force in the world liquor scene. The supposedly excessive debts incurred in his expansion have been greatly reduced and the family battle has a happy ending. Following Hériard-Dubreuil's death in 2002 the two sisters were reconciled, as their daughters had already been, and both have been successful, for the Cointreaus, led by Max's daughter Béatrice and her brother Jean-Pierre, not only restored Frapin to a prosperity and reputation even greater than it enjoyed under their great-grandfather Pierre Frapin, but also bought and resurrected Gosset, the oldest firm in Champagne.

Nik Schuman, as lean and weather-beaten as a first-mate in one of Conrad's novels. Not surprisingly the new regime was soon presenting a major threat to Martell and Hennessy. They had always hated Renaud, claiming that he was merely a typical member of a family of shady operators – and refused to receive his successor socially. Yet throughout the1970s both families were transfixed, obsessed by Rémy's success. Salesmen would return to Cognac paralysed by the success of its VSOP Fine Champagne and unable to mount any form of counter-attack. They could merely hope that its ever-increasing debt burden would result in its downfall.

Worse, the very idea of a successful VSOP which boasted of its origins in the Champagnes challenged their vision of cognac. Traditionally they had relied almost exclusively on their brand names while Rémy was emphasising the importance of individual *crus* and their special *terroir*. Martell and Hennessy continued to rely on blends even for their superior qualities like Hennessy's XO or Martell's Cordon Bleu, historically the biggest selling premium cognac. As Maurice Hennessy had put it: 'doubtless some *terroirs* contribute their own special taste to well-made products but quality can be found anywhere if you look for it. And [quality] is the result of man's work', i.e. that of the owners of the brand name. So they counter-attacked; in late 1970 Courvoisier, Martell and Hennessy took the offensive by removing the etiquette Fine Champagne from the labels of their better brandies, claiming that the standard had greatly deteriorated.

The step merely provided Hériard-Dubreuil with an unrivalled marketing opportunity. He promptly resigned as president of the Syndicat des Exportateurs which grouped the eleven most important firms in Cognac and set up a rival grouping which he called 'Tradition and Quality'. Helpfully he was followed by Otard and two smaller firms, Boulestin and Gaston de la Grange, a new brand created by Martini. His aim, he declared in a superb public relations exercise, was to 'protest against the efforts of the Big Three to disgrace and to standardise their unique product', thus emphasising his firm's unique links with the growers. The resulting dispute, which the press naturally labeled the 'Cognac war', provided splendid publicity for Rémy. It was also music to the ears of the growers in the Champagnes, always afraid of the permanent majority of growers from lesser *crus* in the Federation which represented their interests.

At first the director of the BNIC, Henri Coquillaud – who had been a senior tax inspector responsible for supervising the movement and taxation of cognac – had tacitly supported the reformers but then made matters worse with a bland statement that 'there is no Cognac war and one is inconceivable...what they're trying to say is that there's only one good cognac, Fine Champagne, and that's ridiculous and could even become dangerous'. The mayors of the canton of Segonzac, heart of the Grande Champagne, immediately protested and the 3,750 growers from the Champagnes walked out of the Growers Federation. Individual growers went further, claiming that the BNIC was involved in a plot with the other three major firms. The Big Three counter-attacked, writing to the papers to refute suspiciously similar articles putting forward Rémy's point of view. But in vain, the reputable magazine *L'Express* painted the dispute as 'on one side industry, on the other craftsmanship, art indeed'. The contrast was particularly useful for Otard, not considered a leader in the quality stakes, which promptly launched its own Fine Champagne Baron Otard.

The war, however absurd it may now seem, was clear evidence of a breakdown in the consensus that had governed the Cognac community since the war. It was partly a matter of generations, for Maurice Hennessy and Pierre Verneuil, the growers' leader, had retired without leaving equally respected successors. Félix Gaillard, a former Prime Minister who was the only local political figure with sufficient stature to act as a mediator, had died in the mid-1960s. So the gap remained unfilled, and the relations between different classes of growers and between them and the merchants, now themselves divided, were strained even before the slump of the 1970s.

In the short term the war was clearly too damaging to the image of cognac to be allowed to continue – in public anyway. Within a few months a truce had been declared. Both sides promised to keep quiet, and 'Fine Champagne' soon appeared on other companies' labels, a tribute to Rémy's efforts. Since sales were rising at 20 per cent annually at the time, no one felt that the episode had done any permanent harm. But it had: greed had weakened the unity forged in slump and war. As Claude Belot, a radical local professor wrote in 1973: 'it is undeniable that in the last few years something has changed in this region of ours, which was so cautious for so long.'[68]

For Hériard-Dubreuil, wittingly or not, and helped by the animosity created by Martell and Hennessy, had divided the merchants' community as never before, a division matched by the ever-deepening gulf between the growers in the Champagnes and in the rest of the region. They divided into two *syndicats* and there were even two different magazines representing them. Both divisions were to prove highly damaging during the troubled decades that followed the traumatically sudden end to the *trente glorieuses* in 1973.

---

68 *Norois* magazine 1973.

9

NOT JUST A DRAMA, A CRISIS

Looked at from outside, Cognac has not suffered too badly since 1973, the first crisis after which so much of the world's disposable income was diverted to teetotal Muslims. In fact, despite an immediate fall of a quarter in sales, by 1980 they had bounced back to pre-crisis levels, relying mostly on the United States, Britain, Germany, Japan and Hong Kong. But somehow the cognac community has translated the stagnation since 1976 into the biggest crisis since phylloxera. For the effects of the relatively unhappy years since the collapse have been exacerbated by the way the Cognacais had assumed, arrogantly, that demand would be limitless.

The story of Cognac during the last forty years can be told from three points of view: the commercial, reflecting the roller-coaster ride in sales; the social, with particular concentration on the growers and the distillers who felt the shocks involved; and, perhaps most importantly the psychological. For it was in the last two decades of the twentieth century that, for the first time in three centuries, Cognac ceased to be a largely independent world. Previously, says David Baker of Brandy Classics 'Cognac had been a very self-contained industry'. 'It was in the late 1970s,' said one jaundiced cognac observer, 'that professional managers took over.' When responsibility for such activities as sales and accounts, as well as the bosses themselves, moved away from the town, this not only reduced the number of managerial-level jobs, but also greatly reduced the morale of a town that was used to being a capital and became merely a series of 'branch plants' for the four major international groups. 'For centuries', wrote Michel Coste, 'Cognac the drink and Cognac the town had been synonymous to a degree unmatched elsewhere.' But over the past thirty years 'the world has evolved so that, insensibly the destiny of the town and the drink that made it famous have separated. This inimitable spirit lives its life elsewhere…and the town becomes an ordinary sub-prefecture'.[69]

---

69 *Cognac les Clés de la Fortune* (Librairie du Château, 2001).

Between 1980 and 2002 thousands of jobs were lost – Courvoisier cut half its workforce, while at Hennessy Gerald Navarre, a former brewer brought in from Hoegaarden to modernise a still-paternalist firm sacked many people, and 'renegotiated' contracts with growers especially in the Champagnes; 'he brought the firm from the nineteenth to the twenty-first century in one fell swoop' says one of his colleagues. Other firms also abandoned many contracts and enabled many growers, above all in the Grande Champagne to realise their dreams of launching their own brand. The result, as you can see from the list of producers (pp.160–192), is that there are an increasing number of producers who sell only cognacs – almost invariably up-market ones – distilled from their own grapes.

Not surprisingly the population started to age – a process accelerated by the fact that the Charentais live longer than most Frenchmen and whereas in 1970 a quarter of the active population had been engaged in agriculture by the end of the century the figure was less than a tenth. Nevertheless, the cognac industry, including the ancillary trades, is still the most important employer in the Charente, though tourism is more important in the Charentes-Maritime, a département which is second only to the Var – the Riviera – as a tourist destination.

But after 1973 because of the forces let loose in the previous years, the Cognacais could not face their new problems with the same solidarity they had shown when invaded by the phylloxera a century earlier. Moreover, and notably unlike the situation in Champagne, the other region of France where brands and blends are dominant, the majors were not prepared to work together for the common good. The stark reality was spelled out in a remarkably frank document 'What future for the economy of Cognac?' written by Jacques Faure, then the director of the BNIC (not surprisingly his contract was not renewed). He asked the fundamental question 'will Cognac continue to be sold, has it got a future?' and went on to pursue the adjustments required: the appropriate size for the vineyard and the number of growers it could support. He came up with the figure of 55–60,000 hectares – half the total in 1976 – which would provide a living for the growers and satisfy the requirements of the merchants. Fortunately for Cognac his analysis, though seemingly realistic at the time, has proved overly pessimistic.

Financially the Cognacais suffered worse than their rivals in the luxury goods business because the cost of holding stocks of maturing cognac led to ever-increasing interest charges, which more than doubled between 1973 and 1982, by which time they accounted for over 11 per cent of sales. To make matters worse, the community had taken steps in the wrong direction. One, which was to haunt the region for thirty years was that the panic that there wasn't going to be enough cognac had led to gross over-planting. The crisis of over-production in the 1960s and early 1970s was intensified by the fact that the average yield rose by two-thirds to over 87 hectolitres of wine for every hectare – up to a record of 149 hectolitres in 1973 when, it was said, 'they filled the swimming pools with wine'. By 1976 the region was producing as much brandy as in the pre-phylloxera years when the vineyard was three times the size. Yet a spring frost could still batter the vineyards, the yield in 1991 was under 49 hectolitres per hectare, the lowest since the

1950s. The major firms were so frightened of lack of supply that they'd even bought firms in Armagnac to provide a second string to their spirituous bow. They had ignored not only the failure of sales to rise inexorably, but, even more importantly, the extent of the growth in vinous productivity.

It took some time for the depth – and length – of the crisis to sink in. In the beginning the growers refused to face reality, claiming that it was up to the industry to get the quota increased. For their underlying assumption, common to all producers under the AOC system, was that if the growers produced a wine or brandy it was up to someone else to sell it. To make matters worse the great majority of the growers had been almost completely sheltered by the major firms from external reality, i.e. the markets, for so long.

During the 1970s Cognac was saved from collapse largely by the steady growth in the American market, which nearly trebled to over 70 million bottles. Until the 1970s the cognac habit had been confined largely to the East Coast. It steadily 'went national' during the decade. A major boost came with vastly increased consumption by the black community; in 1980 the depressed, but largely black, city of Detroit, one-quarter the size of New York, drank two-thirds as much cognac. This ethnic predisposition to brandy was explained in all sorts of ways. The most vivid, libellous and unreliable vignette is of black – not white – drug dealers carrying half-bottles in their hip-pockets to make 'black-smack', cognac and cocaine.

Inevitably, marketing efforts were concentrated on the United States. Rémy Martin even introduced a VS quality both there and in Britain. By this time the star system had become so devalued – Salignac even had a Five-Star – that the Cognacais substituted the VS label to try to associate their cheaper brandies with the VSOP quality. The figures tell the story of cognac's bumpy ride during the last decades of the twentieth century. In 1985 world sales were just under 9 million cases, by 1990 they had risen to nearly 12.5 million and by 2001 were down to 9.5 million. It did not help that sales in Europe steadily declined – from 5 million cases in 1985 to 3.6 million in 2001. In France the situation was, if anything, rather worse. Sales in France had started to fall in the 1970s as Scotch whisky started its remorseless climb – almost as much Scotch, 150 million bottles of it, is sold in France alone as cognac world-wide.

In 1983 François Mitterrand, the first French President born in the region,[70] greatly increased the duty on cognac and by the end of the century the state was taking just under half the price of a bottle of cognac, paying nearly sixty times as much tax per bottle as does wine. The remaining costs, like transport, publicity and distribution left less than a third of the cost of a typical bottle of cognac in the hands of the producers. In France today cognac is overwhelmingly sold in supermarkets which rely on anonymous, and by no means distinguished, cognacs. Cognac was not the only spirit to suffer. Within a decade of the tax increase sales of all native brandies, from Calvados to Armagnac represented

---

70 His father had been the station master at Jarnac, his mother came from a family of well-known vinegar manufacturers, but he never wanted to promote the idea that France was merely a producer of luxuries – when he went to Japan he concentrated on selling planes from Airbus rather than attempting to obtain a reduction on the duty imposed on Cognac!

less than 14 per cent of total spirits consumption. Moreover the slump in sales of up-market *digestif* cognacs was demonstrated clearly in early 2013 when the historic Parisian restaurant the Tour d'Argent sold off many of its older cognacs because it was only selling the brandy at a rate of a single bottle a week.

The decline in French consumption has continued. A study by the BNIC in 1999 showed that the number of regular cognac drinkers had nearly halved in the previous five years and that the fall was even steeper in the under thirty-fives who were looking for lighter drinks like rum and vodka. It was also unfashionable; cognac was not perceived as a 'modern' drink. As a result the regulars were largely older males, drinking at home, for cognac was still overwhelmingly perceived as a *digestif*, to be drunk neat at the end of a good meal. Worse for cognac's image was that more was used in cooking than was drunk and that in most cases the same cognac was used in cooking as for drinking. By contrast whisky was perceived as more modern, more fashionable and preferred by heavier drinkers. Today France accounts for sales of a mere 4.4 million bottles, less than 2.5 per cent of the world market and, moreover, decidedly unprofitable consisting very largely of sales to supermarkets unconcerned with quality. The lack of informed consumer interest is reflected in that of the professionals. When the BNIC held a 'summit' in January 2009 to work on, among other aspects of the 'cognac experience', the tastes evoked by the brandies, fewer French than American enthusiasts turned up

The roller-coaster ride in overall sales was largely due to events in the Far East, where they were predominantly of cognacs of VSOP quality and above. Between 1985 and 1990 sales to Japan more than doubled from 570,000 to 1,250,000 cases and in 1990 the BNIC stated confidently that they were bound to increase, since cognac accounted for a mere one per cent of the money spent on hard liquor. Nevertheless by 2001 they had fallen back to under 500,000 cases. The decline was largely due to the steady darkening of Japan's economic outlook during the decade. Cognac firms panicked at the loss in sales and tried to counter the reduction by discounting, thus transforming cognac from a luxury product to just one among many competing spirits.

So the 1990s witnessed a serious slump. Sales of brandies of above VSOP level had nearly trebled in the last five years of the 1980s while sales of VS were below those of superior brandies, whereas by 2000 they accounted for 57 per cent. Naturally the price of land declined and as the market for the better cognacs suffered the gap between the Grande Champagne and the Fins Bois narrowed, indeed disappeared. Between 1994 and 2000 the cost of a hectare of vines in the Grande Champagne dropped by three-fifths while that in the Fins Bois fell by only a third. By 2010 Grande Champagne had recovered to its 1994 level but that in the Fins Bois in the Charente – as opposed to the Charente-Maritime – were nearly a third above their 2004 level – a distinct gap had opened between vines from the same appellation in the two departments.

The ride was even bumpier among the overseas Chinese where sales nearly trebled in the last five years of the 1980s from 636,000 to just over 1.7 million cases by 1990, only to slump to 450,000 by 2001. By contrast, mainland China looked more hopeful. The rise was later – culminating in sales of nearly a million cases in 1995 – but even in 2001 was 440,000 cases, two and a half times the figure fifteen years earlier. This impressive rise came despite the crackdown on excessive expenditure by government officials – notably on luxuries like cognac – that had marked the mid-1990s. Throughout the Far East cognac suffered temporarily from the Asian crash of 1997.

Cognac was also been caught up as an innocent sufferer in trade disputes between the European Union and the United States, based on American hostility to the Common Agricultural Policy. The so-called 'Yuppie wars' of the mid-1980s were based on the EC's restrictions on American exports of agricultural products like cheese, olives and cognac that were consumed only by Yuppies, while the 'soya war' in the early 1990s led to a dramatic fall in shipments to the United States in 1991 and 1993 before peace was declared. And, as so often in the past, the Cognacais have also had to cope with fluctuating exchange rates since the dollar floated in 1971. Since 2002 they have at least been spared the problems within the Eurozone but can do very little when – as happened in early 2003 – the euro strengthened by nearly a fifth against the dollar.

The whole cognac community had always hoped that theirs would no longer be considered a luxury product. Just after the war Maurice Hennessy had expressed the hope that cognac would be regarded as a normal article of consumption for ordinary people. Unfortunately in Britain much of this sector of the market was taken by 'French brandy' made of neutral spirit blended with very strong *esprit de vin*. Obviously the confusion harmed the image – and the consumption – of cognac. By contrast the Scots had had the sense to provide the ignorant majority of drinkers with a double support, not just the brand but also its exact age. As one Cognacais put it: 'People want an age statement... numbers on the bottle.' I realised the importance of exact age when holding a tasting with a group of Japanese sommeliers in the late 1980s. I was overwhelmed by questions, which obviously I could never answer, as to the exact age of the brandies being tasted. Nevertheless, apart of course from Rémy, the major cognac firms in their arrogance relied exclusively on their brand name. To make matters worse, until the last years of the twentieth century the Cognacais were limiting their market even further by refusing to promote cognac's mixability.

One obvious result of the increased pressure on costs and the switch to cheaper cognacs was the increasing concentration of the business. As Faure pointed out in his 1986 report, by the mid-1990s the number of firms had fallen by three-quarters since 1900 and by a half since 1945 and the Big Four accounted for four-fifths of the total, as against only a half fifty years earlier. This does not leave much for the 270 or so other 'merchants' as well as the region's ten co-operatives. The worst effect was the disappearance of many of the medium-sized and generally under-capitalised family firms which had brought considerable stability to a business which demanded continuity, if only to allow time for the precious stocks of cognac to mature. For instance Hardy, owned by the Hardy family and the French bank Crédit Commercial de France had depended acutely on the French market and went bankrupt after its sales in France had dropped by nearly nine-tenths from a peak of 87,000 cases.

In the words of Michel Coste the 'globalisation' of cognac persuaded the owners of

MICHEL COSTE, THE OPPORTUNIST

An accountant by training, Coste was drawn to Cognac primarily because his beloved yacht was moored at Arcachon. For a decade or more he worked at Otard, rising to become managing director. He realised that there was no hope of creating a new major brand, 'Rémy Martin caught the last train' he once said, and always looked for niche markets. Then, in the mid-1970s, he made his bid for independence and took the opportunity of buying up many of the firms stranded by the slump. His group, CCG (Compagnie Commerciale de Guyenne) took over Meukow with its stocks of old cognacs, he bought Lucien-Foucauld from Allied Domecq with spacious premises in the centre of Cognac, while Richard Frères contributed a well-equipped warehouse and bottling complex at Saint Jean d'Angély. Since Coste's death in 2015 his daughter has continued the business.

family firms that 'only such multinational firms could cope with all the changes'.[71] The dominance of the Big Four was reinforced because they, and they alone could afford to cut out the middlemen through wholly-owned subsidiaries outside France. Nearly forty years ago the late Sir Anthony Tennant of International Distillers and Vintners remarked that he was sick of allowing so many of his foreign agents to become millionaires. The general attitude was that 'we don't want to confer our product to anybody. We need to accompany it right down the chain'. In doing so they often formed alliances with other giants. Many family brands which had been absorbed by larger groups, were simply dropped as surplus to requirements over the years. Denis Mounié, Augier and Jules Robin are only three well-known names no longer available. Groups are concentrating on single brands, using others for specific purposes, like selling to supermarkets, and individual markets rather than trying to sell a sprawling, often undifferentiated, range. Of course there were exceptions. The most significant was probably Coste, the very archetype of the mood of gritty realism that seized the region after 1973, who benefited from the policies of the bigger companies.

Camus, number five in the pecking order, albeit far behind the Big Four – and by far the biggest family-controlled company – has survived despite two major blows. It was heavily dependent on the duty-free business in the Far East, where sales collapsed by four-fifths, more completely than those of any other company anywhere. It was also at risk when Hennessy's parent company LVMH[72] bought Duty Free Shoppers in the mid-1990s at the top of the market although Camus was so entrenched in duty free that LVMH had to continue to feature its cognacs. Of other well-known brands Otard was lucky. It had been floating for some years, since Martini – which had bought the brand from Bass – showed no great interest in it. Today it is benefiting greatly from sharing distribution with its parent company, Bacardi-Martini.

---

71 *Cognac Les Clés de la Fortune* (Librairie du Château, 2001).
72 Louis Vuitton Moët Hennessy.

Nevertheless, it still depends for a large proportion of its sales on the thousands of visitors to the Château itself, its magnificent banqueting halls still used for major events.

The events of recent decades showed most dramatically in the very varying fortunes of the Big Four. The big winner was Hennessy, whose sales virtually doubled in the period, increasing its market share from 17 per cent to well over 30 per cent. Hennessy was helped by the backing it received from its ever-expanding owner, but more by the many mistakes made by its competitors. By the end of the millennium Hennessy's only real rival was Rémy Martin. In fourth place as late as 1985, it increased its sales by a half, and market share from less than 9 per cent to 16 per cent in the following fifteen years. This was a remarkable achievement given that the vast bulk of its sales remained VSOP rather than VS.

Despite Rémy's problems Courvoisier was the back marker in the four-horse race with sales down by 15 per cent in the late 1980s and 1990s. Its problems were partly due to successive takeovers. In 1981 Allied Breweries merged with Hiram Walker. For some years the management was preoccupied by the merger – and by the further take-over which created the Allied Domecq group in the early 1990s. This was never well-run or successful and Courvoisier suffered for over two decades, though its position has greatly improved over the past fifteen years since it was taken over by the American firm, Jim Beam.

But the real disaster was Martell. It had been number one as late as 1985 with nearly a fifth of the market. It was already starting to slip – Hennessy had overtaken it – when in 1988 after a long bidding war with the British firm Grand Metropolitan it was sold to Seagram at a ludicrously inflated price. Seagram made every mistake in the book, indeed people now talk of 'ten years in no man's land'. The group as a whole was drifting because the young chairman, Edgar Bronfman Jnr, was far more interested in music and show business in general than in the family's historic liquor interests. Dozens of new products were introduced without any real planning but they were never backed by adequate promotional expenditure and in key markets like the Far East Martell was grossly neglected in favour of Seagram's Chivas Regal Scotch whisky, while its profits and profile both suffered from heavy discounting.

Sales in the 1990s fell by nearly 40 per cent and Martell fell to number three in the pecking order, a relegation unheard of since it first came to prominence in the middle of the eighteenth century. As sales declined stocks rose to reach an extraordinary eleven years, partly because of the perpetual optimism required of its sales force, and Martell had to cut its purchases by a half. This threw the Borderies, in particular, into confusion and enabled Hennessy and Courvoisier to make further inroads into a region which had been largely Martell's fiefdom for two hundred years. In 2001 the break-up of Seagram led to the take-over of Martell by Pernod-Ricard. The changeover was delayed by interminable regulatory problems, which made the loss of momentum even worse.

Pernod soon realised that Martell was in a parlous state. The new management admitted that it had 'missed the train' in the United States but hoped to catch the next one and was basing its hopes on Cordon Bleu, once the world's leading premium cognac – emphasising the particular qualities of the brandies from the Borderies. On the production side the new management found that Martell had been operating out of no fewer than nine premises which Pernod decided to reduce to three. The key change was to transfer the bottling line at Martell's fortress in the centre of Cognac to Rouillac twenty miles to the north where Bisquit already had a modern plant which had proved far too big because of Pernod's failure to expand sales of the brand – the other major houses had already moved their bottling lines away from the centre of town to the suburbs. Inevitably, the move involved 140 redundancies on top of hundreds of others which the workers had suffered under fifteen years of mismanagement by Seagram. They promptly went on strike with three of them going on hunger strike. The management stood firm and after one of the hunger strikers had been taken to hospital they gave up. The fissiparous nature of the cognac community was shown by the total failure of the growers to support their fellows. The growers' attitude was simple: 'they didn't do anything to support us,' one of them told me, 'when we made our major protest a few years ago' – a three-day demonstration launched by the growers in 1997.

Martell's troubles threw a spotlight onto a perpetual problem – how the cognac growers could cope with the boom and bust mentality which had afflicted the region over the ages. In the late twentieth century the problem had been exacerbated by the increased productivity of the vineyard, as well as the new toughness shown by the Big Four which, apart from Rémy, contained not a shred of the industry's historic paternalism. Only cold-bloodied managerial calculations now decided the livelihoods not only of 6,000 direct employees but of 29,000 growers and their families as well. But if the firms continued to go their very different ways, the same applied in spades to the growers and distillers. As stocks rose and interest rates remained high they were caught in a web of increasing financial commitments, and in any case the 'cognac war' had divided them.

In the early 1970s stocks had dropped to a dangerously low figure of 4.4 years' sales, but had reached seven years' sales a few years later. The growers and *bouilleurs de cru* were helpless, all the merchants had to retrench, and the easiest way was to reduce their commitments to them, although the handful of major independent distillers, like Boigneau, survived relatively unscathed. Hennessy and Martell merely cut down the amounts they took from 'their' growers, but other firms (notably Bisquit) had to cancel some of their contracts. The trade also managed to shift the financial burden to the growers (who enjoyed relatively cheap loans through the Crédit Agricole). As a result in the late 1970s the growers actually had more cognac in stock than the trade – a potentially dangerous situation that was to recur on a larger scale in the1990s.

As the reduction in acreage and yields kicked in stocks gradually dropped to reach just over five years' sales in 1988–89, triggering one of those false alarms of lack of grapes so characteristic of cognac's history. Then came the crunch: in 1990–91 800,000 hectolitres were distilled, and a mere 350,000 were needed as the Japanese crisis took hold – yet the growers had been tempted to break their contracts because of the – short-lived – boom in the Far East. Ten years later they were back up to an average of eight years' worth, subsiding to a steady seven or so years by the millennium. But the age structure, was more worrying than the size of the stockpile. In the early 1990s only a fifth of the total was of Compte 6 or above, but the many – usually inferior – young cognacs rejected by the major firms were supplemented by the reduction in sales of older brandies. In the late 1990s three of the big four reduced their stocks. Nevertheless, with the exception of Martell, the Big Four managed to limit the number of contracts they broke – for instance Courvoisier had to cut purchases by a third, but abided by three year contracts.

In 1976 production of brandy was running at 10 hectolitres for every hectare. Over the next five years, thanks to the Common Agricultural Policy, more than half the region's production – not only of spirit, but also of wine – was destined to go for re-distillation into industrial alcohol. New plantations were forbidden until at least the end of 1986 and a programme of *arrachages* inaugurated. Premiums were being given to growers prepared to dig up their vines, although they could replant within eight years if conditions permitted, a policy which did indeed reduce the total under vines by over a quarter to 78,000 hectares – over a fifth had gone by the end of the 1980s, the remainder after a further campaign at the end of the millennium. At the same time two-fifths of the stills, which in 1974 held an average of a mere 16 hectolitres, were replaced, generally by larger ones. Nevertheless, Cognac is still one of the largest wine regions in France and probably the largest in the world devoted virtually exclusively to white grapes. Moreover, *arrachages* were always slow because growers took a long time to decide to abandon their traditional means of livelihood and their precious plots.

Production even on the reduced acreage was severely restricted. Only a certain amount of alcohol could be distilled as cognac from wines whose production was itself limited. Growers were allowed to sell only a proportion of even their limited crop on the market. By 1982–3 they could sell immediately only about half their production, 4.5 hectolitres for every hectare of vines; the rest had to be stocked at their expense. They received some help from ORECO, the co-operative initiated in the early 1970s by Coquillaud, to stock surplus brandies and provide a sort of buffer stock. The merchants did not escape the burden: they now have to buy 10 per cent more stock than they sell in the course of a year – an obligation that obviously weighs particularly heavily on the smaller concerns. The same sort of pressure was being felt by the *bouilleurs de profession*, subject to a squeeze by the bigger firms.

The growers did not show much, if any, social cohesion. This was understandable because they were in such different circumstances. There were many growers who could rely solely on producing grapes and wines for transforming into cognac and could still make a decent living. By contrast growers from the outer regions needed help, not just to uproot their vines but also to find other outlets for their grapes for table wine, table grapes, or for transformation into fortified or sparkling wines. Indeed the shorthand description of the battle was that it was between 16 and 17.[73] The double requirement was summed up in the catch-phrase: 'for each market its [appropriate] production and for each parcel of vines its outlet' together with the need to find 'an alternative product which will exploit the know-how of our growers'.

---

73 Until recently cars registered in the Charente had 16 on their number plates, Maritime had 17.

NOT BY COGNAC ALONE

Many growers in lesser *terroirs* have to rely for sales on 'alternative outlets'. Grapes have always been grown for other uses and when the region's vineyards were at their post-phylloxera height around a tenth of production went into red and white table wines, most of which, not surprisingly, were produced in the Bois Ordinaires and Bons Bois, and which must have been at best mediocre. Today – apart from table grapes – the two most obvious outlets are for Pineau des Charentes and Vins de Pays. Pineau is mostly sold to the hundreds of thousands of tourists attracted by the region's many fine beaches. Pineau is a *mistelle*, a type of drink familiar all over rural France in which the fermentation of fruit juice (not just grape juice, in Normandy they use apples to make their *Pommeau*) is stopped by the addition of brandy. To be legally entitled to the name Pineau des Charentes must contain between 16 and 22 per cent alcohol and has to be matured in wood for a year before it is sold. But it can happily age for up to ten years in cask, at which point the red – in fact it's pink – variety has far greater depth and subtlety than virtually any other *apéritif* I know.

Other outlets vary widely as growers weigh the difference in price between selling their wine for compulsory distillation, as *vin de table*, or as a base for low-grade sparkling or fortified wines (*vins vinés*), all of them increasingly unprofitable. Some varieties – notably Merlot, Colombard and Sauvignon Blanc – can produce wines that are excellent value for money and production trebled in the 1990s.

Not surprisingly it was the far-sighted André Hériard-Dubreuil who did the most to encourage production of table wines. A couple of years before his death he set up the region's first proper wine business by planting 350 hectares round the family's former country house at Saint Même, where the gravel banks round the Charente were far better suited to Merlot, a Bordeaux variety, than to Ugni Blanc. These wines have proved something of a disappointment. The BNIC had hoped that table wines would account for 5,000 hectares but they are unlikely to cover more than 3,000 hectares within the foreseeable future. Nevertheless, this is over three times the size of small appellations like Pomerol, a fact which highlights the task facing the diversifiers simply because of the sheer size of the cognac appellation

The idea of selling cognac-based mixed drinks was not of course new, just think of Cointreau and Grand Marnier. The amounts used by these historic outlets doubled in the last decade of the twentieth century to account for over a tenth of total sales. More of them are steadily being launched on what appears to be a receptive market. One substantial success, above all in the United States, was Alizé, a blend of cognac and passion fruit juice, launched by the Lafragette family which also sold some very decent cognacs, proving that there is no incompatibility between the two markets. Unfortunately M. Lafragette himself has been convicted of fraud, though the drink is still sold by its American owners, Kobrand.

In theory the steady reduction in the number of holdings – and the consequent increase in the average acreage – should have helped. But in the last decades of the twentieth century the growers seemed to be running up a down escalator. Fifty years ago, according to one observer, it was thought that you needed at least four hectares of vines to support a family. By 2000 the figure had risen to fifteen hectares – and the average exploitation was less than ten – though of course expectations of lifestyle had risen dramatically.

In the late 1990s the government weighed in with mixed results. In 1998 Jean Glavany, the Minister of Agriculture in the Socialist government of Lionel Jospin, had visited the region together with a senior civil servant Jacques Bertommeau. Unfortunately they both descended on the Charentes with their ideas already formed. One, as we shall see was extremely useful: to allow the BNIC to have a local president. The other, for the region to have a single union (*syndicat*) representing the growers was more dubious since the visitors from Paris seemed to have no idea of the ever-increasing divide between the two classes of growers.

10

FIGHT-BACK

In the last decade of the twentieth century the Cognacais started to fight back, patchily yes, belatedly certainly, but with increasing effectiveness, and by the end of the first decade of the twenty-first century the booming market for fine cognacs in the Far East, above all in China, had led to record sales of over 180 million bottles. But almost as important was the recognition that they could not stand loftily above the fray and would have to behave like the producers of lesser spirits, above all Scotch whisky. Above all, perhaps, was the general acceptance that cognac had to compete in both its markets, for use as a cocktail or long drink – still over two-thirds of sales – as well as a *digestif.*

One early step was the sorting out of the previous mess of competing *syndicats* representing the vignerons. Today, for the first time in history, there is a single *syndicat* of growers facing a single organisation representing the merchants. But this did not help the argument centred on the amount of alcohol a distiller could extract from his wine. The 'democrats' in the outer regions wanted the misery to be shared equally by limiting the yield of spirit. To placate them the legal limit of brandy production was cut severely – by two-fifths of normal to 6 hectolitres for every hectare between 1996 and 2002. Yet potential productivity had risen from 120 hectolitres of wine to 180 for every hectare – a potential of triple that amount – with the more professional distillers, naturally concentrated in the region's heartland, claiming, rightly, that the limit was far too low to allow them a decent living, let alone profitability.

It also proved inadequate to cope when demand rose by a third in the five years up to 2006 after production had been so severely curtailed. But even in 2007, after allowing for evaporation, stocks never fell below 5.69 years – and were stable up to Compte 8. Nevertheless, the surge created an unsatisfied demand for brandies, particularly the four- and five-year-olds so vital for VSOP, a shortage which obviously had the worst effect on smaller firms without adequate stocks. As sales rose there was an increasing shortage of cognac of between ten and fifteen years old. By the end of July 2012 stocks of brandies over five years old were a mere 310 million bottles, in other words only three years' sales. Fortunately the much higher production level now being allowed has cooled the situation.

The shortage was exacerbated by the producers' tax situation, since individual growers did not want to sell too many of their precious casks and then have to pay tax on the profits. This has had a major impact on the price of land, up from €40,000 per hectare to €100,000 in the best regions. The BNIC has succeeded in calming the boom by copying the situation in Champagne and authorising two types of stock. As the name implies the *réserve climatique* is designed to provide for years when the climate reduces yields. The brandies are kept in stainless steel so do not mature and can be drawn on only when the distiller involved has been unable to fulfill the normal yield for the year. The *réserve de gestion* is a stock of cognac deliberately allowed to be sold only when it is Compte 4 or over to relieve the pressure on stocks of older cognacs. Both reserves will be necessary because the productivity of the vines is steadily decreasing because so many of them were planted in the late 1960s and early 1970s and are now above the age at which they are normally replaced.

This is an example of how, over the past fifteen years, the BNIC has grown in stature. In 1996 a new director was appointed from outside the region, Alain Philippe, with a long and successful career in the construction business behind him. After 2010 Philippe's work was continued by his successor, Catherine Lepage. The president had always been a bureaucrat 'parachuted' from Paris, but in 1998 cognac 'was emancipated' says one insider. They were also lucky in their first local president, Bernard Guionnet, 'the only grower with a broader vision of the future' as one of his colleagues puts it. He was not your typical peasant for he had studied at the top agro-engineering schools in Montpellier and Toulouse and had been president of one of the major growers' groups. Quiet and decisive, he had been running an 80-hectare family estate in the Grande Champagne and the Borderies but was open-minded enough to understand the problems faced by the whole region. After his premature death he was accorded the traditional French tribute of having the road outside the BNIC renamed in his honour.

Progress was even made in the tricky task of extending the official definition of age of maturing cognacs beyond Compte 6. During the 1990s the BNIC gained clearance for up to Compte 8 which came into force in 1999 followed by ages 9 and 10 – changes like this are delayed by the need for official approval of texts from the EC as well as the French government. But the twelve-year delay until 2018 to ensure that XO cognacs should be at least ten years old was due to the unwillingness of some of the smaller firms, who complained that the new requirement would favour the bigger firms, although the real winners will be small producers and firms relying on quality rather than price. Moreover, during the past decades the BNIC has enjoyed considerable, if largely unpublicised, success in defending the name of cognac. Above all it has set up stronger defences against fakes, working with the WTO (World Trade Organisation) in Brazil, Russia and Central Europe. It has also become the first AOC recognised in Vietnam.

The BNIC also stepped up its promotional efforts. Since the early 1960s it had been organising a film festival devoted exclusively to detective films. The Festival was the idea of the late Colonel Gerard Sturm, for a long time the BNIC's public relations director.

The major firms never liked the idea and in 2005 they gained an unlikely ally, the thirty-two year old Jérome Durand, recruited from the champagne industry as the BNIC's first director of marketing and communication. He soon saw that the festival was a less effective use of funds than the more populist jazz and blues festival, which every summer turns both Cognac and Jarnac into hives of thoroughly enjoyable and relaxed musical activity. He also helped to start an annual charity dinner the *Part des Anges* which brings together over 500 people from the Cognac community who vie in offering for sale one of their finest old bottles.

Durand managed to find funds to bring the world's sommeliers to Cognac, to promote cognac-based cocktails and to take part in the great cocktail festival held every August in New Orleans – promoting above all the Sazerac, the earliest cocktail based on brandy. He also had the bright idea of holding seminars for the world's cognac professionals to discuss the whole question of cognac's aromas (discussed on page 150) and decide on the most suitable shape of glass – which, not surprisingly, turned out to be the tulip!

The BNIC was also early on the scene when it came to promoting cognac as a long drink, as was the small firm of Godet, which promoted their Sélection Speciale as a base for many of them (the firm is now blending cognac with tea for the Taiwanese market). Whisky was always welcome because it was sold and appreciated as an *apéritif*, a long drink. And indeed a great deal of cognac was already being drunk with Coca-Cola or lemonade. Moreover the enquiry into the French market revealed that a quarter of cognac drinkers took their cognac with ice and the same proportion in cocktails although the idea of it as a long drink had not yet caught on – even though Gilles Hennessy had launched iced Hennessy on the French market as early as 1988. The BNIC still plugs away at promoting cognac in France as a long drink.

But the great growth in sales over the first twelve years of the twenty-first century has been outside of France, where sales now account for a mere 2.6 per cent of the total by volume and 2 per cent by value. It has been driven by two seemingly incompatible surges. The first, led by Hennessy, has been in sales – mostly of VS – in the United States and of superior cognacs in the Far East, above all in China. In the United States, and despite its elitist image, Cognac had always been largely a drink of the ghetto – official figures say that around two-thirds of cognac drinkers are African-American and the real percentage is probably higher. Luckily Cognac formed an important element in the rise of African-American rock, rap and hip-hop artists (see box on page 142). Stars like these simply cannot be bought. Even if they were willing, their fee would simply break any promotional budget.

Realising that the image of cognac could have been hurt by its association with these performers Hennessy has gone in for supporting charities while Martell's 'Rise Above' advertising campaign featured classier African-American heroes. Fortunately for the firms some of the rappers and hip-hop artists have become mainstream like so many other outré entertainers in the past – remember that crooners like Bing Crosby were considered cultural outlaws in the 1930s – and sales have recovered steadily since a slump in the wake of the 2008 banking crisis.

RAPPIN' – AND DRINKIN'

The rappers, proud of their background in the ghetto, called cognac 'gnac' as part of the way they separated themselves from the 'good ole [white] boys' of country music fame who generally stuck to native whiskies. Typically, to Jay-Z it was a 'classy, sophisticated and really smooth thing to drink'.

Hennessy – now also known as Henn, Henny, Hen-Roc or Henn Do – was the first to understand the potential; as Eminem put it 'what's gotten into me? Drugs, rock and Hennessy'. It was the first firm to sponsor parties for rap artists and their fans and promotes the Mobo music awards. The brand's fame is such that it became the number one brand mentioned in the US Billboard singles chart. But the competition is hard on its heels. Indeed de Fussigny even launched a brandy called NYAK, after the way the rap community pronounces cognac to distinguish it from the more pompous, more whitey cognac. Courvoisier – which is doing well in the US with its VSOP as well as its VS – has been more systematic. The firm has also been exceedingly lucky in that its cognac featured in a hit by Busta Rhymes that reached the top five of the American rap charts called simply 'Pass the Courvoisier'.

> Give me the Henny, you can give me the Cris
> You can pass me the Remi, but pass the Courvoisier

And yes he is equating the cognac he drinks – from Hennessy, Rémy Martin and Courvoisier – with Louis Roederer's Cristal, that most up-market of champagnes.

He was not alone. Puff Daddy and Snoop Doggy Dogg have also serenaded the charms of 'gnac' while Devino Fortunato, a popular Californian rapper, first achieved success with a little number called 'Cognac Loungin'. But perhaps the rap atmosphere is best conveyed in 'So Much Pain' (featuring 2Pac) by Ja Rule:

> *Feel the rage this world has bestowed upon me*
> *And I don't give a fuck 'cause they don't give a fuck 'bout me*
> *So I keep – drinkin Hennessy, bustin at my enemies*
> *Will I live to see twenty-three? There's so much pain*

Fortunately, in a much less well-publicised trend it is moving steadily upmarket. The statistics tell a story of a move upwards in quality, price, and thus revenue thanks largely to the increase in sales in Asia. In the first fifteen years of the twenty-first century sales of VS cognacs represented just under half of the total in quantity and a mere two-fifths in value, to the great benefit, above all, of VSOPs, with obviously favourable effects on profit margins. Exports in cask, almost invariably low-grade cognacs, a full fifth of the total in 1980–81, are now down to a mere 2 per cent by quantity and half a percent by value.

The top four markets – the United States, Singapore, Britain and China – account for nearly two-thirds of total sales. Like so many other luxury products cognac has benefited from the increasing prosperity of the Far East and above all the broader Chinese market, not only China itself but including Hong Kong and the Chinese diaspora in Taiwan, Malaysia and Singapore where the average price is 40 per cent higher than in the United States.

Oddly the most dramatic rise since 2001–02 has not been in the Chinese market but in sales to Singapore, and thus in South East Asia as a whole, where sales have quadrupled. Yet, over a longer period, the China story is even more dramatic. Sales were a mere 360 bottles – just a single hectolitre – at the start of the great Chinese expansion in 1977–78, a year after Mao's death, and only 400,000 bottles in 2003, yet by 2009 they reached eleven million bottles – still less than a sip per inhabitant and with all the Big Four employing agents in a dozen or more major cities. By 2011–2012 they had soared – there really is no other word for it – to 25.5 million. Sales to Singapore, the centre for re-export all over South-East Asia surged ten-fold in thirty years reaching 25.5 million. Much of it was seriously expensive. The most extreme example perhaps came in early 2010 when a single Chinese casino bought 500 bottles of the 1858 vintage recently on offer from Croizet at a mere £25,000 a bottle – I found it a trifle woody but still very much alive.

Then sales dropped by a dramatic forty per cent in a couple of years, partly because of overstocking but mostly as the massive habit of present-giving, mostly of prestige cognacs, was rudely disturbed by the continuing anti-corruption drive. But sales are now recovering and even now most of them are of VSOP or, more often, XO (by contrast sales of VS to the historic British market account for over four fifths of the total). No wonder these sales account for two thirds of the money the Cognacais receive from outside France. But although overall sales have been growing, three quarters of the total income is received from only three markets: the USA, China and the Far Eastern market served from Singapore.

Despite the recent problems the importance the Chinese attach to cognac is best illustrated by a little-noticed decision by the Chinese Administration of Quality Supervision, Inspection and Quarantine. In the four years after 2005, when the CAQSIP had accepted the idea of Protected Geographical Indication awarded by European governments to products ranging from Roquefort cheese to Yorkshire Forced Rhubarb, the Chinese provided only locally produced items – nine hundred of them, including Maotai, the favourite Chinese spirit – with this protection. But in December 2010, after fifteen years of efforts by the BNIC they added cognac as their first non-Chinese product to the list, thus, as it were, providing it with its Chinese naturalisation papers. Moreover, the nationalised Maotai company expressed its desire to work with the BNIC to fight against imitations, a battle already fought by a hundred Maotaists. Clearly the Chinese have adopted cognac as a unique example of a drink worthy of protection from fakes and imitations, a fundamental recognition of its importance in Chinese life, now and, above all, in the future.

The Cognacais have, albeit belatedly, responded to the challenge presented by the Scots – and the Armagnacais – with their single vintage brandies. Avoiding the 1962 ban on single-vintage cognacs – apart from those matured in England – was boosted by the Royer law of 1975, named after the then Mayor of Tours. The formula it created allowed distillers to describe cognacs as coming from a single vintage, provided that they could produce documents showing their origin, unless someone objected – previously producers were assumed to be guilty. The law was national, overriding local regulations if firms could prove the age of the brandy. As a result, a number of reputable firms – notably Hine, Delamain and Croizet – were able to sell single vintage cognacs because they had stocks of cognac under a double lock and key which had been supervised by the French authorities. Nevertheless, only one major firm – inevitably Rémy – is taking advantage of the relaxation by launching a single vintage – the first was a superb 1965 followed by a 1989.

The local restrictions were lifted in 1987 (carbon dating should have been able to help although the ban on atomic explosions in the atmosphere as a result of the 1963 test ban treaty greatly reduced the ease with which brandies could be dated precisely after that date). From then on firms could stock cognacs designed to be sold as single vintages – so that the first of the 'new' single vintage cognacs were the 1988s, now followed by a steady flow of newer brandies.

Nevertheless, the increasing number of single-vintage cognacs, while helping the image of cognac, will be very marginal in terms of sales. Despite the general loosening Ragnaud-Sabourin, one of the most reputable of all growers, was prosecuted for putting an age statement on some of its cognacs. But many companies get round the ban on providing an exact age by giving hints in their promotional literature or even on their labels. The most blatant instance is the Tesseron family, famous for their incomparable stocks of old brandies, who number their cognacs according to the date they were distilled (e.g. 90 for the 1990). For its part Moyet, another firm famous for its stocks, gets round the ban by attaching a separate label to each bottle giving the approximate age of their cognacs.

In recent years a far more important development has been the major effort – visible in their entries in the producers section – by all the Big Four to provide new brandies to fill gaps in their ranges. Indeed, over the past few years the Big Four have introduced more new cognacs, often genuinely interesting ones, than in previous decades. A number of cognacs, frequently very up-market ones, have been produced exclusively to cater for the preference of Far Eastern customers for richer brandies.

Most obviously they have replaced their 'Napoleans' with other cognacs to fill the gap between VSOP and XO. For instance, Hennessy has introduced its excellent Fine de Cognac, while Rémy has gone further with three cognacs; Coeur de Cognac, 1738 and Club for different markets – Europe, the United States and the Far East respectively. Many firms are also paying much more attention to the design of their bottles and labels. They are getting away from the frosted glass bottle first made famous by Rémy Martin's VSOP which had become ubiquitous, even conferring a spurious legitimacy on 'French brandies'. But even a simple rethink can help. Otard for instance, found that sales of its XO leaped when an elegant, light new bottle replaced its rather forbidding darker predecessor – 'it changed people's perception of the brandy' they say (it helps that the cognac is smoother). The Big Four have even imitated the Scots by despatching their *maîtres de chai*, and even specially trained experts, as brand ambassadors throughout the world to spread the gospel of cognac, a policy initiated by Rémy with Robert Leauté.

The most startling story, however, has been the remarkable comeback by Martell, returning the firm to its historical position as the biggest contender to Hennessy, especially in China. A few years after its takeover by Pernod–Ricard, Martell started to reduce its emphasis on VS, largely to increase profit margins, a policy far more important than the obsession with volume characteristic of old-time liquor salesmen – and their bosses. Martell's deliberate policy of concentrating on superior brandies has meant that in the past few years the rise in the value of sales has vastly outpaced the increase in their quantity. It does not seem to worry even about being overtaken by Courvoisier in Britain where it has been market leader for generations. Martell's commitment to up-market brandies was most expensively demonstrated by its purchase in early 2010 of an enormous stock – enough to fill more than two million bottles – of superb old brandies owned by a well-known octogenarian broker. Three years later it bought the venerable house of Augier, presumably with the intention of launching new upmarket cognacs.

The Big Four are too big to have room in their portfolio for smaller, niche products, a tendency similar to that in other industries where the rule is 'the bigger the groups, the bigger the gaps in the market'. Delamain, now partly controlled by Bollinger, is becoming more dynamic but Hine has had its ups and downs. For a few years it was owned by Hennessy, mainly in order to acquire access to the firm's stocks of old brandies. It was then sold to CL, a Caribbean-based conglomerate which went bankrupt so that Hine fell into the hands of the government of Trinidad. But in 2015 Hine was bought by a French family used to a long-term corporate outlook – they can also take a steadily increasing advantage from the brandies produced from an 80-hectare estate in the heart of the Grande Champagne, bought in 2006.

The once-famous firm of Croizet has enjoyed a far more improbable return to relative prosperity. Its owners, the Eymard family, were hopelessly divided and in 2006 the company was bought by M. Varshavsky, a Russian steel tycoon and cognac lover. Despite financial problems typical of other oligarchs he bought more land and his team – headed by Jean-Emanuel Roy, one of Rémy Martin's best distillers – has returned the firm to its historic policy of selling only cognacs made from their own vines in the Champagnes. Its new-found respectability is reflected in its membership of the Syndicat des Maisons de Cognac which groups the top dozen cognac firms.

There have also been a number of initiatives by new entrants. The biggest success story started improbably with one Pierre Voisin, the agent in the region for Fiat and Volvo, who had a passion for cognac. He started to mature some from the Premiers Fins Bois and in the early 1980s launched Léopold Gourmel, a brand given his wife's maiden name. Since then the firm has suffered a number of vicissitudes but recovered under Olivier Blanc, M.

Voisin's son-in-law, thanks to a range of brandies all still from one of the best sub-regions in the Fins Bois.

M. Voisin was not the only outsider to have bright ideas. After his retirement, a Swedish businessman, Otto Kelt, a former maker of crisp diet rolls, had the apparently mad idea of copying the eighteenth-century habit of selling cognacs only after they have been round the world in casks in the hold of a ship. The result is a speedier maturation and a well-integrated cognac. Other newcomers – like two French businessmen Marc Georges and Pierre Dubarry of Moyet, and Ferry de Bakker, a former advertising executive – are searching out cognacs from individual regions. The Finnish group Arriva has bought Larsen and Renault, but the biggest newcomer is Distel, the South African drinks giant, which bought Bisquit-Dubouché from Pernod-Ricard.

The way the Big Four sometimes behaved to their suppliers over the past forty years has led to declarations of independence – including that of the Grande Champagne itself. Thirty years ago the *panneaux* proclaiming *Grande Champagne – Premier Cru de Cognac* were rusty – they'd been put up by *le commerce* but no one bothered to spend any money on them. Today the locals have ensured that the panels are shining bright.

The specialist producers now include an increasing number of growers, not only in the Grande Champagne, but also in the Petite Champagne, the Fins Bois and even the Bon Bois. The biggest is, of course, Frapin, while its neighbours, Raymond Ragnaud and Ragnaud-Sabourin have also been selling their splendid cognacs directly for several generations. But the unreliability of the contracts with the Big Four since 1973 has greatly increased the number of direct sellers. Moreover a more confident younger generation is taking over, far more prepared than their parents to launch themselves into direct selling. Unfortunately these growers suffer from a major disadvantage as against their equivalents in other wine-making regions. Most private clients – the base of any direct sales network – are simply not going to buy cognac in the same quantity that they do say, champagne.

I am reasonably sure that the Far East will ensure that Cognac's present prosperity will continue. But remember, Cognac is a luxury drink, the first thing on which drinkers will cut down in straitened times. It leads to advice first enunciated by Jean Martell. He was, he said 'less ambitious to do things on a large scale than to do them little and well'. His words remain to this day a suitable motto for the town.

COLIN CAMPBELL

In 1962 a young Scotsman had found that Oxford University did not have enough to offer him and was doing not very much in Paris when he was hired, more by accident than design, as a guide at Hennessy. Well before he retired forty-four years later he had acquired a well-deserved legendary status, not only in the firm but within the broader Cognac community. After a short apprenticeship sorting out the firm's businesses in East and South Africa he moved on to what became his life's work, building up Hennessy's business in two markets, the United States and the Far East which proved the key to Hennessy's decades of supremacy in the Cognac business. He also proved the crucial link between Moët-Hennessy and its British partners, once DCL and now called Diageo. For Hennessy owes its present dominance largely to the partnerships

Colin Campbell, the man who ensured that Hennessy remained number one for a generation.

he engineered – notably that in the Far East with Jardine Mathieson, the giant trading firm – and the subsidiaries Hennessy acquired through him, most obviously Schieffelin, its American agents for nearly two hundred years which he bought in 1981.

Knowing Campbell's notorious reticence about his work he will probably hate this paragraph.

PART III
ALL ABOUT THE COGNACS

THE COGNAC AROMA WHEEL: PRINCIPAL AROMATIC NOTES

Cognac's wealth of aromas is depicted here as a seasonal cycle.

Almond
Vine flower
Menthol
Rose

Acacia
May blossom
Iris
Jasmine
Lilac

Wild carnation
Orange
Lime blossom

Apricot
Banana
Lemon
Fresh fig
Peach
Plum

Hay
Passion fruit
Mango
Rose petals
Pear

Butter
Honeysuckle
Orange blossom
Violet

COGNAC HARMONY

Spring Summer Winter Autumn

Cedarwood
Oakwood
Sandalwood
Orange zest

Dried apricot
Caramel
Mushroom
Chocolate/cocoa
Dried fig
Apple

Candied fruit
Lychee
Hazelnut
Walnut
Prune

Coffee
Leather
Smoke
Toasted bread
Pepper
Vanilla (wood)

Cigar box
Humus/Oak moss
Underwood
Tabacco
Truffle

Cinnamon
Clove
Ginger
Coconut
Nutmeg
Liquorice
Toffeee
Vanilla (pod)

Muscat grape
Saffron

11

THE ENJOYMENT OF COGNAC

The enjoyment of cognac, like everything else about this miraculous drink, is a complicated matter. It does not help that, as David Baker of Brandy Classics says with a sigh, 'today people are as ignorant about cognac as they were about wine thirty years ago'. Fortunately it is benefiting from the fact that people don't share their parents' tastes – which is the problem facing blended Scotch in many of its traditional markets. Helpfully, for today's younger generation cognac is a drink associated with their grandparents, so they are open to exploring its qualities.

Cognac's flagships are what Americans would call 'sippin'' brandies, essentially the XOs and above, though including some of the best VSOPs. In the words of Charles Walter Berry, for long Britain's greatest expert on brandy 'it is ideal after dinner; it cleanses the palate and its superfine qualities appeal to all that is best in the human mind'. The novelist Jacques Chardonne provides a wonderful and – for him – unusually precise description of one M. Pommerel. This master taster 'poured a drop of cognac into a cristal glass shaped like a half-opened tulip…he took the glass and then delicately between two fingers, he lifted it up without agitating it, breathing the fumes gently as if, through slow and silent exhalations. He was absorbing all its flavours.' A professional guide to tasting published in the 1970s states firmly that the sense of smell plays by far the most import role in sensory examination of a cognac.

In the past, and sometimes even today, the enjoyment of fine cognac has been bedevilled by its image. In a famous scene in his novel *Brideshead Revisited* Evelyn Waugh provided the tasting of old brandy as one example of the insufferable snobbery which permeates the whole book. The hero, Charles Ryder, is dining with the upstart Rex Mottram at a restaurant in Paris clearly identifiable as the Tour d'Argent. The cognac offered to them is 'clear and pale and it came to us in a bottle free from grime and Napoleonic cyphers. It was only a year or two older than Rex and lately bottled. They gave it to us in very thin tulip-shaped glasses of modest size.' Predictably, Rex does not like it: he 'pronounced it the sort of stuff he put soda in at home'. So 'shamefacedly, they wheeled out of its hiding place the vast and mouldy bottle they kept for people of Rex's sort...a treacly concoction,' which left 'dark rings round the side of his glass...a balloon the size of his head' (still often seen in pretentious surroundings the world over, but never in Cognac itself).

Waugh was being deliberately, outrageously snobbish. But he had clearly distinguished the separate markets which developed amid the cigar smoke and lush living of Edwardian England: the older, 'purer' tradition, of aristocratic sips of light, intense, delicate cognacs shipped early and bottled late, and the newer and more vulgar novelties symbolised by 'vast grimy bottles' and 'Napoleonic cyphers' – a phoney association which still survives. Indeed Christies' catalogues over the years provide numerous examples of brandies labelled not just with the name Napoleon but also with such associative names as *Grande Armée, Impératrice Joséphine* and *Maison de l'Empereur* fetching exaggerated sums at auction. As Charles Walter Berry put it with typical bluntness, 'Napoleon brandy is a snare and a delusion'. Virtually no cognac distilled before 1800 is drinkable as their storage over the centuries is suspect.

Waugh had also isolated a major element in the snobbery which deters younger drinkers, the glasses used. The vast balloons still regularly offered to diners not only lend an air of absurdity and snobbery to the drinking of fine brandy, but their very size precludes proper appreciation of the aromas. In the words of Georg Riedel, the glassmaker: 'with large glasses you have large surfaces and lots of evaporation and this means that the fruit disappears, so all you have left is the alcohol.' Basically you need a glass with a top that is narrower than the bottom to concentrate the aromas, but, unlike balloons of whatever size, is not too large to allow the flavours to be lost. I've even used a champagne flute, but the best is one used by professional tasters, the bulbous 'tulip' glass described by Chardonne which has a small chimney on top of the bulb. This has the desired quality of combining small quantities of spirits with the maximum capacity to entrap and concentrate the bouquet.

Riedel, ever the perfectionist, offers two types of glass – as well, rather shame-facedly, a balloon for old-timers. His VSOP glass is taller than the usual tulip glass and is designed to play up the fruitiness of the brandy and minimise the fiery harshness, the burning sensation so evident in most VSOPs. The idea works, a VSOP nosed in this glass is warmer and less fiery than when tasted in the tulip-shaped glass used for older brandies. Because these should have lost their youthful harshness, the glass can be designed to maximise the power of the complex aromas of rich chocolatey fruitiness and nuttiness typical of the best cognacs. (Of course Riedel is not alone in offering well-designed cognac glasses, Baccarat and Jenkins, for instance, both offer similar ones.)

Chardonne's description of a glass 'shaped like a half-opened tulip' was confirmed in a fascinating session held by the BNIC in early 2009 for professionals from all over the world. Their preference was indeed for such a glass. The shape was found easiest to use, best for judging the colour but also, critically, concentrated the nose of the brandy because of its wide bowl and narrow neck and thus allowed the taster to understand the subtleties and layers of aromatic complexity in the brandy. Nevertheless, the traditional balloon was judged excellent for serving young cognacs, over crushed ice for example.

Of course the brandy should be at the right temperature. The ideal is about 18°, since too warm a brandy evaporates too quickly and thus tastes too alcoholic. Better to start with a relatively cold glass rather than the warmed ones traditionally used – and if the brandy is already the right temperature, it's obviously sensible to hold it by the foot or stem to avoid over-heating.

Tasters obviously have to rely almost exclusively on their sense of smell, for even the strongest stomach cannot survive the small sips ingested when sampling fifty or more cognacs in a row, especially freshly distilled or immature ones. They, like the rest of us, are judging on three criteria: age, *cru,* and the general style which results from the combination of the age, the *cru* and the oak. They will instantly reject the harsh oiliness imparted to both nose and palate by the raw spirit used in even the best grape brandies. The *cru* is more difficult to distinguish. Most cheap cognacs are relatively anonymous, the better will, however, have a certain character. With less routine cognacs it is immensely enjoyable to look for the nuttiness provided by cognacs from the Borderies, and to try and detect the age of the cognac employed in different Champagne brandies.

Compared with wine, the colour of the brandy is of little importance, since most cognacs are coloured with caramel to provide the element of standardisation important in maintaining the brandy's vital 'brand image'. Indeed in Cognac itself the tasters use blue-coloured glasses to eliminate the colour factor entirely. Nevertheless, it is pretty safe to say that brandies which are too deep in colour are overly viscous, containing too much caramel. I've not come across many dark cognacs which offer any elegance while all the best older brandies have a golden streak. You can also judge – roughly – the age of a brandy by the traces, the 'tears' as the professionals call them which fall down the inside of the glass, for the older the cognac the slower they fall.

Tasting cognac is a more complex matter than tasting wines – many wine writers simply refuse to taste brandies because they are so strong. Inevitably amateurs can cope with a far smaller number than professionals. Personally I will taste five or six in a flight, accompanied by large doses of water – which I spit because swallowing would involve some of the brandy. I try not to do more than twenty in a morning.[74] Tasting for enjoyment should still be done in two stages to separate the more volatile constituents from the heavier ones. So the first impression should be gained by holding the glass still with the nose slowly approaching its rim. The glass can then be slowly rotated, rather than swirled, to capture the depth and variety of the more volatile elements which should be emanating from the spirit. This first 'nosing' should not be too near the glass or the strength of the flavours will be overwhelming. You then pause to catch your breath and put your nose into the glass to capture the more alcoholic components. Only then do you actually taste. Now the glass has to be twirled, just like a wine, to check for the individual taste components – the fruit, the balance, the length, the finish – which should be far longer than with wines.

Whatever the sensations, the drinker can generally be guided by the style of the house which blended the cognac. Most are commercial, for few blenders can afford the attitude

---

74 My greatest achievement, which I hope never to have to repeat, was to taste thirty-two South African brandies – a few of which were excellent – in a morning. But I was much younger then.

of Alain Braastad, the former chairman of Delamain, who says simply: 'I blend what I like.' These house styles are a strange mixture of the taste for which customers developed a fondness in times past, of the personal favourites of the blenders, sometimes of a deliberate, almost perverse complexity: 'The more you simplify cognac, the easier it is to imitate' said Robert Leauté of Rémy Martin. Once you rise above the VSOP level, the choice is almost infinite. As might be expected, Martell and Hennessy have very different house styles: Martell, as we have seen, is almost obsessively dry and clear on the palate; Hennessy goes for a much richer, almost voluptuous, taste in its blends. The theme of richness, of a desire to extract as much of the grapiness as possible from the fruit, is also involved in Rémy's distillation policy.

'There are two snobberies associated with cognac,' says Bernard Gauthier who produces excellent cognacs in the Grande Champagne, 'age and new oak.' It was Warner Allen who provided the most accurate rant about old cognacs, which is just as valid today as it was sixty years ago: 'Too many unscrupulous dealers' he thundered, 'dress up a young cognac with sugar, darken it with caramel perhaps add a few drops of really old cognac to give it a purely fictitious date … Bottles with monograms mean nothing … Bottles of brandy that claim to have been in the cellars of the First Napoleon and his contemporaries may multiply themselves like the fragments of the True Cross, but the wise man will give them a wide berth.' Even then you should avoid the brandies strong and forceful enough to cope with the taste of cigars produced by a number of firms, even reputable ones like Hine.

Truly old cognacs, those that have absorbed all they can from the wood, are a class apart. But the most satisfying can often be as young – in brandy terms – as thirty-five years old when they have already developed their vital *rancio*. Indeed the idea of 'beauty before age' so far as cognac is concerned has recently received a major boost thanks to the universal, and deserved praise – and trophies – awarded to Frapin's Multimillésimes, which are composed of three cognacs none more than thirty years old. Whatever their age the best brandies 'expand inside the mouth'. Once they are fifty years old, the best of them have acquired an inimitable, golden-bronze colour and feel: a harmony achievable only with age.

Age can also bring with it a kind of anonymity, blurring the original distinctions between different styles, so some of the real golden oldies, like Rémy Martin's Louis XIII and Hennessy's Paradis, resemble each other more than they do their makers' less distinguished offerings. Style applies more to younger, mid-range blends. The contrast between two widely respected cognacs, Frapin's Château de Fontpinot and Delamain's Pale and Dry, is striking. The Frapin is infinitely more woody; the oak, though dissolved and matured, is still emphatically present. In pre-feminist language, it is a 'masculine' cognac, where the infinitely more delicate Delamain is 'feminine', all lightness and elegance. To my palate, the best balance is achieved by a single-vineyard cognac, that of the Fontvieilles from Ragnaud-Sabourin, which somehow combines the strength and delicacy of the two extremes. But a cognac like this is rare enough to prove the rule that the only way to establish a reliable house style is to blend the products of many stills.

Beware, above all, the oldest cognacs. I've been lucky to sample some superb very old cognacs, but after fifty years quality depends on luck, chance, the skill of the producers and the care with which they have been stored. They may be very intense, very deep, but only too often they are not to my taste because there is no sign of fruity life. My comparison is with drier tawny ports at forty years of age, as opposed to the delicious fruit-and-nut mix at twenty. I've now found support for my lack of enthusiasm for very old cognacs from Edward Bate, the cognac specialist at Berry's and Neil Mathieson who imports such delights as Ragnaud Sabourin. In any case some of these cognacs are far too woody, many may well have been blended with younger brandies, and the strength of some of them can have fallen to well below the statutory 40 per cent and some, of course, were never very good in the first place. Nevertheless, the oldest cognacs will have started as more concentrated spirits since they will have been distilled in much smaller stills – probably not more than 3 hectolitres, an eighth of today's normal size.

The older the cognac the truer these points. Cognacs bottled before 1857 had to be blended and sold without a producer's name and much was poorly aged. Even the cognacs from the Grande Champagne will not age for longer than about 70–80 years and must be taken out of the barrels to stop them deteriorating. Corks will also taint the cognac and need to be changed at least every twenty years, preferably more often.

There has always been a well-founded suspicion as to the accuracy of the ages given to cognac. In 1864 Charles Tovey put it bluntly: 'We place but little reliance upon the cognac shippers' declarations with regard to vintages; and the only security the merchant has is to get his vintage brandy over to England into his own bonded stores as soon after the vintage as is convenient.'[75] Maurice Healy described how some merchants operated a sort of *solera* system: 'Bisquit Dubouché offered to supply apparently unlimited quantities of their 1865, their 1834 and even their 1811. If a cask of 1811 brandy had got down to its last tenth, and was then refilled with brandy of a younger but sympathetic vintage, say 1834, the cask became, within a few days a full cask of 1811, the older vintage having endowed the younger with its quality, while receiving the strength and virility of the other.'

Obviously, says David Baker, 'Provenance is important' but he's not only looking for their genuine date – though even carbon dating can only be accurate to within ten or twenty years. Mere age is not enough, he has to make sure 'that they are still alive', finding that too many of them are 'watery' or woody because they've been kept in casks too long. The worst are those from iconic vintages, above all the many allegedly from 1811, the 'Year of the Comet'. Taste is all. In the words of Charles Walter Berry: 'names and dates stand for little – the veritable article will speak for itself'.

And my own personal tastes? Like the locals – a long-lived bunch – I drink relatively little of it. For me a good or great cognac is more than the sum of its parts. I am looking for bitterness, its length on the palate and the finish – is it long? Too burny? In the end I am looking for the greatest possible impact from the fruit from which the cognac was made. This can be richer or leaner, for it is no more ridiculous to talk of the 'backbone' of a good Martell, the 'elegance' of a Delamain, the 'fruitiness' of a Hennessy cognac than it is to attribute the same qualities to clarets from Pauillac or Saint-Emilion. For the best cognacs have one advantage denied even to the finest wines, because of the sheer strength of the

---

75 *British and Foreign Spirits*, Whittaker.

drink its qualities linger longer. You can taste for hours and still keep finding new depths, new flavours – even next morning when the glass has been empty the whole night long. But no one has put the experience better than the politician – and Bishop – Talleyrand:

> *At the end of a sumptuous supper, one of the guests tossed down his glass of Fine Champagne in one gulp in the Russian manner. Talleyrand took the liberty of advising his friend quite quietly: 'That is not how you should drink cognac. You take your glass in the hollow of the hand, you warm it, you rotate it with a circular movement so that the spirit gives off its aroma. Then you carry it to your nostrils and inhale...and then, my dear sir, you put down your glass and talk about it.'*

DON'T BE AFRAID OF MIXING

You can, of course, dilute cognac with ice, or soda water or other sparkling waters, or exploit its unique complexities by combining it with any compatible mixer. Indeed for several hundred years the British aristocracy usually drank cognac with soda – often last thing at night. Typically, President De Gaulle replaced port and Scotch as *apéritifs* at the Elysée Palace with *fine à l'eau*, brandy and water, which had also been a favourite of Frenchmen sent out to rule France's then-extensive empire. For such a drink you need stronger cognacs; VSOP made from brandies from the Champagnes are ideal for long drinks because they will be tough enough. There are those who claim that by far the best way of drinking cognacs from the Grande Champagne which are less than ten years' old is with ice. But the ice should be made with pure, bottled water to avoid the chloriney taste inevitable with so many waters from taps around the world. Fizz need not necessarily be simply soda water. Personally I prefer Perrier as a mixer, finding its slight saltiness an agreeable counterpoint to the richness of the brandy, but other brandy-bores find it too salty and prefer Badoit or other sparkling waters.

Other key mixers are based on ginger. British pubs used to sell masses of brandy and Stones Ginger Wine. I prefer a dry ginger mixer which must be dry like Canada Dry and not the sweeter American ginger ale, for the brandy is quite sweet enough. Cognac lovers may have noted one absentee on my list of suitable mixers: tonic. The BNIC deliberately chose tonic as its mixer of choice but I am not alone in thinking that the tartness, the aggression of the tonic does not form the same agreeable contrast with cognac as citrus fruits. It does not blend, it clashes, the qualities of the two are incompatible, though, to be fair to the BNIC there is proof that tonic was used as a mixer in the nineteenth century, probably in France's far eastern colonies.

THE COGNAC COCKTAIL GAME

Cognac is an ideal base for cocktails, as Pierre Szersnovicz of Courvoisier puts it: 'other spirits provide purely alcoholic support for cocktails whereas cognac brings a definite character to any blend'. Every cognac brand offers such a complexity of taste that all a professional mixologist has to do is to identify one of the many flavours and aromas in the spirit and enhance it by blending it with complementary flavours. Because it is made from grapes, cognac is eminently suitable for cocktails that will not react too violently with the wine to be drunk later in the evening. The old wives told the right tale: grain and grape really do not mix. I can attest to the ill-effects, felt the next morning, of even the smallest tincture of whisky before drinking wine in any quantity. Cognac-based cocktails *are* healthier.

Cognac's virtue as the spirit of choice for cocktail makers has come at a time when Britain has emerged as the cocktail centre of the world, replacing the rather smug, unadventurous long-time capital, New York. The reasons are many: 'They don't make bad cognacs,' says Dick Bradsell, London's cocktail pioneer, aware that there is less quality control in the making of competing spirits. He and his colleagues are discovering that cognac is mellower and softer and has the necessary smoothness and balance. It helps that you don't need relatively expensive VSOP, VS does fine for cocktails. Moreover, cognac was due for a revival because it had been out of fashion for so long. In Bradsell's words, cognac 'missed out on all the funny drinks of the 1970s and so doesn't have any gimmicky connotations'. It also helps that, in the United States anyway, drinkers believe that cognac is stronger than competing spirits, possibly because it has more character and far greater complexity.

The basic formula for most of these drinks is relatively simple: something sour with something sweet to exploit the flavour and strength of the cognac, together with a touch of character from bitters or the like. The flexibility of cognac is also important. 'Any mix is fine,' says Dave Steward, a cocktail expert, 'provided you can taste the cognac' – a direct contrast to the distillers' attempts to make a competitor like vodka as anonymous as possible and, as he points out 'we hope that these mixes will lead us back to the better cognacs – drunk neat.' Also in its favour is its capacity to provide a more interesting twist on classic whisky-based cocktails – barmen sometimes admit that they're often doing the equivalent of merely reinventing the alcoholic wheel. But then some of these – notably the julep – were originally based on cognac only to be usurped by bourbon.

If you're using lemon or even orange then obviously you want a richer style of cognac – say Courvoisier or Hennessy – to compensate for the bitterness of the citrus fruit. Ready made ones like Grand Marnier or Cointreau which combine orange and brandy can be replicated – after a fashion. There are obvious mixers apart from citrus fruit and other fruit like apples, such as cream, chocolate and coffee. Just think of the Brandy Alexander favoured by Anthony Blanche, another character in *Brideshead Revisited* – though Waugh is clearly painting him as a bounder. The Alexander normally uses dark crème de cacao and grated nutmeg, though Blanche obviously wanted cream with his. Either way it's fine because although it's inevitably sweet, you're not overly conscious of the individual constituents but only of the blend.

Cocktail books provide dozens of recipes for cognac-based cocktails – these are a few of the best:

Brandy Alexander: equal measures cognac, heavy cream, brown crème de cacao.
Brandy Cobbler: 1 tsp caster sugar and equal measures of cognac and soda.

Brandy Collins: also called brandy fizz and much the same as brandy sling or brandy sour, 1 tsp caster sugar, small measure cognac, juice of ½ lemon, soda.

Brandy Highball: cognac with ginger ale or soda.

Brandy Julep: 5–6 mint leaves, 1 tsp caster sugar, measure cognac, put ingredients into collins glass (a small but tall tumbler) and stir until mint rises to the top.

Brandy Manhattan: same as one made with whisky, that is at least 3 parts cognac to 1 part sweet vermouth.

Breakfast Nog: from Jacques Sallé, combine cognac, Grand Marnier or Cointreau, milk and an egg.

COGNAC, EXCLUSIVELY WITH CHOCOLATE?

The British automatically associate cognac exclusively with such delights as brandy butter – the essential accompaniment to such dishes as mince pies. Yet cognac is the perfect accompaniment to any dish containing chocolate – and no, I don't know why! But recently the French have been exploring brandy's use with many, some unlikely, dishes. The high priest of the new cult is Thierry Veyrat, who owns La Ribaudière, a deservedly Michelin-starred establishment on the banks of the Charente, who now sells fifty special *menus gastronomiques* a month which pairs brandy with such unlikely ingredients as red mullet. But even Veyrat insists that 'it's vital to remember that in meals cognac shouldn't be considered a drink, but a seasoning. You taste only a little at a time, holding it in your mouth a few seconds, just long enough to awake the palate and bring out the cognac's various flavours.'

In 1999 Rémy Martin did the first experiments in matching cognac with food and has come up with some surprising results; 'our cognacs,' they declare proudly, 'have enough concentration to cope with any food'. Among the successes: a rich firm shellfish with as little sauce as possible to go with a VSOP with its full flavour; XO goes really well with *ris de veau and morilles*,[76] you need something strong to cut through the richness of the dish; and the same applies to *foie gras* where the cognac provides the dish with some structure; the 1738 is excellent with *vieux mimolette*, a cheese which – like old Gouda – goes so well with claret.

As is inevitable with any suggestions by a French company some of the ideas, like *foie gras* with Szechuan pepper, are, shall we say, slightly off the wall, though iced XO goes surprisingly well with *foie gras*. Nevertheless, other blends are calculated to make you think. These include dishes such as sushi and blue cheeses, which need the strength and tartness of the cognac, as well as lobster or serious game dishes. But what Rémy is really doing is not suggesting specific marriages so much as insinuating in the mind the general idea that it is not inconceivable to associate food and cognac. The best parallel is with champagne firms like Krug when it was owned by Rémy which encouraged the association of their beverage not with mindless enjoyment and a seductive atmosphere but with serious appreciation of a serious wine – such as Krug.

---

76 Sweetbreads and deep-flavoured mushrooms.

12

THE PRODUCERS AND THEIR BRANDIES

Because of the prevalence of wholly unremarkable cognacs I have chosen only to highlight those which have some distinguishing features or a noticeable house style, at whatever level.

* Indicates a particular favourite of mine, in other words, what the *Guide Hachette* calls a *coup de coeur*.

Where possible British stockists are indicated with the abbreviations shown below.

BC: Brandy Classics, 87 Trowbridge Road, Bradford-on-Avon, Wiltshire, BA15 1EG. Tel: 01225 863986, db@brandyclassics.com. David Baker imports several small and reputable producers and has his own brands, Hermitage and Siècle d'Or (qv).

Edevie: Marussia, 225–231 Old Marylebone Rd, London, NW1 5QT. Tel: 0207 724 5009.

SEC: Single Estate Cognacs, 59 Thornhill, South Marston, Swindon, Wiltshire, SN3 4TA. Tel: 01793 831 756, www.secognac.com.

Abbreviations

GC   Grande Champagne
PC   Petite Champagne
FC   Fine Champagne – at least half GC, the rest exclusively PC
FB   Fins Bois
BB   Bon Bois
VS   A minimum of two years old
VSOP   A minimum of four years old
XO   Napoleon Extra, etc. At least six years old, though the cognacs from reputable firms will average above that age.

Figures representing the ages of the cognacs are supplied by the producers. Inevitably they are approximate averages because most of the cognacs involved are blends. All cognacs are 40 per cent unless otherwise stated. Visitors are generally welcome in even the smallest firms and producers provided they phone up to give due warning and show real interest in the producer's cognacs. The Big Four all welcome visitors to their distilleries, as do other firms. The telephone numbers given are for callers outside France.

ABK6

SNC du Maine Drilhon
Domaine de Chez Maillard
16440 Claix
Tel: +33 545 66 35 72

In 2002 Francis Abecassis, a prosperous rice farmer from the Camargue, set up in the Petites Champagnes de Blanzac, one of the best parts of the Fins Bois. Since then he has bought up a number of brands including Leyrat and Le Reviseur.

VSOP: nice grapey feel, a hint of caramel and burn.

Family Reserve 55%: FB the rest PC. Fresh, peachy on nose and palate, lots of liquorice on the finish.

Ice Cognac: As the name implies, designed to be drunk over ice

Les Antiquaires du Cognac

Lartige
16200 Jarnac
Tel: +33 545 36 55 78

Unique set-up. The Pinard family, themselves distillers, offers a range of single *cru*, single vintage cognacs as well as a range of blends.

GC: long, flowery, dry with a hint of spice.

FB: very long, complex, fruity.

Audry

H Boisson & Cie
12 Rue St-Vivien
17103 Saintes
Tel: +33 546 74 11 72
audry@cognac-audry.com

Family business founded in 1878. It stopped selling any of its – inevitably growing – stock of cognacs for half a century until Bernard Boisson took over in the mid-1980s.

Audry XO: nice fresh grapey, floral feel, a little *rancio*.

*Reserve Speciale 15: round, creamy buttery.

Memorial FC 35+: 42%, great concentration, fruit-cakey, very long but a touch woody.

Exception FC: kept in wood for about fifty years. Seriously old and concentrated.

Très Ancienne: 50%, single vineyard GC. Lots of spice and *rancio*.

Bache-Gabrielsen

32 rue de Boston
16100 Cognac
Email: bache-gabrielsen@bache-gabrielsen.com
Tel: + 33 545 320 745

XO FC: light gold colour; fresh, fruity nose and palate, which is deep, concentrated and richly grassy.

1971 Borderies: light lemon colour; rich, earthy nose; light and floral on the palate.

Jean Balluet

1 Rue des Ardillères
17489 Neuvicq le Château
Tel: +33 546 16 64 74
jean.balluet@wanadoo.fr

Distinguished family (including Hippolyte, a resistance hero). They have been distilling cognac from their 35-hectare estate in the Fins Bois since 1845, and have been selling their own for fifty years, since a major customer reduced its order.

VSOP 8
Très Vieille Réserve 26

Banchereau (C du C)

Puy Mesnard
16120 Eraville
Tel: +33 545 97 13 54

Daniel Banchereau took over the family's 23-hectare wine estate at Eraville in the east of the GC from his family in 1968. In 1991 Daniel Banchereau with his children Frédérique and Laurent set up their own distillery to produce cognac for themselves. Today the estate has grown to 45 hectares.

GC XO: fruity and floral, with nice overtones of coffee and nuts.

GC 40 years: incredible depth and richness but an old-style cognac and thus the finish is a little dry and woody.

Hors d'Age: good rich *rancio*, ends a little woody.

Michel Barlaam

Les Landes Rioux Martin
16120 Chalais
Tel. +33 545 98 17 75

With 7 hectares of vines, one of the few growers in the Bons Bois selling brandies to private clients.

Michel Barlaam VSOP 12+

Paul Beau

Michel and Colette Laurichesse
18 rue Millardet – BP 17
16130 Segonzac
Tel: +33 545 83 40 18
michel.laurichesse@wanadoo.fr

Paul Beau has won seven medals for their Hors d'Age cognac in the last ten years. Housed in Segonzac itself, Beau is one of the most distinguished distillers in the Grande Champagne with a hundred hectares of vines. The firm was founded by Samuel Beau in 1895 and he built the distillery, which is still used today. His son Paul Beau expanded the vineyard and installed their own still and bottling equipment. In the 1970s, the family, now headed by their daughter Colette, married to Michel Laurichesse, started to sell their own cognacs.

VSOP: clean, floral nose with a little *rancio*; long, but a trifle woody.

Vieille Réserve: long and complex but a little hard on the finish.

*Hors d'Age Vieille GC: 43°, complex brandy with *rancio*, overtones of eucalyptus, exotic fruits and spice and a long finish.

*Extra Vieille Borderies: the family sold their Borderies vineyard in 1964 so all of the constituents are at least 45 years old. The real McCoy. Rich fruit-and-nut chocolate, very dense and long.

1906: allspice and candied fruits in an endlessly complex cognac.

Jan Bertelsen

Brand created by *Léopold Gourmel* and named after their Norwegian agent.

VSOP Prelude 8: young, fresh, floral nose, a little short.

XO Symphonie 13: rich, some *rancio*.

Extra Orchestra 23: 42°, rich, floral, long.

Bertrand

SARL Bertrand & Fils Reaux
12 rue Les Brissons
17500 Reaux
Tel: +33 546 48 09 03

The owner of the estate Brissons de Laage, Jean-François Bertrand, comes from a long line of growers and merchants. All the brandies come from an 80-hectare estate in the heart of the Petite Champagne owned by the family since 1731. The style is dark and intense because the cognacs are kept longer than usual in very old cognac casks.

VSOP 15+: good floral/fruity nose slightly hot and alcoholic but good fruit.

Napoleon 20–23: rich *rancio* nose, nutty but a trifle leathery and woody.

Vieille Réserve 20–30: dark apricot, nice round *rancio* but also fresh.

XO: slightly heavy but very long, fruity and chocolatey.

PC: 30%, delicious despite some sugar and caramel.

Bisquit Dubouché
90 Boulevard de Paris
16100 Cognac
Tel: +33 545 83 10 83

Founded in 1819 by an enterprising local, Alexandre Bisquit, who was mayor of Jarnac before being deposed by the Emperor Napoleon in 1851. His daughter married a M. Dubouché, who added his name to the firm – and followed his father-in-law as mayor of Jarnac, rising to becoming a senator. Their daughter married a local 'notable', Maurice Laporte, who promoted sales in the Far East. In 1965 the family sold the business to Paul Ricard of Pernod-Ricard, who also bought Château Lignières, the largest estate in the region with 200 hectares of vines. He built a vast distillery and ultra-modern *chai* but in 2009 when the group bought Martell he sold it to the South African group Distel, which produces fine brandies in South Africa. Distel has bought and renovated the palatial former headquarters of Pallisson and has found better sources of cognac.

VS: light colour; clean, fresh nose; clean and floral on the palate.

VSOP: again, light, clean and floral; long but some burn.

Prestige: for the Far East. Richer – and silkier – than the others.

XO: deeper on the nose with some spice, and long, thanks to older brandies.

Roger Blanleuil (C du C)
Chez Beillard
16300 Criteuil la Magdeleine
Tel: +33 545 80 52 01

Roger and Martine Blanleuil and their sons Nicolas and Jérome represent the eighth generation to produce Grande Champagne cognac here. The original family settled in this region in 1800 and commenced wine production. Today Cognac Blanleuil cultivates 45 hectares of vines in the heart of Grande Champagne. They make a good value VSOP and XO as well as a Vieille Réeserve plus their white and rosé Pineaux. They have won both gold and silver medals at the Segonzac concours.

*VSOP: light colour, light floral nose, elegant like a superior Fins Bois.

*XO: good rancio, a very civilised and buttery digestif.

Boissons de Laage
Domaines de Boissons de Laage
17500 Reaux
Tel: +33 546 48 09 03
cognac@cognac-bertrand.com

10: clean colour, light floral nose. Soft and delicious on the nose, but not long.

18/20: chestnut colour; rich, rather simple nose. Rich and commercial.

Daniel Bouju

Chez Lafont
16130 Segonzac
Tel: +33 545 83 41 27
cognac.daniel.bouju@wanadoo.fr

Goes his own way in a lovely valley in the GC which he claims has a very special micro-climate. 'Declared my independence' from the big boys to whom he had previously sold his brandy in 1974 and now has 25 hectares of vines. Distils hot on lees ('a GC without lees is not a real GC' he says) and immediately reduces to 55% 'to conserve the richness'. New casks so some find his brandies rather woody and lacking in elegance.

*Sélection Spéciale: lovely round, fruity nose; round and rich with some wood behind, but one of the best VSs from the Champagnes.

VSOP: rather spirity nose, less fruity, lots of wood.

Napoleon: wood well absorbed, rich, some *rancio*.

XO 25: very rich chestnut colour, rich *rancio*, no apparent wood.

Extra 35: round, complex, *rancio*, good example of a GC.

Brut de fut 40: 50%, characteristic rich woodiness hides the strength.

Royal: 60%, one of the strongest on the market; very concentrated so appears to be 'only' 50%!

Louis Bouron

SA Château de La Grange
189 avenue de Jarnac – BP 80
17416 Saint-Jean d'Angély
Tel: +33 546 32 00 12
Infos:cognac-louisbouron.com

Family business housed in a fourteenth-century castle blending fine cognacs from 90 hectares of vines, 40 each in the Borderies and Petite Champagne and 10 in the Fins Bois.

XO: surprisingly light but plentiful aromas, round, long.

Très Vieille Réserve: long, complex, touch of – natural – sweetness.

Bernard Boutinet

Le Brissoneau
Breville
16370 Cherves de Cognac
Tel: +33 545 80 86 63
cognac.boutinet@wanadoo.fr

Brandies of quality exclusively from a family-owned 26 hectare estate north of Cognac in the best Fins Bois.

*Fine (VSOP) 6: supple but firm in the mouth; long, with some power on the finish.

Vieille Fine/Napoleon 12–14

Très Vieille Fine XO

Coeur de Fins Bois 6: 50%, deliberately aged in very old casks. As a result the brandy is very fresh with overtones of dried fruits and is suitable for long drinks.

Extra Complex: long, rich.

Domaine Breuil-Brillet

BP32

16130 Segonzac

Tel: +33 545 83 41 79

VSOP: easy to drink, suave but a trifle sugary on the end of the palate.

XO: rich, vanilla-y, old-style, i.e. rather woody.

Brillet

Les Aireaux

16120 Graves/Cognac

Tel: +33 545 97 05 06

In theory a merchant, but in practice M. Brillet relies mostly on grapes from the family's 60 hectares of vineyards in the Petite and Grande Champagne. Distils – on the lees – in the family's four stills in his delightful, albeit rather ramshackle property.

Réserve PC: good floral richness, long, the burn disappears leaving pear fruit.

Très Vieille Réserve XO GC: candied fruit, nutty nose, seriously elegant, long, plum fruit.

Très Rare Heritage GC: serious *rancio* on nose but fresher and fruity on the palate. Again very long.

Domaine des Brissons de Laage

(*see* Cognac Bertrand)

Brugerolle

Business established in the early nineteenth century and now part of CCG, which uses the name only for a few unremarkable cognacs sold in European markets.

Camus

Camus 'La Grande Marque'

29 Rue Marguerite de Navarre BP19

16101 Cognac

Tel: +33 545 32 28 28

See also Chabanneau and Planat.

The fifth largest firm in Cognac, and the biggest still family-owned. The founder, Jean-Baptiste Camus, started the business as La Grande Marque, a consortium of growers, and later added his own name. Camus relied largely on sales to Tsarist Russia and thus suffered very badly from the Russian Revolution. By the 1960s it was virtually bankrupt but was saved by a deal struck by Michel Camus with the two young Americans who founded Duty Free Shoppers. In the past few years has risen again with the arrival of Michel's grandson Cyril who studied in the United States and China, married a Chinese girl and, with the help of a new production director Patrick Leger, has tripled sales to 150,000 cases within a few years thanks to the Chinese market. Now the biggest owner in Borderies with 180 hectares which adds to the richness of the firm's brandies.

Camus Elegance VS: clean, warm, some burn on finish.

Camus Elegance VSOP: light and floral on both nose and palate, good concentration, long.

Camus Elegance XO: deep and round, good 'fruit-and-nut' feeling, lots of Borderies.

Borderies XO: deep colour, nutty, woodily reminiscent of almond kernels, rich chocolate nose, deep, relatively young, dry and spicy.

Extra Old: just above XO. GC and Borderies. Long, rich, natural sweetness.

Josephine: introduced in 1995 for sale in duty-free to 'young Japanese office ladies' who continue to appreciate its light floral qualities. Sold in a slim, elegant 50cl bottle enhanced by a label from the great Art Nouveau artist Mucha.

Fine Island: Camus has also has worked with the co-operative on the Ile de Ré to produce the only serious cognac from the island. A real curiosity, tastes extremely salty.

Castel Sablons
Le Bourg Saint Maigrin
17520 Archiac
Tel: +33 546 70 00 30

The Roux family owns 26 hectares of vines in an excellent part of the Fins Bois just south of the Petite Champagne. Recently, has specialised in enterprising new products.

Crystal Dry 3: deliberately young and virtually colourless, designed as a base for cocktails.

Brûlot Charentais: 58%, designed to be used in the traditional drink of the same name, when the spirit is ignited over a cup of coffee to make a fine pick-me-up.

Chabanneau
Historic firm founded in 1830 by a Dutch cognac trader selling to the Dutch East Indies, and M. Pierre Chabanneau, manager of the wine cellars of the Grand Hotel in Paris. Flourished until Indonesia declared independence in 1954. Now a subsidiary of *Camus* and used as a second label for cheap cognacs.

Denis Charpentier
59 Avenue Théophile Gautier
75016 Paris
Tel: +33 145 27 86 07

Specialises in cognacs for the South East Asian market.

Château de Beaulon
17240 St Dizant-du-Goa
Tel: +33 5 46 49 96 13

The most remarkable – and beautiful – estate in the whole region within sight of the Gironde estuary opposite the Médoc. The château itself is an historic monument dating back to 1480 and in the seventeenth century was owned and managed by the Bishops of Bordeaux who introduced 'Bordeaux' varieties. The present owner, Christian Thomas continues the tradition.

The quality of the brandies – and the Pineaux which are among the finest in the region – made by the Thomas family provide proof that this corner of the Fins Bois is capable of producing brandies comparable with the Champagnes, especially when, as here, they are made from Montils, Colombard, Sémillon and Folle Blanche and very little Ugni Blanc.

FB: 7 y/o, 100% Folle Blanche, young but very long with a delightful floral finish.

FB: 10 y/o, rich, fruity nose, some plumminess, long, densely concentrated, ends a little woody.

Grande Fin 12: mostly Folle Blanche, Colombard and Montils. Elegant, lots of FB on nose and palate, tangy ornate feel.

Napoleon: 20 y/o, all four major appellations round, rich – one American taster compared it to a Renoir.

Extra: around 50 y/o, all the complexity of a great FB, long, fruity, raisiny, because of the number of varieties involved. Is proof that some brandies from this sub-region can age as well as those from the Champagnes.

***1971:** a model cognac; clean, pure, long.

Château de Montifaud (BC)
17520 Jarnac-Champagne
Tel: +33 546 49 50 77
vallet@Château-montifaud.com

Estate of 50 hectares in the Petites Champagnes d'Archiac owned by the Vallet family for a century and a half. Looking for a light unwoody style they distil on the lees, and include 10% of Colombard in the blend.

***VSOP 10:** lovely floral feel, like a good FB de Jarnac but richer.

Vieille Réserve: full bouquet of flowery aromas, dry and smooth, long.

XO: a single vintage XO with pronounced aromas, hint of dark chocolate and spice, round and very long.

Hors d'Age: a superb mix of fruity and flowery aromas; dry, round and extremely long.

Château Paulet
Domaine de la Couronne
Route de Segonzac BP24
16101 Cognac
Tel: +33 545 32 07 00

Owned by the Cointreau family (*see* Frapin) and now not seen much.

Château de la Raillerie
Recently bought by Rémy and likely to disappear as a separate brand.

VSOP: good roundness and warmth, bit of burn.

Extra Old: middle aged, nice balance and fruit, clean and sparky.

Château St-Sorlin
Saint-Sorlin de Cognac
17150 Mirambeau
Tel: +33 546 86 01 27

Madame Castelnau-Gros is the great-granddaughter of one of the nurserymen who provided the vines for replanting the region after the phylloxera. She slightly sweetens the cognacs she makes from her 20 hectare estate on a chalky patch opposite the upper Médoc with syrup.

Chollet
16100 Boutiers-St-Trojan
Tel: +33 545 32 12 93

In 1977, after Salignac stopped buying Jacques Chollet's cognacs he started selling them himself. He likes his cognacs soft.

Resistance 3577: nice light apricot colour, light floral nose with just a touch of *rancio*. Good floral richness on the palate, a little short.

306: 25 year old – is this GC? Deep, raisiny, slightly woody nose, warm and fruity on the palate but not very concentrated.

307 XO: again, GC? Very good appley nose, warm and ripe; a nice mouth-filling cognac.

Pascal Combeau
Owned by *Marie Brizard*.

Compagnie Commerciale de Guyenne
26 rue Pascal Combeau
16100 Cognac
Tel: +33 545 82 32 10

Now a major group founded in 1976 by *Michel Coste*, one of the most remarkable figures in the recent history of Cognac, who bought up a number of firms like Brugerolle, Lucien Foucauld and *Meukow*, now its principal brand.

Cognac du collections
(*see* La Gabare)

André Couprie
La Roumade
16300 Ambleville
Tel: +33 545 80 54 69
couprie@club-internet.fr

Laurent Couprie's family has been settled on the same 22-hectare estate at Ambleville since 1730 and continues to sell only its own cognacs. Like so many grower's cognacs from the GC, the VS & VSOP have simply not had the time to lose their rough edges.

Napoleon 12+: rather woody and leathery, short and dry on the finish.

XO 20+: not much complexity, rather hard, ideal with a cigar.

*Hors d'Age: 41.5%, 40 years old, some Folle Blanche and it shows in the florality and elegance of a fine cognac; mellow and very long.

1936: all the qualities of a rich, *rancio* cognac.

1903: like so many old, old cognacs this is too woody for comfort.

Courvoisier

Place du Château
16200 Jarnac
Tel: +33 545 35 55 55

Most untypical of the Big Four. Has never owned its own vines, has always relied on outside distillers, a dependence which cost the firm its independence in the early 1960s. Its brandies have always been rich and round and over the past twenty years the quality has continued to rise. In *Skyfall* M drank Courvoisier. She has died but they're hoping her successor will follow her example.

VS: rich, typical of the firm throughout the ages. Excellent for mixing because of strength.

VSOP Fine Cognac: very elegant and aromatic but a trifle alcoholic.

VSOP Le Voyage de Napoleon: produced exclusively for the Far East duty-free market. A lot of old Borderies and it shows, but also floral and spicy.

Emperor VSOP: very complex; rich, with deep florality, aromatic on the palate, a little wood.

VS Global Travel Retail: 100% Fins Bois 'for those who want a bold style'.

XO: GC and PC and some old Borderies; deliberately richer for the Far East market.

GC: very strong and rich *rancio* combined with toffee on nose and palate but still elegant.

Emperor For the Chinese market. Dark gold colour; rich, chocolate fruit-and-nut on the nose; rich but no caramel on the palate

*Initiale Extra: GC and Borderies; although only half Borderies they dominate the blend especially on the nose. A very natural richness with a feel of *sous bois* – the fresh, wet, earthy, mushroomy feel.

Essence: their answer to Hennessy's Richard and Rémy's Louis XIII with the same deep leathery woodiness and concentration.

Croizet

BP3
16720 St-Même-les-Carrières
Tel: +33 545 81 90 11

The most extraordinary story in the recent history of Cognac. The Croizet family had owned vineyards in the Grande Champagne since the seventeenth century and founded their firm in 1805. In the late nineteenth century Léon Croizet was awarded the Légion d'Honneur for his work replanting the vineyard with grafted vines. Until 2006 the firm was run by the Eymard family – descendants of a Mselle Croizet who married a M. Eymard in 1892. With Hine and Delamain, Croizet was one of only three firms allowed to sell individual vintages before 1985.

The firm decayed because of family quarrels, relying on selling cheaper cognacs. In

2006 this sleeping beauty was bought by M. Varshavsky, a Russian steel tycoon and cognac lover. His team – headed by Jean-Emmanuel Roy, one of Rémy Martin's best distillers – now sell cognacs exclusively from the firm's 150 hectares of vines in the Champagnes. His pride and joy is the Cuvée Léonie based on a stock of 1858 cognacs largely forgotten by the previous owner.

VS GC: rich, fruity, floral on nose and palate, very long for a VS.

VSOP: 7–8 y/o, light apricot colour, complex on the palate, a little *rancio*, some vanilla, a little fruit.

*XO: 20–30 y/o, serious *rancio*, good complexity, long, concentrated.

*Extra: Very rich, notes of freshly-made marmalade – Seville not ordinary oranges! – on the nose, dry.

Comte Audoin de Dampierre

Château de Plassac
17240 Plassac
Tel: +33 546 49 81 85
Châteaudeplassac@9business.fr

At first sight, the Comte, clad in suitably worn but distinguished country clothing and standing in front of his delightful eighteenth-century château, seems like a character straight out of the novels of PG Wodehouse. This is misleading; he's a real wine and spirits man who founded a successful champagne firm. Not surprisingly his two cognacs are both well made.

Napoleon: nice light gold colour from the borders of the FB and BB, floral nose, rich summer flowers on the palate.

XO: deep apricot colour, again summer flowers on the nose, rich fruit-and-nut on the palate, long.

Davidoff

One of the first cognacs designed to accompany cigars. Blended by Hennessy for the cigar company of the same name. The cognac is too rich for a non-smoker.

Delamain

Rue J & R Delamain
PO Box 16
16200 Jarnac
Tel: +33 545 81 08 24
delamain@delamain-cognac.com

The firm and its brandies are both unique. The brandies have always been the favourites of the English aristocracy, the first customer for the best cognacs. Many of them were 'Early Landed, Late Bottled'. Their quality has been unquestioned since the early eighteenth century, and the firm is still run by the family – a Mselle Delamain married a M. Braastad, great-grandfather of one of the present directors. The firm still buys only from the Grande Champagne and then only brandies of at least ten years of age, matured in old casks, thus giving all the firm's brandies their unique elegance.

*Pale & Dry: floral, delicate, long.

Vesper: deliberately completely different from Pale & Dry, with a natural richness comparable to a Hine.

*Très Vénérable: combines the delicacy and richness of the two 'lesser' offerings.

*Très Vieille Réserve de la Famille: classic GC with flowery overtones. Long, complex.

Also offers one single vintage at a time which they select when they buy the young cognacs. Since they're individual casks they can vary. At the moment it's a 1973, slightly richer and rounder than the blends but a remarkable, pure cognac.

Delaunay

(*see* Lebecq)

Delisle

Chez Genin
1 Rue des Distilleries
16200 Bourg Charente
Tel: +33 545 35 40 90

The Cabanne family has been producing cognacs since the late seventeenth century but has been selling its own cognacs only since 1999.

VSOP: FB and PC. Nice floral nose, some nice fruit on palate.

XO: Rich, rounded nose. Classic well-balanced cognac with good nutty candied fruit.

Club Cigare: very dark chocolate with less of the harshness than is usual with a 'cigar' cognac.

1965: 60.5%! Very rich, fruity nose; a little woody and dry but not too alcoholic despite its strength!

Jacques Denis

Le Maine au Franc
16130 St Preuil
Tel: +33 545 83 41 22
cognac_denis@hotmail.com

The estate in St Preuil in the heart of the Grande Champagne has been owned by the family for several generations.

10 ans: very typical of the GC; light and well rounded.

XO: 20 y/o, rather short but its chocolate overtones make it an ideal accompaniment to a chocolate dessert.

Extra: very elegant nose with good fruit on the palate, not very long.

*Vieille Réserve: 50 y/o, 55%. The nose may be slightly alcoholic but hides its additional strength through sheer depth and complexity.

AE Dor (BC)

4 Bis Rue Jacques Moreau
16200 Jarnac
Tel: +33 545 81 03 26
AE.Dor@wanadoo.fr

Family firm best known for its fabled – but alas inevitably now diminishing – stock of historic brandies, many bought by M. Dor soon after he had founded the firm in 1858. In 2015 Dor was bought by a local cooperative alliance.

VSOP: FC, complex, clean, floral, delicious.

Drouet et fils (SEC)

Patrick and Corrine Drouet
1 Route du Maine Neuf
16130 Salles d'Angles
Tel: +33 545 83 63 13
contact@cognac-drouet.fr; domaine.drouet.et.fils@aliceadsl.fr
web: www.cognac-drouet.fr

Well-equipped family producer in the Grande Champagne, bought by the Drouet family in 1969 and now run by Patrick Drouet. They use around 8% of Colombard in their cognacs.

VSOP: rich clean non-burny nose, a little wood on the finish.

XO: good fruity-wood blend on the nose, a little lighter on the palate, long and clean, well balanced and elegant.

Hors d'Age: rich *rancio* nose, slightly woody but ditto on palate.

Paradis de Famille: woody but very serious *rancio* with good fruit and nut chocolate.

Duboigalant

Former name of brandies made by the *Trijol* family.

Dupuy (SEC)

32 Rue de Boston
16100 Cognac
Tel: +33 545 32 07 45
cognac-dupuy.com

Founded in 1853 by Auguste Dupuy. In 1905 his son Edmond sold it to two Norwegians, Peter Rastad and Thomas Bache-Gabrielsen whose family still owns the firm. As well as Dupuy they now sell their own Bache-Gabrielsen brand to Scandinavia.

Luxus Tentation GC PC and FB: light floral nose, very pure.

Extra FC: slightly alcoholic, *terroir* nose but very elegant and well balanced.

*XO Tentation PC, FB and Borderies: excellent and unusual blend, a model XO.

Hors d'Age GC

Famille Estève

Les Corbinauds
17520 Celles
Tel: +33 546 49 51 20

Serious family growers in the Petite Champagne but very near the boundary with the Grande Champagne so produce excellent brandies of great delicacy.

Jacques Estève Très Vieux Cognac de la Propriété XO: 35 y/o, very rich and *rancio*-y on the palate, but still a bit woody throughout.

Jacques Estève Hors d'Age Excellent: balance of fruity and flowery aromas; nutty with a trace of wood; round and very long.

*Jacques Estève Réserve Ancéstrale 50: an excellent example of an old PC; lighter, more elegant and less *rancio*-y than an old brandy from the GC, about as good as you can get from the PC.

Exshaw

An old-established firm, once famous in Britain – and India. Post-war decline led to sale to *Otard* in 1975. No longer produced.

Pierre Ferrand

Alexandre Gabriel
Château de Bonbonnet
16130 Ars
Tel: +33 545 36 62 50

In 1989 two business-school friends bought the rights to use the name of Pierre Ferrand, an old-established producer (who has set up as Pierre de Segonzac (qv). Also using stock from a nearby distiller in the Grande Champagne they could offer an excellent range of GC cognacs. They then bought the Logis d'Angeac, a 37-hectares estate in the Grande Champagne now extended to 102 hectares where they make all the Ferrand cognacs: Ambre, Reserve, Selection des Anges, Abel and Ancestral All Grande Champagne, distilled on the lees. A small range of small estate cognacs often in limited editions is distilled by *bouilleurs de cru* under the label Gabriel & Associés (G&A). The firm is now owned exclusively by Alexandre Gabriel.

GC Ambre 10: light colour, very agreeable overtones of pear on nose and palate.

*Reserve 20: delicious, crisp, baked-appley.

Borderies Light: manzanilla colour, light style but unmistakable Borderies nuttiness.

Selection des Anges 30: light agreeable *rancio* nose, a little wood but still fresh and delicious.

*Ancestrale Light: apricot colour, long, rich, good *rancio*, but not too heavy.

XO: sprightly, light floral nose, no *rancio* but very agreeable.

Also sells cognac from four small estates: Ch de Clam FB 8 y/o; Domaine Varennes Borderies 15 y/o; Domaine Fleuret PC 25 y/o, 42% and Domaine de Communion GC 35 y/o, 43%. Also a second brand, Landy, for the Far East.

Jean Fillioux

Domaine De La Pouyade
16130 Juillac-le-Coq, France
Tel: +33 545 83 04 09
e.mail: cognac-jeanfillioux@orange.fr

Founded in 1880 by an independent-minded member of the Fillioux family, the company was a distiller for Hennessy for a century and a half. Since then they've been selling cognacs from their own twenty-two hectare estate in the Grande Champagne as well as those from two other estates in the region. All their cognacs are pure and clean with no trace of caramel!

*La Pouyade: light lemon colour, very fresh with a clean grapey feel on nose and palate.

So Elegantissime XO: again, light lemon colour, fresh floral warmth on nose and palate.

1992: light gold colour; full roasted pepper feel on nose and palate,

Tres Vieux: light gold colour; full, rich but fresh *rancio*-y nose and palate.

Reserve Familiale GC: fruity aromas dominate; dry, round, long, classic well-aged.

Michel Forgeron (BC, C du C)

Chez Richon
16130 Segonzac
Tel: +33 545 83 43 05
cognacforgeron@wanadoo.fr

Classic GC producer, established a few miles east of Segonzac in the mid-nineteenth century. In the 1960s the independent-minded Michel started turning what had been a largely agricultural estate into a vineyard. He built his own still in 1965 and started selling direct in 1977, largely through his dynamic wife Françoise.

2000: clean, fresh, chocolatey but only a little burn on the finish thanks to very slow disillation.

10: deep apricot nose, fresh, clean and floral, a little burn.

20: fresh candied fruit on nose and palate.

30: deep baked pineapple nose, rich, *rancio*-y but a trifle alcoholic.

*VSOP: 43%, nice, rich, well-balanced at twelve years. Any other producer would have called it a Napoleon!

XO: 45%, over twenty years, rich and long but still some burn on the finish, probably due to the strength.

1975: 47%, very rounded, slightly woody nose, complex with good *rancio*.

*Hors d'Age: a truly serious fifty-year-old, exceptionally concentrated and complex with overtones of candied fruits and sandalwood.

Lucien Foucauld

Old established firm now part of *Compagnie Commerciale de Guyenne*. The name is used only for brandies sold to German supermarket group Metro.

Cognac Frapin

Soc P. Frapin & Cie
Rue Pierre Frapin
CS 40101 - 16130 Segonzac
Tel: +33 545 83 90 51
Email: anne@chateaufontpinot-frapin.com

Frapin, with its rose-haunted courtyard, is the only major firm to be based in Segonzac. Its brandies all come from the biggest single estate in the rolling chalky heartland of the Grande Champagne, and is a key element in the history of Rémy Martin [qv]. Since 1984, when the Cointreau family took over what was then a forgotten brand, they have been selling increasing quantities of brandies – even so their stocks represent eighteen years of sales.

VS 5–6: light colour, delicious florality on the nose.

*VSOP 10–12: nice colour, feels even older than it is – I would have guessed a 15-year cognac, i.e. between Napoleon and XO – because of the number of older cognacs in the blend.

XO: Fontpinot made exclusively from grapes from the fabled vineyard of that name. Relatively young – 20–25 years – light, gold colour; rich, oily fruitiness on the nose; rich, vibrant, fruity on the palate.

VIP XO: older – around 35 years, old gold colour; light rancio on the nose; rich, dry and fruity on palate.

Extra 40–50 years: very rich, concentrated, fruity nose. Very concentrated fruit-and-nut on the palate.

*Plume Frapin: up to 80 years old, kept in even older casks; deep, rich *rancio* on nose and palate; very long and satisfying.

Over the past few years they have offered a series of 'multi-Millesime' blended from three excellent vintages, none more than thirty years old, none produced in quantities of more than 1270 bottles, and all different though they all combine *rancio* with complexity and fruitiness. They are matured carefully with only six months in new wood, a much shorter period than is normal with other Frapin cognacs. Some years – like 1984 – were not considered good enough for the blend. The latest selection, the fifth, is of the 1982, 1986 and 1989 vintages.

A de Fussigny

23 Place Jean Monnet
16100 Cognac
Tel: +33 545 36 42 60
cognac@a-de-fussigny.com

Founded by Alain Royer, of the Louis Royer family, to sell small lots of fine cognacs. Since then it has passed through a number of hands.

NYAK: the way the rap world pronounces cognac. Not your average VS. Rich, lots of brandies from the Champagnes.

VSOP FB: Pale lemon–gold colour; light, floral feel on nose and palate; a bit short and lacks concentration.

VSOP Borderies: Unusual cognac. Light, gold colour, typical Borderies nuttiness on the nose and palate.

VSOP PC: Light, gold colour, woody nose, rich but rather young.

VSOP GC: Fresh, elegant, floral nose; rich on palate but inevitably a trifle young.

Selection: Sharp, floral nose, nutty but young.

Superieur: Light colour, fruit-and-nut nose, but rather short and dry.

Cigar Blend: has the requisite chocolate richness to cope with a good cigar.

Cognac de Collection La Gabare
16370 Cherves de Cognac
Tel: +33 493 99 72 52

The result of a happy partnership between Ferdinand de Bakker, a retired PR executive and Jean Grosperrin, an experienced Cognac broker and his son Guilhem who own the majority of the company and manage it. They select small lots of fine – and often old – cognacs. Their best offerings – which obviously change from time to time – include:

1972: FB, fine and floral.

1944: BB, a remarkable brandy. Very pure nose, and like a fine bourbon whiskey on the palate.

Gaston de La Grange
Brand invented by Martini, and now part of *Otard*.

VSOP: rather sharp.

XO: rouge; nice, round, fruity nose; good commercial cognac.

XO: black, GC, rich fruitcake nose, candied fruit.

Gauthier (C du C)
Chez Nadaud
16120 Malaville
Tel: +33 545 97 53 19
gauthier.earl@wanadoo.fr

Bernard Gauthier's family was first established at Le Petit Gauthier near Malaville in 1750. Yet he is far from being a traditionalist, his ideas make him one of the most original producers in the Grande Champagne. He grows his vines high as *hautes vignes* for extra protection of the grapes against scorching by the sun as well as other weather damage. They have also been practising organic farming for over 25 years.

*Réserve de la Famille: round and rich with overtones of vanilla pastry.

GC Très Vieux (20 year old): a lovely, fruity, *rancio* richness.

Gautier
28 Rue des Ponts
16140 Aigre
Tel: +33 545 21 10 02
Now part of the Belvedere group which includes the Marie Brizard empire. Housed in a picturesque eighteenth-century water mill in Aigre, in the heart of the Fins Bois.
VS: nice floral feel on nose and palate. ISC Bronze 2003.
Myriade: FC crisp and round, not very long, but easy drinking; an excellent introductory cognac.
XO Gold & Blue 15+: again, easy drinking, round, unremarkable.
Pinar del Rio: hard and rich to cope with cigars, named after the leading cigar-making 'appellation' in Cuba.

Jules Gautret
Brand from *Unicognac*.
Rois des Roi XO: rich, fruity, 20+; a little caramelised.
Extra: very old, virtually no reduction in strength, traditional style, very long, concentrated but a bit woody.

Geffard
16130 Verrières
Tel: +33 545 83 02 74
The family of the present principal, Henri Geffard, has been making cognac for five generations at their property at Verrières in the heart of the Grande Champagne since 1840. He and his two sons cultivate 29 hectares of vines between Verrières and Juillac-le-Coq.
VSOP: very round on the palate, overtones of coffee and spices but lacks concentration.
Vieille Réserve: despite its slight resinous woodiness it's also long, rich and deep.

Godet
1 Rue du Duc
17003 La Rochelle
Tel: +33 546 41 10 66
Email: godetexport@cognacgodet.com
The only survivor of the numerous families of Dutch origin who settled in La Rochelle in the sixteenth century when it was the leading port for exports from the region. Originally, like their competitors, they exported cognac only in cask, but now sell in bottle. Bought by the British giant, Grand Met in 1989 then bought back by Jean-Jacques Godet, an enthusiast for Folle Blanche, six years later.
VS de Luxe: as the name implies it is indeed a superior VS with some Borderies.
Séléction Spéciale 10: a superior VSOP; nice, refreshing, floral nose; good length, no burn.
*Folle Blanche Epicure: floral roundness, very deep but light, exceptionally elegant.

Gastronome FC: especially bracing, refreshing, tonic cognac, unripe gooseberry on nose, no apparent wood.

Excellence: Some Borderies and it shows, nutty but not heavy, refreshing. ISC Gold 2000.

XO FC 35: classic, light, *rancio* nose and on palate.

Reserve de la Famille GC Vieilles Borderies: a single lot, deep, characteristically nutty

Reserve de la Famille GC Extra Vieille

Reserve de la Famille GC d'Ambleville

Vintages: 1965 GC, 1970 PC, 1971 FB, 1972 FB, 1975 FB, 1979 GC.

Léopold Gourmel

BP 194

16016 Cognac

Tel: +33 545 82 07 29

Leopold-Gourmel@leopold-gourmel.com

One of the handful of firms exploiting the very special qualities of the best brandies from the Fins Bois. It was founded by the late M. Voisin, who owned the franchise for Volvo and Fiat in the region and was a passionate cognac lover. He discovered a couple of suppliers of fine brandies in the mini-region called the Petite Champagne de Blanzac in the south east of the Fins Bois, stored casks of their cognacs and then started to sell them under his wife's maiden name. Today the business, run by his son-in-law Olivier Blanc, exploits the very different qualities of the brandies as they mature, starting off floral, then fruity and then getting more complex and spicy as they age well for far longer than most brandies from the Fins Bois.

Petit Gourmel 8: no malolactic fermentation, orangey, nutty–peary nose.

Age des Fruits 13: relatively rich and round with strong overtones of almond kernels.

*Age des Fleurs 16: vanilla, floral, delicate, long, rich.

*Age des Epices 22: oily, grapey, peppery, with a lovely roundness and complexity.

Quintessence 30+: changing this to younger casks after a decade in older wood gives it a delicious lightness and freshness as well as complexity – but no *rancio*.

*Bio Attitude: One of very, very few organic cognacs. They are all single vintages and the 2004, 2005 and 2006 all share qualities of youth, cleanliness, a delightful floral nose, while being refreshingly light; almost appley–peary on the palate.

La Fontaine de La Pouyade

La Pouyade

16120 Bassac - France

Tel: +33 (0)5 45 81 92 88

www.plantevigne-dubosquet.com

La Fontaine de La Pouyade Classic: mature GC with plenty of *rancio*.

La Grolette

(*see* Ordonneau)

Gronstedts

House brand of the Swedish alcohol monopoly. Excellent basic quality cognacs, VS and VSOP.

Jean Grosperrin

La Gabare SA
17460 Chermignac
Tel: +33 546 90 48 16
ggrosperrin@yahoo.fr

One of the regrettably rare reliable firms selling old cognacs dating back to the 1940s from the whole region, e.g. a 1940 Bons Bois, together with some truly aged treasures.

Guillon-Painturaud (SEC)

Biard
16130 Segonzac
Tel: +33 545 83 41 95
info@guillon-painturaud.com

The Guillon family has been living on this 18-hectare 'farm' in the GC near Segonzac since 1610, run by Madame Line Sauvant who sells cognacs of specific ages, all GC.
VSOP: 5 y/o, light, slightly burny, floral on nose and palate, long.
Vieille Réserve: 20 y/o ; nice rich grapiness on nose; young and sparky for its age.
*Hors d'Age: 30 y/o, good *rancio* on nose, some fruit, sprightly.
Renaissance single vintage: 40 y/o, mature, nutty, a little wood, rich *rancio*.

Hardy

142 Rue Basse de Crouin
16100 Cognac
Tel: +33 545 82 59 55
info@hardycognac.fr

A family firm founded in 1863. In the 1980s it went into administration and was bought by a cooperative. Now, having made a considerable recovery, it has been bold enough to launch a range of luxury cognacs.
*VSOP FC: Apple, flower and fruit on the nose, with excellent baked apple on palate.
XO FC: Rich and nutty on nose and palate.
Noces d'Or: One of the range of luxury cognacs. Deep rancio, nut–chocolate nose, rich on the palate.

Hennessy

1 Rue de la Richonne
16101 Cognac
Tel: +33 545 82 52 22
www.hennessy.com

One of the two dominant forces in the cognac trade since the French Revolution and today the unquestioned world leader – its VS alone accounts for about one bottle in four of all the cognacs sold in the world. Family-owned until 1971 when merged with Moët & Chandon it is now part of the giant LVMH-Louis Vuitton combine. Its cognacs, still blended by a member of the Fillioux family which has been responsible for over a hundred and fifty years, generally combine richness with a certain structure. They are rarely labelled as coming from the Champagnes, although it has a major distillery in the region.

VS: nice, warm, round, grapey nose and palate, relatively mature, typical traditional Hennessy.

Classium VS: designed for the Chinese market. Nice and spicy, round with a little wood.

Pure White: a triumph of technical achievement to have produced a cognac which is clean and elegant, not fiery, yet without any of the colour associated with any brandy. Now sold exclusively in the Caribbean.

Fine de Cognac VSOP: light, elegant, young, clean – no new wood and it shows.

Privilege VSOP: traditional, rich, warm, grapey nose; good concentration and depth, but still clean. Strong enough to drink with an ice-cube.

XO: very rich, long and caramelly.

*****Private Reserve:** As the name indicates it was indeed originally blended from a mere fourteen brandies for the Hennessy family. Very elegant and long, made from 20–30 year old brandies.

Hennessy Black: has a nice flowery nose and good non-cloying richness on the palate. Long. No indication of origin, probably lots of the best FB. Advertised as 'made to mix'.

*****Paradis Imperial:** Long with some *rancio*, more elegant than normal house style.

*****Richard:** the – incredibly expensive – sum of their brandies, richer but less elegant than the Paradis.

*****Paradis Extra:** a superb brandy, long, with some *rancio*, more elegant than normal house style.

Hermitage (BC)

A range of single vintages from 1900 to 2000 from small firms and individual growers, scrupulously selected by David Baker of *Brandy Classics*. These are his tasting notes.

Chez Richon, Grande Champagne: flavours of pineapple, toffee and burnt almonds; unusual for so young a cognac.

10 y/o Jarnac Champagne, GC: Mostly Ugni Blanc, but unusually also some Colombard and Folle Blanche. The aroma is predominantly dried apricot and peaches.

1993 Ambleville, GC: pale and delicate in colour and taste. On the palate, lots of yellow fruit, melon and pear, followed by a fresh peppermint and eucalyptus.

1991 Ambleville, GC: pale and delicate in colour and taste, with a flavour reminiscent of agave, aloe (gripe water), and almonds.

1988 Chez Richon, GC: a fruity flavour with citrus and spicy tones, slightly sweeter than the others of this era.

25 y/o GC, Segonzac: long and complex.

30 y/o PC, Réaux: smooth and rich, toffee and chocolate.

1975 Chez Richon, GC

43 y/o GC, Segonzac: rich and tangy.
Provenance 10 Complex
Provenance 25: *Cognac Masters 2014 – Masters Award.* The wonderfully complex flavours of this cognac are result from it having been kept in oak barrels in damp cellars for over 25 years.
Provenance 30

Hine
16 Quai de l'Orangerie
16200 Jarnac
Tel: +33 545 35 59 59

Founded in 1782 by an immigrant from Dorset who married a Mselle Delamain. For nearly two centuries the firm's brandies, like those of Delamain, were British favourites, many of them 'Early Landed, Late Bottled'. The family sold to the Distillers Company which itself was taken over by Guinness in 1986. Now owned by a private French family firm, it offers a few beautifully balanced, rich but elegant brandies which have been distilled and blended under the watchful eye of Bernard Hine, the last member of the family to be involved in the firm.

H by Hine PC: can be used for cocktails. Florality – and liquorice – on the nose, nicely rich, slight burn.
*Rare & Delicate: an up-market VSOP – the average age of the brandies, at around ten years, is far above that of the usual offering.
*Hine Antique XO Premier Cru: a unique, raisiny concentration with an unobtrusive touch of wood that holds the blend together.
Triomphe and **Mariage:** classic examples of the rich, chocolate fruit-and-nut qualities found in classic mature cognacs from the GC.
Homage: Like *Frapin*, Hine has produced a cognac formed from three vintages (1984, 1986 and 1987) and twenty cognacs, three of them Early Landed. Very flowery and fragrant, fresh and young on the palate – no *rancio* – but no alcoholic burn.
Bonneuil 2006: after Hine bought some superb vines in the heart of the GC it made a deeply satisfiying, deeply floral nine-year old brandy.

Also offers a number of single vintages, an early landed and an older one matured in Cognac as well as a vintage pack with three 20cl bottles from the 1957, 1975 and 1981 vintages.

Jenssen
Jenssen SARL
Le Maine Pertubaud
16120 Bonneuil
Tel: +33 545 96 02 78
info@jenssen.fr

In 2000 and 2001 a Norwegian, Espen Schulerud Soland, bought all the buildings in this hamlet together with the vines. He used the grapes – and some bought in from other properties in the Grande Champagne – to launch a range of distinguished cognacs called, for some unknown reason, Jenssen

Carte Blanche GC: fresh, floral, fruity nose, a trifle young but refreshingly grapey.

XO GC: darker colour, slightly woody on the palate, losing its fruit and a little leathery but long and satisfying.

Hors d'Age: 41.6%, rather dry on the palate, a truly old, woody, leathery cognac – but some dried fruit.

L'Epiphanie Hors d'Age: 42%, very deep *rancio*, real rich fruitcake on the nose, very well balanced.

Arcana: 43%, the model of a very old cognac that, for once, has not been left in the wood too long.

Kelt

Château de St Aubin
32800 Réans
Tel: +33 562 09 98 18

In 1987, after his retirement, a Swedish businessman, Otto Kelt, a former maker of crisp diet rolls had an apparently mad, but splendidly successful idea: to copy the eighteenth-century habit of selling cognacs only after they have been round the world in casks in the hold of a ship. The result is a speedier maturation and well-integrated cognacs.

VSOP Tour du Monde: one of the rare VSOPs from the GC and it shows.

XO GC Tour du Monde: rich and powerful but not cloying or blowsy.

Lafragette

L & L Cognac SA
17 Rue des Gabariers
16100 Cognac
Tel: +33 545 36 61 36
organic.lafragette@wanadoo.fr

One of the rare organic producers – made in an organic distillery from organic growers' wines from the Champagnes.

Fins and Bons Bois: lovely, pure, floral nose combined with excellent bite.

Landy

(*see* Pierre Ferrand)

Larsen

66 Boulevard de Paris BP 41
16100 Cognac
Tel: +33 545 82 05 88
frederic.larsen@wanadoo.fr

'Viking' firm founded by immigrants from Norway and specialising in ceramic containers – including Viking ships. Very enterprising, one of the first firms to sell on the net and has a shop in Jarnac. Sold to Rémy Martin in 2012 and in 2015 to major Finnish spirits business Altia.

*VSOP: elegant, floral, delicious.

Alain Lebecq (C du C)

16300 Criteuil la Magdeleine
Tel: +33 545 80 56 27
lebecqassocies@wanadoo.fr

Alain and Laurence Lebecq have 21 hectares of vines in the commune of Criteuil la Magdeleine in the heart of the Grande Champagne with four centuries of family knowledge behind them. Alain is also a passionate huntsman (hence the availability of their VSOP in a hip flask for someone on the move) with a pack of hounds. The cognacs of Delaunay were originally named for the other branch of the family but are now sold by the Lebecqs.

VSOP: elegant, nutty, well balanced, but lack of concentration on the finish. Chosen for the *2010 Guide Hachette.*

XO de M. Delaunay: very round and civilised.

L'Exigence de M D: delicious, slightly fruity nose, not great concentration.

Leyrat (Edevie)

Same owner as *ABK6.*

Cognacs from the same 'Petites Champagnes de Blanzac in the Fins Bois' as exploited by *Léopold Gourmel.*

Lot no. 10: no new oak; nice, clean, floral nose; not burny but sparky.

*VSOP: warm, clean, buttery nose, fruit-and-nut chocolate on palate.

XO: fresh, floral, grapey no *rancio.*

*1971: 43% but it doesn't show! A truly fine FB. Lovely floral nose, fresh but a little *rancio,* excellent dark chocolate feel.

Guy Lheraud

Domaine de Lasdoux
Angeac-Charente
16120 Châteauneuf
Tel: +33 545 97 12 33

A typically long-established – in their case since 1639 – family which now owns 62 hectares on some of the best chalky slopes in the Petite Champagne. Uses a little Colombard and Folle Blanche to enrich the family's best brandies. Uses new oak but no caramel, boisé or syrup so all their brandies are clean and true to their origins.

20 PC: warm and rich, yet not caramelly. Excellent fruit.

*Paradis Antique: distilled in 1942. Lovely, light, well-balanced nose, everything well-absorbed. You forget it's 45%.

Logis de la Mothe

16300 Criteuil
Barbezieux
Tel: +33 545 80 54 02

Since 1865 the Jullien family has owned 61 hectares of vines in the Grande Champagne centred round a beautiful *logis,* a fortified farmhouse.

*VSOP: lovely, round, plummy nose and palate with the depth of a Napoleon.

Trois Ecussons VSOP

XO: serious *rancio* nose but younger and less full than the VSOP.

De Luze

Domaine Boinaud

16130 Angeac-Champagne

Tel: +33 545 83 72 72

De Luze was a famous name in Bordeaux with a business in Cognac based on the Domaine de Chaine in the Grande Champagne. In 2006 the name was bought by the Boinaud family. Distillers since the seventeenth century they now own over 100 hectares of vines and forty-one stills, the second biggest distillery in the region. Until 2006 they had remained out of the public eye, 'to live happily live hidden' being their motto.

S: two-thirds from their own vineyards, nice and oily and very round.

XO: 43%, brandies between ten and thirty years old, warm and rich.

Marcardier-Barbot (C du C)

Le Pible

16130 Segonzac

Tel: +33 545 83 41 18

marcadierbarbot@wanadoo.fr

VSOP: nice overtones of sandalwood but a trifle young and woody.

Napoleon: nutty, with candied fruits, but ends rather dry.

XO: charming new style but a little perfumed.

Hors d'Age: incredible concentration and length, classic old-style, slightly woody cognac – Louis XIII at a tenth of the price.

Martell

Place Edouard Martell

16101 Cognac

Tel: +33 545 36 33 33

For two centuries one of the two family companies which, with Hennessy, dominated the world of Cognac. Unfortunately in 1989 the family sold the company to the American group Seagram which promptly proceeded to wreck it, introducing hordes of new cognacs without much success. Since 2001 it has been restored to profitability by the Pernod-Ricard group.

Throughout its history Martell has gone its own way in the style of its cognacs. For over a century they were blended by the Chapeau family who had always relied on a relatively neutral style of brandy, made from wines from the Fins Bois and the Borderies which provided their unique qualities. The brandies' character was largely formed by maturation in casks made from oak from the Troncais. The result was a dryer style than most.

VS: powerful, some fruit, good mixer.

VSOP: very powerful, some PC, raisiny, ideal for the cocktail Horses' Neck.

Caractère: light gold colour; deeply nutty on both nose and palate

Distinction dark gold colour; very deep nose with some *rancio*; very long and nutty but rather dry

Noblige VSOP+: the old FB give complexity and nice dried fruits, a little wood.

***Cordon Bleu:** historically Martell's major up-market cognac, first produced in 1912. Over 30% cognacs from the Borderies, complex, very aromatic, rich but not dry, spiced bread, a real mouth-filler.

XO: a sumptuous cognac with all the deep rich fruitcake characteristic of the *rancio*. Much longer than Cordon Bleu.

Chanteloup Perspective: from all four major regions. Natural richness, lots of candied fruit, very long, a touch of *rancio*.

***Creation 'Grand Extra':** lots of old GC, so rich and *rancio*-y, fruit-and-nut dark chocolate, orange and lemon peel. A little wood at the end palate.

L'Or de Jean Martell: quintessence of the Martell style, 10–100 y/o GC and Borderies, very well-balanced and concentrated, spicy, a touch leathery, very long, deep and aromatic.

Martell is now offering some single vintage cognacs in its 'Millésime Collection', available only in duty-free in Asia.

Menard

BP 16
2 Rue de la Cure
16720 St Même-les-Carrières
Tel: +33 545 81 90 26
menard@cognac-menard.com

Long-established 80 hectare family estate at the unfashionable eastern edge of the Grande Champagne.

VSOP: a very fresh and agreeable blend, a very commercial cognac.

Ancestrale: 45%, again a very agreeable thirty year old cognac, lots of fruit-and-nut.

Merlet

Chevessac
17610 Saint Savant
Tel: +33 546 91 50 36

Family firm making liqueurs as well as cognac, which it started to sell under its own name in 2010.

Brothers Blend VSOP: designed to be the base for cocktails; rich and clean – no caramel.

Saint Savant XO: warm, rich fruit-and-nut on nose and palate.

Mery

1T Route de Pruneau
16130 Salles d'Angles

A twenty-three hectare estate in the heart of the Grande Champagne. Formerly a Remy Martin supplier and now one of the few biodynamic cognac producers.

VS: nice, fresh, floral nose, light and elegant on the palate.

VSOP: rather dumb on the nose; woody but concentrated on the palate.

XO: good fruit-and-nut on the nose; a fresh richness on the palate.

Extra: 40 years old and it shows; elegant with candied fruit.

Meukow

Old-established firm now part of, and flagship brand of, *Compagnie Commerciale de Guyenne* .

VSOP: good warm nose, a little caramely, a nice commercial cognac.

XO: specially blended for the Russian market; crisp, floral, appley feel.

Extra: a light, delicate brandy.

Rarissime: 41.3%, seriously well-balanced floral/fruity cognac.

Monnet

16 Quai de l'Orangerie

16200 Jarnac

Tel: +33 545 35 59 59

info@monnetcognac.com

XO: a little *rancio* and very agreeable. Good value.

Logis de Montifaud

16130 Salles d'Angles

Tel: +33 545 83 67 45

info@logis-montifuad.com

Family estate still run by Christian Landreau whose family bought this seventeenth-century farmhouse in 1999 after having made wine at Criteuil for over a century.

Mounier

(*see* Unicoop)

Moyet

62 rue de l'Industrie BP 106

16104 Cognac

Tel: +33 545 82 04 53

An old firm rescued by two businessmen, Marc Georges and Pierre Dubarry. When they took over in 1984 Moyet was a sleeping beauty, home to splendid casks of old cognacs and a cellarmaster, Honoré Piquepaille, who had cherished them for seventy years. Their qualities were discovered by some leading Paris restaurateurs and since then Pierre Dubarry has built up a deserved reputation for providing fine cognacs.

Cognac des Fins Bois: nice floral nose, elegant, spring flowers on the palate though some *brûle*.

VSOP: FC, delightful cognac, well above the average VSOP; chocolatey with a little *rancio* – unusual in a VSOP and due to some age.

Cognac de PC: agreeable florality.

Cognac FC: rather heavy, not as delicate or elegant as the firm's other offerings.
*Cognac des Borderies: 43%, the real nutty stuff, tastes over 20 years old.
Cognac FC XO: 35ish y/o, round, fat, oily nose with real chocolatey *rancio*.

They also always have a number of special offers that are well worth tasting.

Normandin-Mercier

Château de la Péraudière
17139 Dompierre
Tel: +33 546 68 00 65
Cognac.normandin-mercier@wanadoo.fr

Family firm founded in 1872 by a broker, M. Normandin, who worked with his mother-in-law Madame Mercier and soon bought the château just north of La Rochelle where the firm is still based. For twenty-five years after 1945 the firm specialised in selling old cognacs to major firms but since the 1970s has specialised in selling fine old brandies. Jean-Marie Normandin buys only from the Champagnes and matures them in his own cellars, because these are damp due to the proximity to the sea the cognacs are not aggressive.
Fine PC: elegant nose, slight burn on end but very persistent light fruit.
Très Vieille GC: elegant, round and long with aromas of flowers; hints of fruit develop with time, magic palate of considerable length.
PC Vieille: rich aromas, dry, finesse, touch of spice, pleasant *rancio*, hints of curry, tobacco and jams and jellies, very long.

Ordonneau (BC)

Domaine de la Grolette
16370 Cherves Richemont
Tel: +33 545 83 80 37
cognacordonneau.com

Long-established estate at Cherves, just outside Cognac. Today it is run proudly by two paraplegics who sell some of the greatest of all cognacs from the Borderies.
Borderies: 25–30 y/o, very clean with overtones of hazelnut toffee.
*Grande Vieille: the epitome of all that is nutty and spicy about the region's cognac, a miracle of complexity; rich, nutty, leathery.

Otard

Château de Cognac
127 Boulevard Denfert-Rochereau
16101 Cognac
Tel: +33 545 82 40 00

Sold to Bacardi in 1975, this was rather neglected at first but has now been relaunched as Baron Otard with more serious and elegantly packaged cognacs.
Baron Otard VS: light gold colour; nice, rich, fruity overtones on both nose and palate.
Baron Otard VSOP: more elegant, deep, rich, flowery nose, long and fragrant on the palate.

Baron Otard XO: gold, densely concentrated fruity feel on both nose and palate.
Baron Otard Extra 1795: deep nutty nose, fresh and nutty on the palate.

Payrault
(*see* Château de Montifaud)

Pierre de Segonzac
La Nerolle
16130 Segonzac
Tel: +33 545 83 41 82

Soon after *Pierre Ferrand* sold his name he set up under a new name to sell brandies from his estate in the heart of the Grande Champagne, owned by his family since 1702. He's the archetypal peasant, complete with beret, and his farm buildings are equally typically Charentais.

Sélection des Anges: well balanced on the nose, a touch of spice, round, very long.
Ancestrale: very deep, elegant and fruity nose. On the palate a serious old cognac with the touch of woodiness; typical old-style cognac.

Planat
Subsidiary of *Camus* which bought it from a certain M. Pionneau who had his own ideas about cognacs, which he liked old-fashioned. The new owners use the brand for some fine cognacs, including a number of single vintage brandies.

XO: nicely floral and fruity.
Extra Vieille XO: classic thirty year old with good *rancio*, long.
FB 1967: heavy, floral nose; baked apple feel on palate.

Prince Hubert de Polignac
In 1947 the Polignac family – which then owned Lanson and Pommery champagnes – licensed the Unicoop co-operative [qv] to use the name of Prince Hubert de Polignac.

VS: nice round nose, fruity, albeit a bit sugary. Ideal for mixing with ice etc.
VSOP: run of the mill, not concentrated enough for mixing.
Dynasty: good *rancio*, complex aromas, round, long.

Roger Prisset
Domaine de la Font de Bussac
16250 Jurignac
Tel: +33 545 66 37 55
florence@bobe.fr

Annie and Roger Prisset are the fourth generation of cognac producers at Puycaillon, set high above the border of the Grande and Petite Champagne. For 104 years, the family has been cultivating and distilling Fine Champagne cognac from their 30 hectares of vines, now managed by Florence of the fifth generation.

VSOP: complex *rancio* with nice, spicy, woody overtones.

XO 35: long and complex, some leather and wood on the finish.
1962 Petite Fine Champagne: rich, lots of *rancio* but fades.

Prunier (BC)

Maison Prunier
7 avenue Leclerc
16102 Cognac
Tel: +33 545 35 00 14
prunier@gofornet.com

Small but highly-regarded family firm whose members have been distilling since 1700. Now run by the Burnez family which was called in by M. Prunier in 1918.

Fins Bois: 20 y/o, delicious.
XO: as delicate and profound as a Delamain.
Twenty Year Old: a model cognac of its age.

Ragnaud-Sabourin (Edevie)

Domaine de la Voûte
Ambleville
16300 Barbezieux
Tel: +33 545 80 54 61
Ragnaud-sabourin@swfrance.com

La Voûte, a prestigious estate just south of Fontpinot (cf Frapin) was established in 1850 by Gaston Briand, a well-known figure who helped to found the INAO and one of the first in the region to push for an establishment of recognised *crus*. But throughout his long life he preferred to sell his brandies to his friends, the Hennessys. In the 1930s he was persuaded by the great French wine writer Raymond Baudoin to sell his brandies to a few select restaurants, but right up to his death – in his eighties in 1957 – the label on each bottle was laboriously hand-written, usually after Sunday lunch, by Briand and his son-in-law Marcel Ragnaud. (I suspect that most of the handwriting on lesser bottles sold by other growers to give the impression that they are of the highest quality is in imitation of their splendid penmanship!) While one son, Marcel, developed Ragnaud-Sabourin, in 1941 Raymond Ragnaud set off on his own brand. Ragnaud Sabourin is now run by three descendants, from grandmother to grandson and granddaughter: Annie, Olivier and Patricia Ragnaud-Sabourin.

VSOP: elegant and agreeable but relatively unremarkable.
Réserve Spéciale: 43%, buttery, rich. Made from all eight permitted varieties. Light, pure, floral nose. Rich and a little nutty – but still floral – on the palate.
XO Alliance 25: a little Folle Blanche but lacks complexity compared with the family's other cognacs.
*Fontvieille Alliance 35: 43%, superbly balanced, elegant, long, *rancio*-y but not heavy. Two-fifths Colombard and Folle Blanche.
*Florilege 45: 46% undiluted. Some of the purest *rancio* I have ever come across; lovely fruitcake feel at the end – 40% Folle Blanche.

Raymond Ragnaud (BC)

Le Château
Ambleville
16300 Barbezieux.
Tel: +33 545 80 54 57
Raymond_ragnaud@le-cognac.com

Classic GC estate of 44 hectares at Ambleville. Already in 1860 the family owned a small estate in the GC. Paul Ragnaud installed himself at the château – in reality a small manor house and in 1974 the family as they put it 'declared its independence' by selling direct. They don't filter so the cognacs are rich.

Selection: 4y/o, lovely fruity nose, round and rich but burns a little, suffers from not being blended.

Reserve: tastes like a 7 y/o; very elegant and pure; fruity, rather over-woody, slightly spirity on the nose.

Napoleon: chestnut colour, wood well absorbed; long, complex, rich nose of candied fruit, some *rancio*.

Grande Reserve: 15 y/o, no new wood.

Reserve Rare: 18-year-old taste.

XO 25: rich chestnut colour, full *rancio*, very little wood, fresh.

Extra Vieux: 42%, around 25 y/o and it shows in this truly classic GC with all the balance and notes of candied and dried fruits appropriate to the age and *cru*.

Très Vieux 40: fat, buttery, concentrated.

*Hors d'Age 43°: 35 y/o, the full complexity of a great GC; rich, immensely satisfying brandy.

Rémy Martin

20 Rue de la Société Viticole
16100 Cognac.
Tel: +33 545 35 16 15

The most extraordinary success story in Cognac during the twentieth century. All the firm's brandies still come from the Champagnes and are still distilled on their lees to provide greater richness.

*VSOP: still the standard by which all others are measured; 15y/o, very spicy, bread, candied fruit, long.

Mature Cask Finish: sold only in Europe. Fruitier, with apricot overtones, rounder and more elegant than Rémy's traditional VSOP.

1738 Accord Royal: (after the year the first M. Rémy Martin got royal permission to plant more vines). Atypically for Rémy it is rich, smooth, concentrated and spicy; would be good with cigars – and chocolate.

*Coeur de Cognac: very smooth, creamy, delicious.

*Club: much richer, for the Chinese market.

*XO Excellence: 85% GC, 10–35 y/o, average 23 years; again, rich *fruits confits* – apricot, orange, prune – so concentrated that you don't even have to put your nose into the glass, so it's okay to put a little ice in the drink.

Extra 35: mostly GC, rich *rancio*, spicy and gingery.

Centaure de Diamant: for duty free; quite dry and woody on the nose but richer and well-balanced on the palate.

Louis XIII: quintessence of the Rémy style in a special Baccarat bottle. There's also the **Louis XIII Black Pearl**, the most intense cognac I have ever tasted, on sale at a mere $32,000.

Vintages: the only major firm to launch a series of specially selected vintages, sold under the name 'The Centaur's Collection', selected from a mere couple of hundred casks out of a total of 200,000.

Remy Tourny
Domaine de Montlambert
16100 Louzac Saint André
Tel: +33 545 82 27 86
remytourny@wanadoo.fr

Family with 30 hectare estate in the heart of the Borderies. Since M. Tourny himself died in 1996 his daughter and granddaughter decided to start selling some of his older brandies.

Fine Borderies 30: deep almond–violet nose, ends nice and nutty though lacks concentration on the middle palate.

Renault
Once a firm famous for its Carte Noire cognac. It was founded by Jean-Antoine Renault, the first to sell cognac exclusively in bottle. Bought by Pernod-Ricard in the 1970s. It was sold to the Finnish group Altia in 2010.

Le Reviseur
Brand owned by M. Abecassis (cf ABK6)

VS: pure and simple.

VSOP: more mature, spicy and appley.

XO PC: from a single estate, Barret west of Barbezieux. Nice, rich but not heavy good, raisiny fruit, bit of burn.

Roullet
Le Goulet de Foussignac
16200 Jarnac
Tel: +33 545 35 87 03

For nearly four centuries the Roullet family has been growing grapes, still including a little Colombard and Folle Blanche, on a 22-hectare estate in the heart of the Premiers Fins Bois de Jarnac. Now sells brandies from its extensive stocks.

Louis Royer
23 Rue Chail
BP 12
16200 Jarnac
Tel: +33 545 81 02 72
cognac@louis-royer.com

Founded in the nineteenth century this firm used to specialise in bulk cognacs, including those treated ('denatured') with salt and pepper for use by butchers. Since it was taken over after a family row by the Japanese drinks giant in 1989 it has been very enterprising, introducing excellent cognacs from different sub-regions in a five-pack of 20cl bottles, called 'Distilleries Collection', a clear and effective imitation of major whisky firms. All its cognacs are exemplary.

VSOP GC
Distilleries Collection
BB: a floral warmth most unusual in a 'mere' BB.

*FB: light milk fruit-and-nut chocolate nose and palate.

Borderies: good nut chocolate on nose but slightly burnt feel on the palate.

*PC: richly floral elegant 'sipping' cognac.

GC: again, the rich chocolately feel with some *rancio* and good concentration.

Salignac
Place du Château
16200 Jarnac
Tel: +33 545 35 55 55

Famous firm, now a subsidiary of Courvoisier making only an unremarkable VS destined for the American market with brandies from the Bons Bois west of Cognac.

Seguinot
La Nerolle
BP21 16130 Segonzac
Tel: +33 545 83 41 73
cognac@seguinot.fr

10 VSOP: very clean, fresh and floral.

Siècle d'Or (BC)
Brand produced by Brandy Classics.

Siècle d'Or Provenance 6 GC: good floral feel, long, slightly fiery.

Provenance 10: agreeable old-gold colour, fruit-and-nutty, still a little woodiness.

20: dark gold, very complex, fruit, nut, chocolate on nose. Very fresh.

A Tesseron
16120 Châteauneuf-sur-Charente
Tel: +33 545 62 52 61

Traditionally a wholesaler holding the region's largest stock of old cognacs. Now sells to some lucky few buyers. They get round the ban on dates by numbering their cognacs with the approximate date (eg 90 for the 1990).

Lot 90 XO Selection: clean, grapey, fresh and fragrant, just a hint of *rancio*.

*Lot 65 XO Emotion: dry, rich, elegant, tannic, long, light *rancio*.

*Lot 53 Topaz Perfection: rich, fruity nose, still very fresh and young, lots of *rancio*. A little *sous bois*.

Extreme: porty nose, as good as a truly old cognac can be, a classic expression of the qualities of a cognac from the GC.

Tiffon
29 Quai de l'Ile Madame
16200 Jarnac
Tel: +33 545 81 08 31

Founded by one Médéric Tiffon in 1875 and bought in 1946 by the Braastad family – *see* Courvoisier and Delamain – and since then has naturally concentrated on selling to the Scandinavian drinks monopolies.

VS: nice summer flowery nose but a bit short and sharp on the palate.

VSOP: rich, floral overtones on both nose and palate.

XO: rich and floral on nose and nut-chocolate on the palate.

Le Domaine de la Tour Vert
Guy Pinard et Fils
16200 Foussignac
Tel: +33 545 35 87 57
guy-pinard.com

The Pinard family have been wine growers and cognac producers for several generations. Today they own 32 hectares (80 acres) of land including a vineyard of 18 hectares (45 acres). Their property is in the little village of Foussignac, in the heart of the 'Fins Bois de Jarnac' a small sub-region which has been renowned for its elegant and floral cognacs for several hundred years. Since 1969 three generations of the family have cultivated their vines organically.

VS: 3+ years and the extra ageing shows in its excellent florality and purity.

VSOP: 6+ years, very elegant with some richness.

Napoleon: 10+ years, again this elegant richness but fruity rather than floral.

Folle Blanche 1999: light and floral on the nose, very rich and elegant; long, with overtones of late summer flowers.

*XO 1990: delicious, no *rancio*, epitome of Fins Bois de Jarnac.

1979: A little *rancio* but still recognisably FB elegance.

Maxime Trijol (Edevie)
17520 St-Martial-sur-Né
Tel: +33 546 49 53 31

The Trijol family has been growing grapes and distilling wine since 1859 and is now a major distiller with twenty stills, so only a proportion of its brandies come from its 30 hectares of vine. Used to sell its brandies under the name of Duboigalant, the maiden name of Madame Maxime Trijol.

Elegence: 4–10 y/o, clean and floral on nose and palate.

VSOP: 10–12 y/o, GC, very good fruitiness, depth and concentration on nose.

*XO 30 GC: rich florality and some *rancio* on nose, well balanced, and grapiness on palate.

70 Borderies: seriously nutty nose, followed through on the palate.

Cigar blend 35 GC: good fruit, some wood on the finish, more new oak than usual, strong structure to cope with cigars.

Unicognac

Route de Cognac
17500 Jonzac
Tel: +33 546 48 10 99

See also Jules Gautret.

One of the major co-operatives in the Cognac region with 3000 members, 250 of them growers owning 5,000 hectares of vines in the PC and FB.

Ansac: a special blend for the American market.

Roi des Rois: a prestige brand bottled in various crystal or porcelain containers.

Unicoop

49 Rue Lohmeyer
16102 Cognac
Tel: +33 545 82 45 7

The other major co-operative in the region, with 3,600 members who distil 250,000 hectolitres between them in all the major regions, although 45% are in the Fins Bois and 35% in the Bons Bois. Its business relies heavily on producing the ultra-premium Grey Goose vodka. In 1947 they bought Prince Hubert de Polignac [qv] and in 1969 they bought the old firm of H Mounier.

GLOSSARY

ACQUIT: official certificate of origin of an alcoholic drink.

ACQUIT JAUNE D'OR: special type of *acquit* required for cognac.

ALEMBIC CHARENTAIS (originally a *cucurbite* and also known as *chaudière d'eau de vie*): literally a spirit boiler. In reality the pot still, vat used for distilling cognac.

APPELLATION D'ORIGINE CONTRÔLÉE: legal guarantee that a wine or spirit conforms to certain provisions as to its geographical origin, the methods used in its production, the varieties of grape from which it is made, the maximum yield of the vines etc.

ARRONDISSEMENT: old name for a *canton* [qv]. Not to be confused with the Parisian variety.

ASSIGNATS: rapidly depreciating monetary certificates issued by the early revolutionary governments after 1789.

BAN DES VENDANGES: official starting date for the grape harvest. Before 1789 a feudal right, which ensured that the landlord's grapes were picked before those of the peasantry.

BARRIQUE DE COGNAC: before 1789 this held 27 *veltes* [qv]. By 1900 it held 275 litres, now usually 350 litres.

BASSIOT BASIN: bucket or other receptacle to catch the newly-distilled cognac as it emerges from the still.

BNIC: *see* Bureau National Interprofessionnel de Cognac.

BOIS: formerly wooded sub-regions representing the majority of the Cognac region. Before they were formally defined they were known by a wide variety of names including Premiers Fins Bois, Deuxième Bois, Bois Communes etc.

BOIS ORDINAIRES: outer semi-circle of the Cognac region with only a few hectares of vines.

BONS BOIS: the middle ring of vines in the Cognac appellation.

BONBONNE: glass jar holding approximately 25 litres used to store old cognacs.

BONNE CHAUFFE: second distillation which produces cognac.

BORDERIES: small rectangular sub-region north of Cognac which produces very special nutty brandies.

BOUILLEUR: distiller.

BOUILLEUR DE CRU: grower allowed to distill only his own wine.

BOUILLEUR DE PROFESSION: professional distiller allowed to distil wines from other producers.

BOUSINAGE: toasting the casks.

BRANDEWIJN, BRANDWIN, BRANDYWIJN: literally 'burnt wine'. Dutch term for brandy.

BROUILLIS: spirit of about 30 per cent produced by the first distillation.

BRÛLERIE: literally 'burning house', in fact, a distillery.

BUREAU NATIONAL INTERPROFESSIONNEL DE COGNAC (BNIC): cognac's ruling body set up in 1946 which supervises the production and sale of cognac.

BUYERS OWN BRAND (BOB): cognacs bottled under their own names by major buyers such as supermarkets and state liquor monopolies.

CAMPAGNE: the Cognac year, which runs from 1ˢᵗ September to 31ˢᵗ August.

CAMPANIAN (Fr: *Campanien*): A type of chalky soil found only in the Grande Champagne.

CANTON ADMINISTRATIVE: district, part of a *département* [qv] once called an *arrondissement*.

CHAMPAGNES: regions which produce the finest brandies, named after the Roman Campania. *See* Grande & Petite Champagne.

CHAPELET: the white circular head formed by newly distilled cognac when poured into a glass.

CHAPITEAU: literally a circus tent, the 'big top', a small, round container which traps the alcoholic vapours from the alembic below.

CHAUDIÈRE D'EAU DE VIE: former name for an alembic [qv].

CHAUFFE: literally 'heating'. Term used for one of the two passes through the still required to produce cognac.

CHAUFFE-VIN: cylinder in which wine is heated before it is distilled, using the heat from the newly-distilled brandy.

CHLOROSIS (Fr: *chlorose*): disease caused by an excess of chalk in the soil which chokes the vines.

COEUR: the heart of the distillation, the only portion which should be extracted.

COL: the neck of the still.

COL DE CYGNE: literally 'swan's neck', the modern shape of the *col*.

COLOMBARD (also called Colombat or French Colombard): grape variety widely planted in cognac in the eighteenth century. Still scattered plots.

COMPTES: term describing the age of cognacs.

COURTIERS: cognac brokers.

CRU: term describing the subdivisions of the Cognac region.

CUCURBITE: *see* alembic.

DÉPARTEMENT: French administrative unit, similar to a British county.

EARLY LANDED: cognacs shipped in cask soon after distillation to Britain where they are aged until bottled (hence the term Early Landed, Late Bottled).

EAU DE VIE: any brandy distilled from fruit.

ESPRIT DE VIN: term dating back to the eighteenth century for especially strong brandy.

ESPRIT DE COGNAC: a rectified spirit of 80–85 per cent in strength which can only be used in the production of sparkling wines.

FINE: French term for any brandy, in cognac the term simply means that a cognac comes from a specific region, as Fine Borderies.

FINE A L'EAU: brandy and water, formerly a favourite French *apéritif.*

FINE CHAMPAGNE: a blend of brandies from the Grande and Petite Champagne, with at least half coming from the Grande Champagne.

FINS BOIS: large and very varied region outside the Champagnes.

FOLLE BLANCHE: grape variety much planted in Cognac before the phylloxera which produced floral brandies. Now rare because of tendency to rot. Also called Folle in Cognac and Gros Plant in the mouth of the Loire valley.

FUREUR DE PLANTER: mania for planting vines that swept through France in the early eighteenth century.

GABARE: barge used for transporting brandy.

GABELLE: salt tax levied from the Middle Ages until 1789.

GROIES: special clay soil found only in the Borderies.

LEES: the detritus, leaves, skins and other solids left in the vat after fermentation.

LIMOUSIN: open-grained Limousin Pedunculata oak, originally from the forests round Limoges (hence the name), major source of wood for brandy casks (*see* also Troncais).

MAÎTRE DE CHAI: 'cellar master' responsible for the distillation, maturing and blending of cognacs.

MALOLACTIC FERMENTATION (Fr: *le malo*): Secondary fermentation in which the harsh malic acids in the wine are transformed into the smoother lactic acid.

MOUT: must, unfermented grape juice.

NAPOLEON: name attached to a – legally undefined – quality of Cognac, above VSOP [qv] and below XO [qv].

OIDIUM: fungal disease that afflicted the Cognac vineyards during the 1850s.

PARADIS: *chai* holding older cognacs.

PART DES ANGES: literally 'the angels' share', local term for spirit lost through evaporation.

PETITES EAUX: mixture of brandy and water employed when reducing the strength of cognac before bottling.

PHYLLOXERA VASTATRIX: 'wine louse' which devastated Cognac and France's other wine regions in the last quarter of the nineteenth century.

PINEAU DES CHARENTES: local *apéritif* made by adding brandy to grape juice and thus preventing fermentation. Legally Pineau must be between 16 and 22 per cent alcohol and be aged in wood for at least a year.

PIPE: (now used only for port) 600 litres.

PREUVE: average strengths of brandy. In the eighteenth century: *Preuve de Cognac* 60 per cent alcohol; *Preuve d'Hollande* 49 per cent; *Preuve de Londres* 58 per cent.

QUART DE SEL: tax of 25 per cent paid in the Middle Ages whenever salt changed hands.

QUEUES: French term for tails [qv].

RANCIO CHARENTAIS: Rich complex flavours combining nuts and candied fruits developed by the best cognacs after twenty years or more in wood.

RIMÉ: a cognac that has been overheated in the still and has developed burnt flavours.

SAINT-EMILION: alternative name for Ugni Blanc [qv].

SAINTONIAN [Fr Saintonien]: type of chalky soil found almost entirely in the Petite Champagne.

SECONDES: low-strength brandy from the later stages of distillation.

SERPENTIN: the cooling coil attached to the still.

TAILS: the modern term for *secondes*.

TERROIR: French term covering the geological, physical and chemical composition of a vineyard, includes the weather and the aspect.

TÊTE: the 'head' or first brandy from a distillation.

TÊTE DE MAURE: old-fashioned type of *col*, supposedly the shape of a Moor's head, complete with turban.

TIERCON: pre-1789 measure holding two *barriques* – then about 404 litres.

TONNEAU: in Cognac this means any large cask.

TONNELIER: cooper.

TONNELERIE: wood-working shop where casks are made.

TORULA COMPNIACENSIS RICHON: fungus that lives off the fumes from cognac and blackens the roofs of *chais*.

THREE STAR: older name for the basic quality of cognac, now called VS.

TRONCAIS: Sessile oak, one of the two types of oak used in Cognac, the other being Limousin [qv]. The grain of troncais is tighter. Its name derives from the Forest de Troncais in Central France.

UGNI BLANC: the basic grape variety used in Cognac where it makes neutral, low-strength and acid wine.

VELTE: Dutch measure which represented 8 *pintes de Paris* or 6 *pintes d'Angoulême* – what we would call an Imperial gallon.

VINS VINÉS: fortified wines.

VS: the basic quality of cognac. Legally the youngest cognac in the blend must be at least thirty months old (i.e. Compte 2).

VSOP: Originally called very Special Old Pale. The quality above VS, the youngest cognac in the blend must be at least four and a half years old (i.e. Compte 4).

XO: stands for Extra Old. A superior type of cognac, generally but not universally, comprising cognacs which are at least ten years old.

APPENDIX I
THE LAW

COGNAC AND THE LAW

The Cognacais are governed by three authorities: the tax authorities (Direction Générale des Impôts), who regulate the quantity distilled; the Direction de la Consommation et de la Repression des Fraudes, which polices the quality of the spirit; and the BNIC, which, among other tasks, issues the *certificats d'âge* stating the age of the cognac being sold.

The basic legislation covering the use of the word 'cognac' is the Decree of 15 May 1936, which provided that the term 'cognac' (and also eau de vie de Cognac and eau de vie des Charentes) could be used only for spirits produced and distilled in the region illustrated on the map (shown below). The sub-appellations (*sous-appellations*), Grande Champagne, Petite Champagne, Borderies, Fins Bois and Bons Bois, on the same map were defined in a series of decrees, the first issued on 13th January 1938, the latest dated 16 February 1978.

The word *Fine* can be attached to any sub-appellation, as in 'Fine Borderies' but is legally meaningless. But 'Fine Champagne cognacs' have to contain at least 50 per cent spirit from the Grande Champagne, with the rest coming from the Petite Champagne. The word 'Grande' is reserved for cognacs from the Grande Champagne. In theory, words such as *cru*, *clos*, *château*, etc. can be used only when all the spirits involved come from a specific plot of land, but merchants have been allowed to use the terms for *châteaux* that do not produce all the spirit in the bottle. Nevertheless, the BNIC exercises strict control over labels, ensuring, among other things, that the addresses given on labels are those of the merchants' or growers' actual establishments and not merely postal boxes.

Permitted grape varieties are divided into two categories. The principal varieties are Colombard, Folle Blanche, Jurançon Blanc, Meslier St François, Montils, Sémillon and of course, the near-universal Ugni Blanc. Folignan and Sélect can be used in up to 10 per cent of the total. Wine making must be conducted according to local custom. The use of continuous Archimedes presses is specifically forbidden. In the Charente itself no sugar can be added to the must. In the Charente-Maritime sugar can, in theory, be added but only to musts destined to provide table or sparkling wines. Growers have to declare the acreage of vines and quantities of wine produced (including wines set aside for home consumption).

Article 443 of the Tax Code (Code Général des Impôts) forbids the movement of any wines or spirits on a public highway without the appropriate documentation. Each certificate must include details of the quantity, the type and the appellation. The cognac also has to be accompanied by an *acquit jaune d'or*, the famous golden-coloured permit used by no other drink and first authorised in 1929.

Newly distilled cognac, already warm and rich.

DISTILLATION

To be called cognac the spirit has to be double-distilled, to a strength of not above 72°. Continuous distillation is expressly forbidden. The *alembic charentais* (pot still) consists essentially of a still heated by a naked flame, with a *chapiteau* (head) with or without a *chauffe-vin* (wine-heater) and a cooling coil. The alembic used for the second distillation must not hold more than 30 hectolitres, nor be loaded with more than 25 hectolitres. Bigger alembics holding up to 140 hectolitres, are allowed for the *première chauffe*. The cognac should be aged in casks made of oak from either the Troncais or the Limousin type.

There are three classes of distillers: the co-operatives, the *bouilleurs de profession* (including the Cognac merchants), who buy the wine from the growers, and the *bouilleurs de cru*, who can distil only their own wines. The use, purchase, sale or repair of the alembics are subject to supervision by the local tax office, whom the *bouilleur de cru* has to inform when he wants to start distillation. Manufacturers and salesmen of alembics have to maintain a register providing details of all alembics bought, manufactured, repaired or sold.

Before it is sold cognac has to be reduced to between 40 and 45 per cent alcohol through the addition of distilled water or weaker spirit (which must also come from the Cognac region). Additives are restricted to caramel, oak chippings and sugar. Sugar, limited to 2 per cent of the total volume, can be in the form of either syrup or sugar soaked in spirit of a strength between 20 and 30 per cent. Such additions may reduce the strength of the cognac to 38°. Colouring matter is limited to two parts in 1,000.

AGEING

The BNIC is responsible for guaranteeing the age of the cognacs on offer. To be sold as XXX or VS brandies have to be two years old starting at the beginning of September, the beginning of the *campagne*, cognac's official year; the *campagne* starts on 1st September, five months after distillation has been completed. Brandies called VO, VSOP or Reserve have to be at least Compte 4 and those labelled XO, Extra, Napoleon or Vieille Reserve must be Compte 6, which will rise to ten in 2016.

All cognacs are registered by age, and the certificates giving the age of any parcel of cognac are an indispensable adjunct to the *acquit jaune d'or*. The age classification is as follows – ageing starts officially only on 31 March each year:

- 00 is for cognacs distilled between the harvest and the following 31st March, at which point they turn into 0 cognacs. Brandies distilled after 1 April retain their 00 designation until the following 31 March.
- 1 is for cognacs more than one year old on 1 April of any given year; 2, 3, 4 and 5 cover cognacs from two to five years old on 1 April. A Compte 6 was introduced in 1979, 7 in 1994, 8 in 1995, 9 in 2000 and now extends to 10.
- The youngest cognac that can be sold must be at least thirty months old (i.e. Compte 2). It can be called only VS or ***.
- To be called Reserve, VO or VSOP, the youngest cognac in the blend must be at least four and a half years old (i.e. Compte 4).
- To be labelled Extra, XO, Napoleon, Vieux, Vieille Reserve and the like, the youngest eau de vie in the blend must be at least Compte 6 – an age which will rise to 10 in 2016.
- There are no official regulations covering cognacs older than Compte 10, though many countries have special requirements, and may demand a certificate of age.

ALLIED PRODUCTS

Esprit de cognac is a triple-distilled cognac, of between 80° and 85°, used when making sparkling wines. Pineau des Charentes consists only of wine from the Cognac region fortified during fermentation, once only, with cognac, to give a beverage of between 16° and 22°. In *fruits au cognac* only cognac can be used. If it is *à base de cognac*, then at least 51 per cent of the total liquid content must be cognac. For a *liqueur au Cognac* the minimum content is 30 per cent. *Vins vinés* (fortified wines) of up to 24 per cent alcohol, mostly for export to Germany, are also covered by German law, which now corresponds to French regulations.[77]

LE BUREAU NATIONAL INTERPROFESSIONEL DU COGNAC (BNIC)

The BNIC is a quasi-administrative joint board, with specific legal rights and financial autonomy. The functions of the BNIC are to study and prepare all the regulations covering the buying, distillation, stocks and sale of wines and eaux de vie produced in the Cognac area; to supervise the preservation of the historic methods of making cognac; to control the quantity of cognac produced or allowed to be sold and to promote any measures likely to improve the production or sale of cognac.

The General Assembly of the BNIC controls its policies. In certain cases the decisions are confirmed by official decree. The BNIC is financed by a quasi-fiscal levy that covers its administration and promotional activities.

The Bureau shares overall control with the Administration Fiscale, which polices the appellation and the quantities of brandy distilled by the *bouilleurs de cru*, and with the Inspecteurs des Fraudes, who test the qualities of the cognacs on sale.

RECENT RESTRICTIONS

In recent decades a number of restrictions have been introduced to reduce the growing surplus of cognac. Since 1975 there have been limitations in the alcoholic yield of a hectare of vines and separate quotas covering the quantity that can be distilled and (a lower amount still) the quantity that can be sold. As a result of EC regulations, in 1982–3 only 100 hectolitres of wine could be produced per hectare under Cognac's own restrictions; only 4.5 hectolitres of spirit could be sold freely; one hectolitre could be stored; a further 3 hectolitres could be kept or sold under certain conditions; and any surplus spirit could not be kept or sold as cognac. In 1980 further plantings of vines were forbidden until 13 November 1986, a ban which has continued since that date and a bonus of 13,500 (€2,000) francs per hectare was provided for growers who pulled up their vines.

---

77 BNIC and Marguerite Landrau, *Le Cognac devant la loi*, Cognac, L'Ile d'Or, 1981.

APPENDIX II
THE FIGURES

SIZE

Table 1: Size of vineyard

Including vines destined for other purposes and vineyards not in production

Year	Hectares
1788	156,000
1877	282,667 – last year before phylloxera
1880	233,110
1885	85,240
1893	40,634 – low point
1913	74,000
1926	77,000 – inter-war peak
1939	63,431
1946	59,219
1959	64,114 – last years before new planting rights were granted
1976	110,331 – post-phylloxera peak
1997	85,495 – plan to adapt the vineyard
2011	78,000

PRODUCTION

Table 2: Production of cognac

Years	Millions of bottles, annual average
1879	107.6 (pre-phylloxera peak)
1889	16.4 (post-phylloxera low)
1891–1900	22.2
1901–1910	32.2
1911–1920	31.1
1921–1930	39.9
1931–1940	38.4

SALES

Table 3: Sales of cognac, averages

Years	Millions of bottles
1947–56	37.2
1957–66	60
1967–76	92.9
1977–84	141
1985–92	142
1993–2002	120

Table 4: Sales by campagne year, September to August

Year	Millions of bottles
2003–4	132
2004–5	137
2005–6	146
2006–7	159
2007–8	153
2008–9	146
2009–10	160
2010–11	176
2011–12	184

BIBLIOGRAPHY

Allen, W., *White Wines & Cognac* (London, 1952).

Mac A. Andrew, *Cognac an Independent Guide* (USA, 1999).

Anon. *A Sad Picture of Rustic Folk* (1786).

Baudoin, A., *Les Eaux de Vie et la fabrication de Cognac* (1983).

Bernard, G., *Le Cognac* (Bordeaux, 2008).

— 'La formation des crus de Cognac' *NOROIS*, 1980, n° 105, pp 89–103.

Berry, C.W., *In Search of Wine* (London, 1987).

— *Viniana* (London, 1929).

Bertall (real name, Arnoux), *La Vigne* (Paris, 1878).

Boraud, H., *De l'Usage commercial du nom de Cognac* (Bordeaux,1904).

Bure, M., 'Le Type Saintongeais'. *La Science Sociale*; Vol 23 (Paris, 1928).

Butel, P., *Histoire de la Société Hennessy* (Cognac, 1995).

Campbell, C., *Phylloxera – How Wine was Saved for the World* (London, 2004).

Caumeil, M., *Pour la Science* (December 1983).

Chardonne, J., *Le Bonheur de Barbezieux* (Paris, 1938).

— *Chronique Privée de l'an 1940* (Paris, 1941).

Coquand, H., *Description physique, géologique, paléonlologique et minéralogique de la Charente* (Paris, 1858).

Coste, M., *Cognac les clés d'une fortune* (Librairie du Château, 2001).

Coston, H., *Dictionnaire des dynasties bourgeoises et du monde des affaires* (Éditions A. Moreau, 1975).

Coussié, J-V., *Le Cognac et les aléas de l'histoire* (BNIC, 1996).

Cullen, L., *The Brandy Trade under the Ancien Regime* (Cambridge, 1998).

— *The Irish Brandy Houses of Eighteenth-Century France* (France, 2000).

Daniou, P. *Annales GREH*, (1983).

Delamain, R., *History of Cognac* (Paris, 1935).

— Lecture given in Jarnac in December 1947.

Demachy, J.F., *L'Art du distillateur des eaux fortes* (Paris, 1773).

Diderot, D., *L'Encyclopédie ou Dictionnaire raisonné des sciences, des arts et des métiers*.

Doléances de la Sénéchaussée d'Angoulême pour les Etats Généraux de 1789.

Duluzeau, F., (ed) *Histoire des Protestants Charentais La Croix* (Vif Partis, 2001).

Enjalbert, *Etudes locales* 1939, no 192–1193.

Flanner J., (Genet) *Paris was Yesterday* (London, 1973).

Forbes, R.J., *A Short History of the Art of Distillation* (Leiden, 1970).

Genet, C. & Moreau, L., *Les deux Charentes sous l'Occupation et la Résistance* (Gemozac, 1987).

Gervais, J., *Memoire sur l'Angoumois* (reprint), SAHC.

Guibert, A., *Histoire des villes de France* (Paris, 1845).

Jarrard, K., *Cognac* (NJ, USA, 2005).

Julien-Labruyère, F., *A la recherche de la Saintonge maritime* (Versailles, 1974).

— *Paysans Charentais*, vol.I (La Rochelle, 1982).

Lafon, R. & J. & Coquillaud, P., *Le Cognac: sa distillation* (Paris, 1964).

Landrau, M. *Le Cognac devant la loi.* (L'Isle d'Or Cognac, 1981).

Leauté, R., 'Distillation', *Alembic American Journal of Enology and Viticulture*, Vol 4, No 1, 1990.

Long, J., *The Century Companion to Wines and Spirits* (London, 1983).

Lys, J., *Le Commerce de Cognac* (Université de Bordeaux, 1929).

Martin-Civat, P. 'La Monopole d'Eaux de Vie sous Henri IV', 100eme Congrès de Sociétés Savantes (Paris, 1975).

Mejane, J., *Annales de technologie agricole* (1975).

Monnet, J., *Mémoires* (Paris, 1976).

Morgan, C., *The Voyage* (London, 1940).

Munier, E., *Essai sur l'Angoumois à la fin de l'Ancien Régime* (Paris, 1977).

— *Sur la manière de brûler ou distiller les vins* (Paris, 1981).

Neon, M., *De la crise viticole en Charente* (Paris, 1907).

Petit, C., *Les Charentes: pays du Cognac* (Paris, 1984).

Plante, R., *La société en Charente au XIX CRDP* (Poitiers, 1976).

Quenot, J-P., *Statistique du Département de la Charente* (1818).

Ravaz, L. & V., *Le pays du Cognac* (Angoulême,1900).

Cyril, R., *Cognac* (London,1985).

Riou, Y-J., (ed) *Cognac cite marchande: urbanisme et architecture* (Poitiers, 1990).

Saintsbury, G., *Notes on a Cellar-book* (Macmillan, 1921).

Savary des Brulons, J. & Sons, *Dictionnaire Universel du Commerce, d'histoire naturelle et des Arts et Metiers* (Paris).

Sepulchre, B., *Le Livre du Cognac: trois siècles d'histoire* (Paris,1983).

Taransaud, J., *Le livre de la tonnellerie. La roue à livres diffusion* (Paris, 1976).

Tesseron, G., *La Charente sous Louis XIV* (Angoulême, 1958).

Tovey, C., *British and Foreign Spirits* (London, 1864).

Verdon, J.A., *Une commune rurale vue par son instituteur d'alors: Malaville en 101 Annales* (GREH, 1982).

INDEX

Company names deriving from their owners' names are listed without inversion, e.g. Pierre Frapin is listed as it appears, under Frapin. Personal names are listed with the usual inversion, e.g. Frapin, Pierre.